THE JASON VOYAGE

Tim Severin was educated at Tonbridge School and was a geography scholar at Oxford University. He was a Harkness Fellow at the Universities of California, Minnesota and Harvard and holds a B.Litt. from Oxford University in Medieval Asian Exploration. He has written seven books on the history of exploration, and has recreated the travels of Sindbad, St Brendan and Marco Polo. His home is in County Cork, Ireland.

The Sindbad Voyage, The Brendan Voyage and *Tracking Marco Polo* are also available from Arrow Publications.

THE JASON VOYAGE

The Quest for the Golden Fleece

Tim Severin

DRAWINGS BY TRONDUR PATURSSON

PHOTOGRAPHS BY JOHN EGAN,
SETH MORTIMER AND TOM SKUDRA

ARROW BOOKS

Arrow Books Limited
62–65 Chandos Place, London WC2N 4NW

An imprint of Century Hutchinson Ltd

London   Melbourne   Sydney   Auckland
Johannesburg and agencies throughout
the world

First published by Hutchinson 1985

Arrow edition 1986

Printed and bound in Great Britain by
Guernsey Press Limited, Guernsey, C.I.

ISBN 0 09 946180 3

Contents

Illustrations

Illustrations

The Jason Voyage

Commemorating *Argo*'s arrival at Colchis★
'Princess Medea'★
Solid gold bangles of the 4th century BC†
A Svan gold-gatherer of the Caucasus Mountains†
Sheepskins trap the gold of the mountain streams†

★Photographs by John Egan
†Photographs by Seth Mortimer
‡Photographs by Tom Skudra

Introduction

To row and sail a twenty-oared galley from Greece to Soviet Georgia, a distance of some 1500 sea miles, was a team achievement *par excellence*. As skipper of *Argo* I feel that there is no more appropriate way to introduce my account of the Jason Voyage than to list the men and women who made up the twentieth-century crew – whether for all 1500 miles plus trials and delivery, or just a single day's rowing. They were the New Argonauts:

Main Voyage

Dave Brinicombe: Volos to Georgia – *sound recordist*
Miles Clark: Volos to Istanbul
Jonathan Cloke: Armutlu to Georgia
Peter Dobbs: Volos to Canakkale
John Egan: Volos to Georgia (also trials and delivery) – *photographer*
Richard Hill: Volos to Georgia – *film cameraman*
Nick Hollis: Volos to Georgia – *doctor*
Adam Mackie: Zonguldak to Georgia – *doctor*
Peter Moran: Volos to Georgia (also delivery) – *cook*
Seth Mortimer: Paleo Trikeri to Georgia – *photographer*
Cormac O'Connor: Istanbul to Georgia
Trondur Patursson: Volos to Abana (also delivery) – *artist*
Tim Readman: Volos to Georgia (also delivery) – *purser*
Mark Richards: Volos to Georgia (also trials and delivery) – *rowing master*
Tim Severin: Volos to Georgia (also trials and delivery) – *skipper/helmsman*

Peter Warren: Canakkale to Georgia (also trials and delivery)
Peter Wheeler: Volos to Georgia (also trials and delivery) –
  ship's carpenter

Greek Volunteers

Costas Ficardos (also delivery) Theodore
Elias Psareas   Antonis Karagiannis

Turkish Volunteers

Ali Uygun   Yigit Koseoglu
Deniz Demirel   Bulent Doveci
Umur Erozlu   Nurettin Kumru
Erzin Yirmibesoglu   Ertunc Goksen
Kaan Akca   Cevdat Tosyali
Mustafa Pikdoken   Mehmet
Husnu Konuk   Yuksel
Ziya Derlen

Bosphorus Volunteers

Ferruh Manau   Yunus Yilmaz
Taner Tokay   Berattin Kokcay
Emir Turgan   Mehmet Burckin
Mehmet Yavas   Ozgen Korkmazlar
Elfi Cetinkaya   Bulent Tanagan
Nejat Akdogan   Engin Cezzar

Georgian Volunteers

Vladimir Beraija   Paata Natsvlishvili
Jumber Tsomaya   Vladimir Petruk
George Topagze   Givi Tskhomarya
Anatoly Akaev   Aivar Strengis
Leonti Negeftidi   Zurab Tsitskishvili

Trials Crew

James Neeves
Jason Hicks
Chris Murphy
Chris Bedford
Andy Stirrup
Paul Owers
Chris Burton

Robin Gwynn
Mac Mackenzie
John Woffinden
Robert Hamlin
Jane Townson
Jannet Tjook

Delivery Crew

Martin Anketill (also trials)
Stematis Chrisphatis
David Gilmour (also trials)
Mike Kerr (also trials)
Mike Kostopoulos
Clive Raymond (also trials)
Tom Skudra (also trials)

Philip Varveris
Tom Vosmer (also trials)
Ian Whitehead

also:
Lou Lyddon
Doreen
Ron

of ARGO

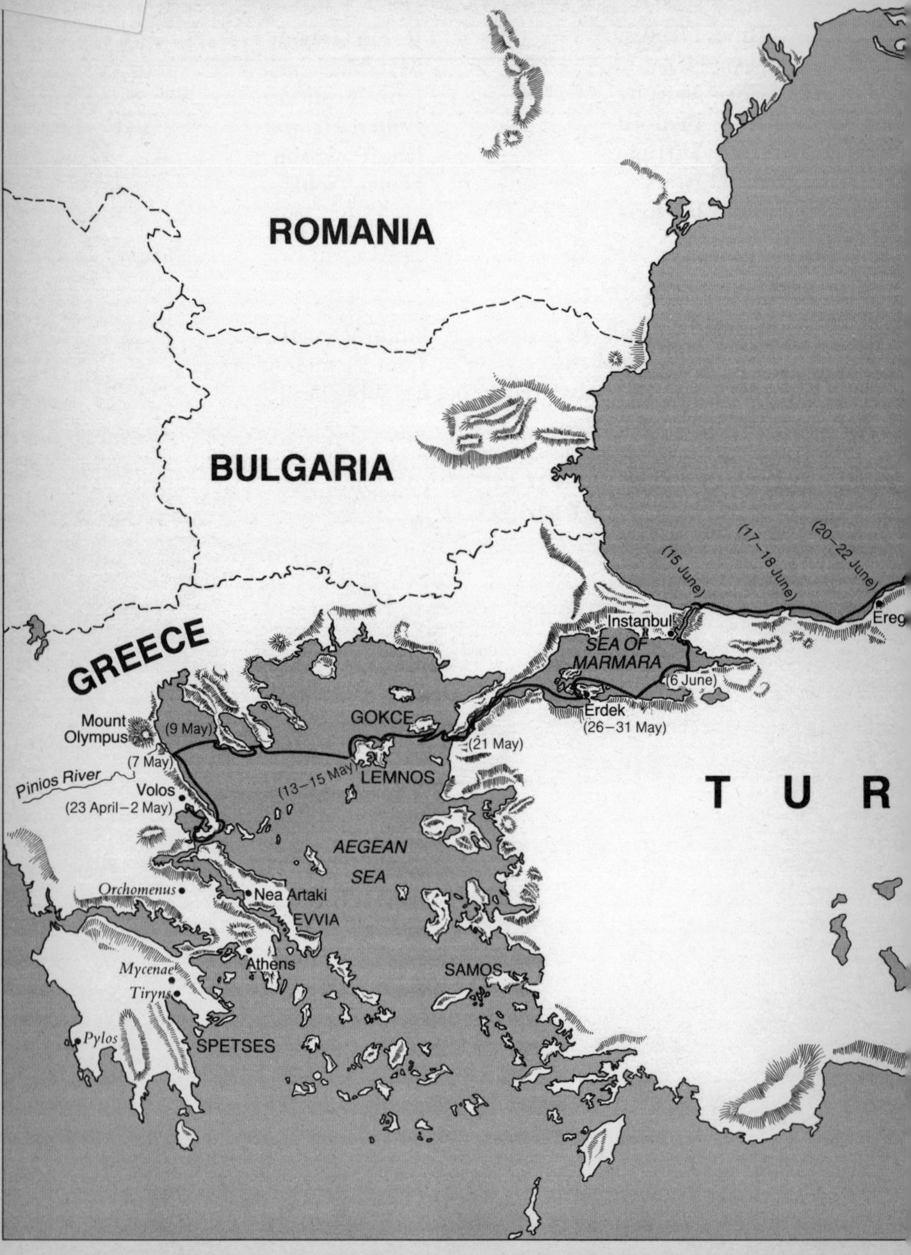

ROMANIA
BULGARIA
GREECE
T U R
Instanbul
SEA OF MARMARA
(6 June)
Erdek
(26–31 May)
(15 June)
(17–18 June)
(20–22 June)
Ereg
Mount Olympus
(9 May)
(7 May)
Pinios River
Volos
(23 April–2 May)
GOKCE
(21 May)
(13–15 May)
LEMNOS
AEGEAN SEA
Orchomenus
Nea Artaki
EVVIA
Athens
Mycenae
Tiryns
Pylos
SPETSES
SAMOS

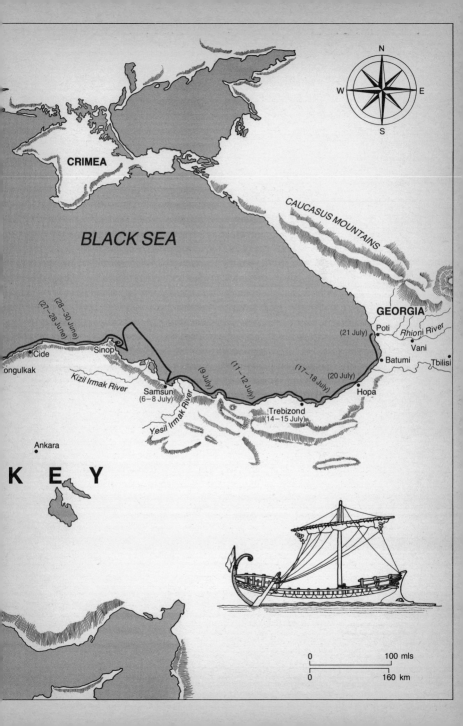

N
W   E
S

CRIMEA

BLACK SEA

CAUCASUS MOUNTAINS

GEORGIA
(21 July) • Poti   *Rhioni River*
• Vani
• Batumi   • Tbilisi

(28–30 June)
(27–28 June)
• Cide   • Sinop
ongulkak   *Kizil Irmak River*
(9 July)   (11–12 July)   (17–18 July)
(20 July)
• Samsun
(6–8 July)
• Hopa
Yesil Irmak River
Trebizond
(14–15 July)

• Ankara

K E Y

0   100 mls
0   160 km

1
The Quest

It was King Pelias who sent them out. He had heard an oracle which warned him of a dreadful tale – death through the machinations of the man whom he should see coming from the town with one foot bare. . . . The prophecy was soon confirmed. Jason, fording the Anaurus in a winter spate, lost one of his sandals, which stuck in the bed of the flooding river, but saved the other from the mud and shortly appeared before the king. And no sooner did the king see him than he thought of the oracle and decided to send him on a perilous adventure overseas. He hoped that things might so fall out, either at sea or in outlandish parts, that Jason would never see his home again.

So begins the first voyage saga in western literature: the tale of Jason and the Argonauts in search of the Golden Fleece. It tells of a great galley manned by heroes from ancient Greece which sets out to reach a land far in the east. There, in the branches of an oak tree on the banks of a great river, hangs a sacred fleece of gold, guarded by an immense serpent. If the heroes can bring home the fleece, Prince Jason, the one-sandalled man, will win back his rightful throne from his half-uncle, the usurper King Pelias. On their voyage, so the story recounts, the heroes meet all manner of adventures: they land on an island populated only by women who are eager to make husbands of the Argonauts; a barbaric tribal chieftain challenges them to a boxing match, the loser of which will be battered to death; the dreadful Clashing Rocks bar their path and only by a whisker do

15

they save their vessel from being smashed to shards. A blind prophet, who is being tormented by winged female demons, gives them guidance; and when the heroes finally reach the far land, the king's daughter, Princess Medea, falls so madly in love with Jason that she betrays her family, helps Jason steal the fleece, and flees back with him to Greece.

Small wonder that such a romantic tale has echoed down through the centuries. Homer said it was already a 'tale on all men's lips' when he came to write the *Odyssey*. Greek poets of the stature of Euripides, Aeschylus and Sophocles based plays upon it. In the third century BC Apollonius Rhodius, head of the great library at Alexandria, wrote the most complete surviving version of the tale in the Greek classical style. 'Moved by the god of song,' he wrote, 'I set out to commemorate the heroes of old who sailed the good ship *Argo* up the Straits and into the Black Sea and between the Clashing Rocks in quest of the Golden Fleece.'

Twenty-two centuries later, my companions and I also set out to commemorate those heroes of old, but in a different manner. Whereas Apollonius had accompanied the Argonauts in verse, we hoped to track them in reality. So we rowed out aboard the replica of a galley of Jason's day, a twenty-oared vessel of 3000-year-old design, in order to seek our own Golden Fleece – the facts behind the story of Jason and the Argonauts. Our travel guide was a copy of the *Argonautica*, the book of Apollonius, wrapped in layers of plastic to guard it from the rain and sea spray aboard an open boat. Pessimists calculated that unless favourable winds helped us on our way, we would have to row more than a million oar strokes per man to reach our goal.

Our galley, the new *Argo*, was a delight to the eye. Three years of effort had been devoted to her research, design and construction, and now her elegant lines repaid every minute of that care. Fifty-four feet long, from the tip of her curious snout-like ram to the graceful sweep of her tail, she looked more like a sea animal than a ship. On each side the oars rose and fell like the legs of some great beast creeping forward across the quiet surface of the dark blue Grecian sea. Two painted eyes stared malevolently forward over the distinctive nose of her ram, and at the very tip of that ram a hollow handhold breathed like a nostril, as it burbled and snorted with the water washing through the cavity.

'What's that over there?' someone shouted suddenly, pointing slightly to one side of the boat's path. 'Looks like the fin of something big, maybe a basking shark.'

'I didn't know there were any sharks in the Mediterranean,' a voice replied.

'What about it, Trondur?' I called forward, from where I stood at the helm. 'Is it worth a try?'

A muscular, bushy-bearded figure seated among the rowers on the oar benches gave a slight nod. Trondur Patursson, seaman and artist-extraordinary, and I had sailed together on two previous expeditions and knew one another so well that it wasn't necessary to waste words. '*Ja!*' he grunted, and leaned down to dig a harpoon head out of the kitbag beneath his oar bench. Then he scrambled forward to the bow of the ship, and a minute later the harpoon head was firmly lashed to its wooden shaft. Trondur took up position, poised on the prow, weapon in hand. He looked like Poseidon himself.

'Everyone pay attention,' I said softly. 'We'll see if we can get that shark for the pot.' The crew began a steady, slow stroke, dipping their oar blades into the water as quietly as possible to avoid alerting the quarry. Now more than ever, the galley was like a sea beast as it manoeuvred into position. It was a predatory animal stalking its prey.

Gently I pushed across the tiller bar so that the nose of the galley swung round and pointed at the black triangle of the great fin dipping slowly up and down in the sea. The shark did not seem to have sensed our presence. Anxiously, I tried to remember the old whaling techniques that I had read about. Was it better to get the crew to take a few hard pulls on the oars and then drift up to the shark with the impetus? Or should we row down on it all the way, pulling stealthily like footpads approaching their victim? The former course seemed more logical.

'Easy, port side oars . . . carry on rowing, starboard side.'

The port side rowers stopped, and held their oars clear, the water dripping from the tips of the blades on to the oily, calm surface of the sea. The starboard rowers took five firm strokes, and then rested their oars as well. The galley slid forward, silently curving towards its mark. We were almost on top of the shark now. I could see its underwater shape, a large blotchy mass, maybe 3 metres long, flickering in the half-light. The shark was becoming vaguely suspicious of the boat's presence, and began to turn away. As the shadow of the galley passed over it the shark began to dive for safety, and at that moment Trondur threw, tossing the harpoon in a short curve.

A hit! The harpoon struck the water with a splash, and stopped abruptly, two-thirds of its shaft sticking out of the water straight up, the harpoon head embedded in the shark's hide. It was as if the harpoon had hit a solid lump of driftwood. Then there was a flurry of spray as the shark twisted, trying to escape. Trondur seized the harpoon line to stop it running out, and there was a moment's pressure. Then the harpoon, which had sunk out of view, bobbed back to the surface and lay flat on the water. The barb had not held firm. Phlegmatically Trondur pulled in the line, and held up the harpoon to show us. The impact had bent the sharp point of the harpoon at right-angles to the steel shank, so that it looked like a gaff hook.

'No good,' said Trondur, shaking his shaggy head in self-reproach. 'Harpoon must be more down,' gesturing that his throw had been too flat. To pierce sufficiently deeply through the shark's tough skin the harpoon should have struck more squarely to its target.

'For anyone a bit wet behind the ears,' announced Peter Dobbs 'there went our breakfast. Shark meat tastes very good, if you cook it right, with fried onions.'

Peter, Trondur and two other men in the galley crew – our doctor Nick Hollis and ship's purser Tim Readman – were old hands at this sort of voyage. They had all sailed with me when we had taken the replica of an eighth-century Arab trading ship 8000 miles under sail from Muscat in the Arabian Sea to Canton in China. On that seven-month trip, investigating the background to the stories of Sindbad the Sailor, our Omani Arab shipmates had shown us the best recipes for cooking shark flesh to supplement and vary our shipboard diet. Naturally, when it came to selecting a crew for an ancient galley to track Jason and the Argonauts, I had first contacted my former shipmates. The response was immediate. Tim and Peter had taken leave of absence from their jobs; Nick had arranged to be between hospital appointments so he could have the summer free; and Trondur, who lived in the Faeroe Islands where he made his living as an artist and a sculptor, only had to pack his rucksack full of artist's materials – as well as fishing hooks and harpoon heads – and make his way to Greece.

There they joined two men who had helped to build the galley: Peter Wheeler, a twenty-six-year-old English engineer, now serving as ship's carpenter, and John Egan, from County Mayo in Ireland, who had been a general handyman at the boatyard and was acting as one of the two expedition photographers. The other photographer, Seth Mortimer, joined at the last minute, and had looked distinctly startled when he first set eyes on the ship's rowing master, who had the job of teaching the newcomers how to handle an oar. Rowing master Mark Richards had shaved his head completely bare, and years of competition rowing had developed his muscles so that he had the torso of a prizefighter. The combination of his gleaming skull and bulging biceps made him look like the slave master in a Hollywood epic. A stranger would have been surprised to learn that Mark had studied classics at Oxford University and could read Latin and Greek with ease, so making him a most suitable companion to help untangle the Greek text of the *Argonautica*.

Alongside Mark on the same rowing bench was a former rowing rival, Miles Clark, who had competed in the Boat Race for Cambridge University, while up in the bows was the most important man of all, Peter Moran, our cook. Having just completed a five-year training course in hotel management, he had

Miles

decided to take a complete break before donning the dark-suited uniform of his profession. Certainly he had his hands full. Grimy and stripped to the waist, with grease smudges on his cheerful face, he ruled a tiny kitchen a few feet square in the very forepeak of the boat where, on a paraffin stove, he was expected to feed up to twenty ravenously hungry galley slaves. He was utterly unperturbed at the prospect.

'If they help me prepare the vegetables and clean up afterwards, the crew and I will get along just fine,' he told me. 'Mind you, I won't let anyone else near the food stores. Otherwise they'd pinch the lot, and we'd have nothing left.'

As I watched this high-spirited crew, it was tempting to compare them with the men who were supposed to have manned the legendary *Argo* on her voyage in quest of the Golden Fleece. The original crew lists differ from text to text, because nearly every city in classical Greece wanted the honour of claiming to have provided a member of Jason's crew, and so the final roster reads like a roll call of all the great provinces and cities of Greece. But certain figures stand out.

For his helmsman Jason had Tiphys, 'an expert mariner who could sense the coming of a swell across the open sea, and learn from sun and star when storms were brewing or a ship might sail'. The lookout was keen-sighted Lynceus who, it was alleged, could see farther and more clearly than any man alive. The ship's carpenter was Argus, who had also been the master craftsman in charge of building the first *Argo*, 'finest of all ships that braved the sea with oars'. The fastest runner in the world, Euphemus of Taenarum, was also aboard. It was said that he could run across the rolling waters of the grey sea without getting his feet wet. Then there were the twins, Castor and Pollux, the one a genius at horse-racing, and the other the boxing champion of Greece, a useful talent which was to save the crew from death on their travels. Two members of the team, Mopsus and Idmon, were seers. They could read auguries, foretell the future and translate the twitterings of birds. Calais and Zetes were sons of the North Wind, from whom they had inherited the ability to fly through the air. Burly Ancaeus, clad in a bearskin, was such a phenomenally strong oarsman that he could balance the rowing power of the strongest man who ever walked the earth – Hercules himself.

Just when and how Hercules joined the Argonauts depends on

which early author tells the legend; and exactly how long he stayed with the expedition is also not clear, as we shall see. But the ancients considered it inconceivable that the great hero Hercules had not taken some part in the quest for the Golden Fleece, and so they wrote him into the tale. Similarly, in the heyday of his popularity as a cult figure the master musician Orpheus was given a major role in the project. Playing his lyre, Orpheus kept time for the oarsmen. His music calmed the storms and soothed the rowers when they quarrelled among themselves; and the charmed sounds of his singing brought fish to the surface of the sea to gambol in the galley's wake.

To me, the tale of Jason and the quest for the Golden Fleece had long held a special fascination. Like most people I first read about Jason in school, in an anthology of Greek legends, among the stories of Theseus and the Minotaur, the Labours of Hercules, and all the spellbinding narratives of the gods on Olympus and their interventions in the lives of men and women in the ancient Greek world. But as a historian of exploration, studying the great voyage epics of literature, I began to realize just how important the Jason story is. It holds a unique position in western literature as the earliest epic story of a voyage that has survived. It predates even Homer's *Odyssey* and – for reasons which I was to learn later – the Argonaut saga describes events that were supposed to have taken place in the late Bronze Age, in the thirteenth century BC. The actual ship that carried the heroes, the immortal *Argo*, is the first vessel in recorded history to bear a name. To a seaman this has powerful appeal: for the first time a boat is something more than an inanimate floating object, an anonymous vehicle. *Argo* is a named, identifiable boat which has a character of her own. In the ancient telling of the story *Argo* could speak with a human voice, and at crucial moments state her own opinions. Even the description of her crew as the 'Argonauts' or 'sailors of *Argo*', comes from the boat herself. In a modern world accustomed to hearing of astronaut, cosmonauts and even aquanauts, it was worth remembering that the Argonauts were the first distant adventurers of an epic.

Yet the study of ancient Greek history and literature has attracted the finest scholars for generations. Could it be possible, I had to ask myself, that they had left anything to be learned about so important a voyage? I felt it was almost impudent to re-examine texts that so many great scholars had studied with such encyclopedic knowledge for so many years. Then, too, there was the problem of the sheer age of the Argonaut tale. In theory the voyage had taken place so long ago that surely there was not enough surviving evidence to enable anyone to retrace their route. And yet, when I reread the *Argonautica* I was struck by the fact that there was virtually no disagreement about the geography of the legend. All the learned scholars agreed that the alleged voyage started in northern Greece and had gone to the far eastern end of the Black Sea, to what was once called the kingdom of Colchis and is now Soviet Georgia.

At that point scholarly accord ended. Some authorities saw the tale as pure fabrication, an engaging myth invented to amuse its audience. Other scholars preferred the theory that the legend had perhaps a minor tap root in the late Bronze Age, but had been altered beyond recognition in the intervening centuries. Some critics pointed out that, although there are passing references to Jason and his voyage as early as Homer, the first full-length version of the story was not written until the middle of the third century BC, nearly a thousand years after the events it describes.

Another school of thought said that the voyage was physically impossible. These critics considered that a boat of late Bronze Age structure could not have survived the 1500-mile coasting voyage from Greece to Colchis. The primitive vessel would have been wrecked or fallen to pieces. Above all, it was beyond credence that such a boat had succeeded in passing through the Straits of the Bosphorus to enter the Black Sea. According to these objectors, the adverse currents in the Bosphorus are far too strong to have been surmounted by Jason's galley. It would require a vessel of at least fifty oars, stacked in two levels one above the other, to row up against the Bosphorus, and maritime historians have no evidence that a boat of this type and power existed before the end of the eighth century BC. As proof, these critics pointed out that, after these boats were invented, there followed a dramatic expansion of Greek interest in the Black Sea and the foundation of many Greek colonies along its coasts. The Argonaut story, they argued, was premature. Jason and his men never got to Colchis or any farther than the present site of Istanbul on the Bosphorus. Not everyone, however, was totally dismissive of at least a kernel of truth in the legend. 'Argonauts,' pronounced the sober and authoritative *Oxford Classical Dictionary*, 'one of the oldest Greek sagas, based originally on a perhaps real exploit. . . .

But was Jason's voyage a 'real exploit'? The only way to settle the matter, at least for practical doubters, was to build a ship of the time, to try rowing her up the Bosphorus against the current, and then to get to Soviet Georgia in her. But long before even considering such an experiment, I had to check the value of the basic Jason text, Apollonius' *Argonautica*. And here I was immediately reassured. Its author was no lightweight. Rather, Apollonius Rhodius was one of the outstanding scholars of his day. He had studied under the great teacher Callimachus, been selected as royal tutor to the Ptolemies, and appointed to the prestigious post of Head of the Library of Alexandria. There he had access to the greatest single repository of learning in the ancient world, its major collection of scrolls and archives, when he came to compose the *Argonautica*. Equally, we know that his fellow scholars scrutinized the *Argonautica*, and were quick to correct its errors and lapses. Indeed, it is recorded that Apollonius first wrote a much longer version of the *Argonautica* which was so severely mauled by the critics that he withdrew the work, left Alexandria and spent several years recasting and shortening his text. This revised version was accepted by the contemporary scholarly community, and even if its critical values were different from those of the modern age, there was no doubt at all that the surviving *Argonautica* of Apollonius was a text of major scholarship, written by an extremely learned man who set out to tell the tale of Jason and the Argonauts in the form in which he had researched it, using the best resources of his day.

So if the written text provided a sound basis for a new Argonaut expedition, what was known about the ships of the time? More particularly, was it possible to assemble enough data to reconstruct a thirteenth-century BC vessel of the right type? Obviously all manner of different vessels had been in use in the eastern Mediterranean in the late Bronze Age – cargo boats, coasting boats, boats operating out of Cyprus and the Levant as well as out of Crete and mainland Greece, rowing boats, sailing boats, warships. And presumably every type of boat had its regional and local variation, depending upon where it was built and what it was used for. Jason's ship, according to every text, was a galley, and this was surely the logical choice for a ship that was going on an expedition that could well have to fight its way through hostile territory. Only a galley could carry enough warriors to undertake what might prove to be a plundering raid if the guardian of the Golden Fleece, the king of

Colchis, did not wish to hand it over.

Painstaking research by maritime historians over the last twenty years has amassed a vast body of knowledge about the early Greek ships, and all the indications are that the Greek galleys were not abrupt new inventions. Like the longships of the Vikings, the Greek galleys evolved gradually over the centuries. Today we are able to trace the line of descent of Viking ships, which in some ways resemble the Greek galleys, over a period of 1300 years, and the alterations in design and construction were very gradual indeed. There is every reason to suppose that the Greek galleys underwent the same conservative process. By assembling and collating all the evidence, I hoped that it might be possible to arrive at a representative ship of Jason's era, a galley of the late Bronze Age.

According to the *Argonautica*, the galley was specially built on a beach close to the city of Iolcos, now called Volos, which was the capital of Jason's royal family. And here I had an excellent stroke of luck. I found that the earliest surviving picture of a Greek galley, painted on some sherds of early pottery, had been excavated from Volos itself. The sherds were small and badly broken, but the Greek archaeologist who found them had been able to piece them together like a jigsaw puzzle and fill in the gaps to form the picture of a boat. It was a modest little sketch, but it was all important because it revealed that as early as the sixteenth century BC, the date of the sherds and several centuries before Jason's time, Greek boats already bore the characteristic ram beak, the upward sweeping stern,

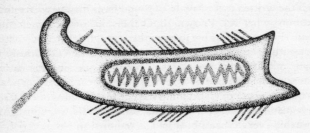

The 'Volos' ship, c. 1600BC

and a side steering oar. Later boat pictures, dating from the seventh to fourth centuries BC, provided a great many more technical details, such as the way the sails were rigged and controlled.

But how big should the galley be? Jason's *Argo* was reputed to be the largest and most splendid ship of its time, her exact size is never stated. On board, according to the different accounts, were anything between thirty and fifty men, or maybe even more, though not necessarily all of them were oarsmen. Early Greek oared ships were not measured by length, but by the number of oars they rowed. In Homer's poems they came in three sizes – the twenty-, thirty- and fifty-oared galleys. I realized at once that building a fifty-oared galley was impossible. I simply could not afford such a large vessel, and where would I find fifty men to row her? On the other hand, if an expedition to the kingdom of the Golden Fleece could succeed in the smallest size of boat – including the task of rowing up the Bosphorus – then my experiment would be all the more convincing. If one could row to Soviet Georgia in a twenty-oared galley, then it would have been even easier for Jason in a bigger ship. So the obvious choice for my vessel was the humble twenty-oared galley. This size of vessel shows up again and again in the early texts; it was the maid-of-all-work of the early Greek fleets, serving as scout, escort and courier ship. It was in a twenty-oared galley, for example, that Telemachus, son of Ulysses, went to seek news of his missing father from the king of Pylos; and this was only a generation after Jason's expedition. If I could build a twenty-oared galley, I would have a representative ship of the age. Aboard her, perhaps, a determined crew of oarsmen could follow in the wake of Jason and his Argonauts.

I knew whom to ask to design the vessel. Colin Mudie, naval architect, had already designed two ancient boats for me. From his drawing board had come the technical specifications for *Sohar*, the eighth-century Arab merchant ship, her planks sewn together with 400 miles of coconut cord, aboard which we had made the Sindbad Voyage. Before that, in 1976–77, Colin's skills had produced the specifications for the skinboat *Brendan*, covered with oxhides, in which three companions and I had made the hazardous crossing of the North Atlantic by way of Iceland, to investigate whether Irish monks could have reached the New World nearly a thousand years before Columbus.

When I telephoned Colin and told him that I was thinking of reconstructing an ancient Greek galley, he seemed not the least surprised. 'Come down and see me,' he said, 'and we'll discuss what can be done.' A week later I was sitting in his office, outlining my idea for an Argonaut expedition, and beginning to realize that once again I was setting him a fiendishly complicated task. To turn my jumble of data into a practical boat shape, Colin cross-examined me about how many men would be aboard, and for how long at a time. Would they spend their nights at sea, or would we always come ashore at dusk? If so, what were the beaches like where we would be landing? What was their angle of slope? In what season of the year would we travel? What was the timber the ancients used for their own boatbuilding, and was it still available? If so, in what lengths and quality? How much of the voyage did I expect to be spent rowing, and how much under sail?

I answered the barrage of questions as best I could, while Colin's pen skipped across the page making notes. I knew from the rapid fire of his questions that this was just the sort of project which he and his wife Rosemary enjoyed tackling as a break from their more normal design work. Whatever I had overlooked during my research, Colin and Rosemary would dig out of their files, applying that genial mixture of scholarship and tradecraft which is the hallmark of all their work. Colin's pen, which was now jotting notes, would soon be making little design sketches, then preliminary drawings, and finally the technical plans of a twenty-oared galley, closing a gap of three millennia. By the time I left their house, we had already touched on such arcane matters as why the early Greeks divided an Olympic cubit into twenty-four finger widths, how many foot pounds of energy a man could exert while rowing steadily for eight hours at a stretch, and whether perhaps ancient Greek shipwrights preshaped their timber by bending over living trees and tethering them to the ground with ropes, so that they grew into the required curves. Design conferences with Colin and Rosemary were always refreshing occasions, and the speed with which Colin came up with a preliminary design study betrayed just how intrigued he was with the problems.

'It's coming together very nicely indeed,' he told me with his next telephone call. 'Everything seems to fit. One solution leads logically to the next.'

'What about the actual construction?' I asked nervously. 'Will the boat be difficult to build?'

'Ah, that will depend on the shipwright you manage to find. This is going to be the most sophisticated of your three historic boats. But then,' he added with a chuckle, 'the harder a boat is to build, the better she usually goes once she's afloat.'

Two weeks later he sent me a drawing of my new ship. '20 Oar galley for Tim Severin, Esq.,' announced the rubric at the top. 'Preliminary Design Study. Drawing No. 365.1.' Sitting on a gently sloping beach was a 54-foot galley with a 9-foot 4-inch beam, benches for twenty rowers, and a distinctly jaunty expression in the roundel that Colin had drawn above her ram nose.

'Show that drawing to your boatbuilder, and see what he says,' Colin told me when I congratulated him. 'Then we'll consider what alterations he feels should be made.'

The trouble was that I hadn't yet found a suitable boatbuilder, nor did I have the slightest idea of where to look for one. Naturally I wanted to build the boat in Greece. But it's not every day that a shipwright is suddenly asked to build a galley from the late Bronze Age, and I knew that I would have to find a very special man. What I needed urgently, I realized, was someone who could point me in the right direction in Greece, someone who could advise me where to search for a traditional shipwright with the skill and imagination to tackle the job, someone to help me with the negotiations, someone to explain to me the proper system of arranging for a boat to be built; someone who possessed a full nautical vocabulary in both Greek and English.

But where could I find such a paragon? In a burst of optimism I decided that the obvious place to start looking was at the annual London International Boat Show just after Christmas, which always includes stands run by charter firms which rent out yachts to summer visitors to Greek waters. Perhaps by asking around I could pick up the name of someone, a charter boat skipper or perhaps a Greek yachtsman, who knew the Greek boatbuilding scene well enough to advise me.

Certainly I had not expected to find the paragon himself at the Boat Show. But at the first charter firm's stand, when I explained my quest, the girl assistant brightened visibly and said, 'Oh, why don't you talk to John Vas?'

'John who?' I asked.

'I'm afraid I don't know his last name properly. It's rather difficult to pronounce, so everyone just calls him John Vas for short. He lives in Athens, and helps us out with any problems in chartering our boats there. He always comes to England for the Boat Show, and he's here now. I saw him only a few minutes ago near the stand. If you'll wait, I'll try and find him.'

Five minutes later I was being introduced to a large, extremely grave-looking man in his sixties, who spoke impeccable English in a deep, deliberate voice. In fact, with his dark blue blazer, grey flannel trousers, yachting shoes and neck scarf, John Vasmadjides could have been mistaken for an Englishman. For more than thirty-two years he had worked for British Airways and its predecessors at Athens Airport, and finished up as their station manager. Recently he had retired to devote himself to his real passion, which was sailing and having as much as possible to do with boats. I surmised that in his long professional career he must have been faced with every conceivable sort of crisis – irate and upset travellers who had missed their planes, or been separated from their baggage, or lost their tickets, or had their flights diverted. In any such calamity John would have been magnificent. Never had I met anyone who had a more calming influence on the people around him. It was partly his bulk, for John was a big and imposing figure, but it was also his careful, deliberate manner. To John no problem was insoluble, no story too long to listen to, no crisis too awkward to handle. His slow-moving appearance was completely deceptive. He got things done very quickly by calling on the help of a vast circle of friends and a huge fund of experience.

From my very first chat with him, I had the impression that John either knew every traditional shipwright, sailmaker, chandler and harbour master in Greece, or at least knew how to contact them. He offered at once to give me all the help he could. I was to get in touch with him as soon as I came out to Greece to search for boatyards, and he would advise me where to look. During the next year and a half of frenzied activity, building and testing the replica of a 3000-year-old galley in a race against time, John was to prove essential. With his knack of untangling difficulties, his avuncular friendliness and his patience, he earned himself the project nickname of 'Uncle John'. If any member of the team ever had a problem in Greece, or needed advice, the natural reaction was to say, 'Why don't you contact Uncle John and ask whether he can help?'

Later that same month, armed with a road map of Greece and a copy of Colin's drawing of the galley, I set out in a rented car to visit the traditional boatyards of Greece that Uncle John had suggested. It was bitterly cold, with deep snow on the central mountain range, and the search very soon made me despondent. Uncle John's list of possible yards was dismayingly short, and the locations seemed to be scattered as widely as was geographically possible around the Greek peninsula. For hour after hour I drove down small side roads which degenerated into potholed tracks, and then ended up on some chilly foreshore, littered with decaying hulks and boats forlornly drawn up for their winter overhaul. I quickly learned that only the owner of the boatyard was qualified to answer my questions, and the shipwrights themselves would shy away from a stranger. Either the owner was absent, or he was half-buried inside the guts of a boat under repair. In the latter case he certainly did not relish being interrupted by a foreigner, talking absurdly about making a ship of the late Bronze Age. Even if I did entice the owner to crawl out from the bilges and listen to my proposal, the conversation usually seemed to be conducted within 6 feet of a bandsaw, whose scream made any sensible discussion well-nigh impossible, particularly when conducted in a broken jumble of Greek and English with confusing interjections from bystanders.

I must have searched out a dozen such country boatyards, driving from one side of the Greek mainland to the other, travelling to the nearer islands, and constantly being disappointed. Uncle John even took me to the vast shipyards of Piraeus where, improbably, a couple of builders of wooden boats still survived. Their workshops were sandwiched between towering hulks of condemned ships that were being torn apart for scrap in a cacophony of fierce hammering and clanking and the hiss of cutting torches. Everything I saw indicated that traditional boatbuilding in Greece was perilously close to extinction. Small fishing boats were being built, but usually they were the work of individual fishermen or part-time carpenters and enthusiasts. Of full-time, professional shipwrights working in timber there was just a handful. At yard after yard only repairs were being made, no new boats. Always I heard the same reasons – lack of suitable timber, no demand for traditional boats, craftsmen retired or moved to better jobs. Sometimes I unfolded Colin's drawing of the jaunty-looking galley and asked if such a boat could be built. The reaction was astonished disbelief or total bewilderment. Why on earth would I want such an odd-looking vessel? Was it something to do with the tourist trade asked the astute ones. When I mentioned the possibility of taking her to the Black Sea, without an engine, people shook their heads at such a crazy idea. What was the sense of it? What a fortune I would have to pay the rowers!

Only near Volos itself, where Jason's *Argo* had been built with timber from Mount Pelion overlooking the town, was there a flash of understanding. A shipwright there glanced at the drawing and remarked casually, 'Oh! You want to build *Argo!*' just as if I was asking him to build an everyday rowing dinghy. Luckily he spoke some German, and I was able to explain haltingly the details of the galley's construction and size. But when I inquired if he felt that the shipyard could do the job, he explained regretfully that it would be very difficult to obtain the right timber, and that he could not guarantee recruiting enough experienced shipwrights to finish the task on time as it was impossible to calculate the man hours required for such an unusual commission. Like most other traditional Greek shipyards, the bulk of his work consisted of repairing old wooden boats, not building new ones.

Feeling rather downcast, I returned to Athens to see Uncle John. Next day was my last in Greece. I planned to fly to another island where, perhaps, there might be a good shipwright. A gale was blowing next morning, and the flight was cancelled.

'Why don't you try visiting the island of Spetses to see if you can find a suitable man there?' suggested John. 'It's rather a long drive, because all the ferries have been cancelled due to the bad weather. But if you drive to a point on the mainland near Spetses, you should be able to get a water taxi to take you across to the island. It's only a mile offshore. I'll ring up a friend of mine there, and see if he can advise a good man for you to meet.'

Spetses seemed to me the most unlikely spot in all Greece in which to find a traditional boatbuilder. I knew it only by reputation as an island which had been popular since the turn of the century with wealthy Athenians who had built summer homes there. Then came the Greek tourist boom. Spetses had been one of the first islands to receive the deluge of package tours. Judging by other towns I had seen, this could mean an ugly fungus of quick-built concrete hotels and apartment blocks along the beaches, the old harbours pillaged by ferry boats disgorging hordes of trippers, and fishermen who abandoned their nets and made a far more lucrative living by taking tourists for day excursions.

My first impression of Spetses confirmed these fears. As I disembarked from the water taxi onto the jetty of Spetses New Harbour, the ravages of tourism were very evident in bleak late January. The inevitable line of cafés around the harbour was tightly shuttered up for the winter. Through the grimy glass hundreds upon hundreds of tatty metal chairs and tables were seen stacked in sad heaps, their legs sticking up like dead insects. Signs advertising the summer's hamburgers, icecreams, rooms to rent, cocktail bars and boat rides were drab and peeling. Ripped awnings flapped wanly in the gale. Spetses had at least been spared the major blight of concrete hotels, and the town's centre was relatively untouched, though that morning its narrow, twisting streets were devoid of life. There was not a living creature to be seen, apart from a couple of half-starved cats crouching under the battered wooden tables in the tiny fish market. Judging by the thin flanks of the cats, there was precious little fish being gutted that winter on Spetses. The driver of the water taxi had tied up his boat and promptly made off, disappearing to his home in the back streets where the population, apparently exhausted from the trauma of dealing with thousands of tourists in a Babel of languages, eighteen hours a day for seven days a week over the entire summer season, had collapsed in their homes to hibernate. The place felt as if it had been evacuated in advance of a tidal wave.

Turning left, I trudged along the coast road which John had told me would bring me to the Old Harbour where the shipwrights still worked. I was to ask for a man called Vasilis Delimitros who, he had been told, was reputed to be the best shipwright on Spetses. Sure enough, as I approached the Old Harbour I began to hear all the usual sounds of boatbuilding – the distinctive whine of electric planers, intermittent hammering, the buzz of drills and the noise of bandsaws. After the complete emptiness and silence of the New Harbour, it was a shock to turn the corner and find the Old Harbour bustling with activity. The place was full of sound and movement. Shipwrights were energetically at work, muffled up against the cold wind, and small motor scooters rattled along the quayside. Electric cables snaked out of the houses across the road to reach at least fifteen boats in various stages of building. These boats were scattered higgledy-piggledy around the harbour, perhaps on a convenient stretch of road as if it were a casually parked car, or in a front garden, or on a gravel path leading to the rocky beach. One boat carcass was even sticking out of a ground-floor garage under someone's house, with the washing on the balcony above and the other half of the garage advertised as a discotheque. This was by far the largest, most active centre of traditional boatbuilding that I had yet seen in Greece, and it struck me as remarkable that this industry, dying elsewhere, continued to flourish in the very shadow of a major tourist centre.

I got curious looks from the shipwrights as I picked my way over the piles of planks and the electric cables, and asked for directions. One advantage about a tourist island was that plenty of people spoke English. Where, please, would I find Vasilis Delimitros? The curious looks became even more pronounced. Keep walking around the harbour, they said. Vasilis has the last boatshed. I couldn't miss it.

Later I was to learn the reason for those odd looks. Vasilis had a ferocious reputation and was generally considered to be a Tartar. Fiercely independent, he worked alone and hated to be disturbed. One story had it that a summer tourist, watching Vasilis at work on a boat, had asked him three times to explain exactly what he was doing. The first two times he got only a grunt for answer; at the third repetition Vasilis whirled on him, scowled menacingly and dumped his tools in the astonished tourist's hands. 'Here! If you're so interested, do the work yourself!' Vasilis is supposed to have growled as he stalked off without a backward glance. The other shipwrights of the Old Harbour must have wondered what sort of reception I would get from Vasilis in the dead of winter, when he could reasonably have expected to be left undisturbed by pestering strangers.

On the far side of the Old Harbour, by a ledge of rocks, I found a lean-to shed attached to the side of yet another discotheque. There were a couple of half-built small fishing boats, a pile of timber and a short, very busy man dressed in working trousers and a heavy jersey. He was scowling, not at me, but at one of the half-built boats. He was attacking it with an adze, a tool like a hammer crossed with a small axe, as though he hated the vessel. Chips of wood were spinning out in all directions as he chopped viciously at his target. Every so often he would stop, take a step back, cock his head on one side and survey his handiwork. Then he would spring back into the attack, grimacing with concentration. On his head was stuck a curious hat, a grubby grey cone of felt with several oil smudges on it, and for a moment I was irresistibly reminded of Rumpelstiltskin in Grimm's fairy tale. He shot one brisk glance in my direction and then ignored me totally. As I stood there watching him, he continued with his work as if I did not exist. He was proceeding with extraordinary speed and clearly he was doing his work entirely by eye. Even as I looked, I could see the curves of several ribs alter into harmony with one another as he chopped pieces away to the precise shape he wanted. He never hesitated, even for a second, but trimmed the excess timber with a staccato series of blows. Then he would abruptly flip the adze onto his shoulder as he stood off to take another look at the lines of the boat.

After watching this virtuoso performance, I went off to find myself an interpreter, for Uncle John had warned me that it was unlikely that Vasilis, as a shipwright building wooden boats almost exclusively for Greek fishermen, would speak any English. Luckily the discotheque owner was inside his building, and he agreed to translate for me. Together we went back to the shipwright.

'Excuse me, *mestri*,' said my interpreter hesitantly. 'This man would like to talk with you for a few minutes about building a boat.'

With an exaggerated air of politeness Vasilis put down his adze and jerked his head to indicate that we should follow him into his workshed. There he fished a cigarette out of the pocket of his jacket, hanging on the back of the door, offered me a smoke, which was declined, and lit up for himself. '*Libon* – well?' he said. It was the first word that he had uttered.

There followed an extremely brief and to-the-point discussion. My interpreter explained that I was looking for someone to construct a wooden boat.

A very special boat, I interrupted, a historic vessel like nothing that had been built for hundreds of years, a copy of an ancient Greek galley.

Vasilis' expression did not change, nor did he utter a syllable.

'Here's a drawing of the boat,' I offered, 'prepared by a naval architect.' I spread out Colin's elegant design study on Vasilis' workbench among the clutter of whetstones, jars of nails and tools. 'Do you think it is possible to build such a boat nowadays?'

With the patient air of someone who would rather be getting on with his job, Vasilis bent over the drawing and studied it. 'How long is it?'

'About 16 metres.'

No reaction.

'The planks,' I added, 'will have to be joined together in the original ancient way, with hundreds of little tongues of wood fitting them together. This is how the old shipwrights did the work. Is that a problem?'

'No.' A single flat statement.

'How long will it take to build?'

'Is there to be a cabin?'

'No, no. It's just an open boat.'

'An engine?'

'No. It will be driven by oars and a sail, just like the original galleys.'

'Four or maybe five months to build,' said Vasilis flatly.

'It won't be just for show,' I cautioned him. 'I want to make a long voyage with this boat, to sail and row her to the Black Sea, to investigate the story of Jason and the Argonauts.'

Vasilis said nothing. The conversation seemed to have no room for hesitation, rather like his work with an adze. So I put the vital question.

'Can you build it for me?'

'Yes.'

'When can you start work? The boat must be ready for a voyage in the early summer of 1984.'

Vasilis considered this for a moment. 'I will start next October.'

He stubbed out his cigarette, strode out of his shed, picked up his adze, and a moment later the chips were flying. The conversation was at an end.

Later, much later, when the completed galley was on the slipway ready to be launched, a newspaper man came down from Athens to interview Vasilis about the building of the boat. Why had he undertaken to build such an unusual and difficult boat, full of unknown problems and not at all the sort of boat that Vasilis normally constructed? Even to agree to undertake the job must have put at risk his reputation as a master craftsman. Why, then, did he do it?

Vasilis looked at the journalist in his usual direct fashion. 'I did it,' he replied, 'for Greece.'

2
Vasilis

Construction drawings arrived at Spetses from Colin. They showed details of how the galley should be made: the width, thickness and length of every plank and beam; the place and shape of those delightfully named items of wooden boatbuilding – stringers, shelves, keelson, knee and futtock. There was a drawing for the precise curve and cross-section of the scorpion-tail keel, and a little sketch showed how the planks might best be joined together with innumerable little tongues of wood. Colin had also worked out how large the sail should be, and what shape. He calculated that a parallelogram of about 300 square feet, a very modest size, should be enough to drive such a slight vessel at a respectable speed. Colin also attached a thought-provoking calculation for my attention – a diagram which warned me, if I pressed the boat too hard, at what angle she would capsize.

Argo's design was made above all to help the oarsmen as they toiled to propel her through the calms. Another of Colin's neat little illustrations depicted three robot-like men, 'standard men', sitting faithfully in their rowing positions to demonstrate how much room they would have to swing their oar handles without knocking one another off the oar bench. But 'standard men', we had agreed, would be hard to come by. Whoever signed up for such a gruelling trip – and I still couldn't guess who would volunteer for hours of sweating at the oar benches – they were not likely to be 'standard men' in any way.

Colin's meticulous attention to detail was vital to the successful building of the galley, but how was I going to coax Vasilis into following such alien ideas? Sheets of paper from a naval architect's office in England meant nothing to him. Vasilis worked from years of experience, from what he had learned as a time-served apprentice, and from turning out so many of his traditional Greek fishing boats that he knew by heart the size and shape of every piece of timber, and just how it should be placed. Vasilis called no man his master, and he certainly did not work from drawings. Clearly I had to find a way of translating Colin's technical drawings into some sort of guidance that Vasilis would accept and follow, but without compromising his fierce pride as a master shipwright. I hoped that I had the answer – I would get a model made of the galley, a superb, millimetre-precise model, so beautifully built that Vasilis would admire it for its craftsmanship, and then use it as his inspiration. I was gambling on the fact that if Vasilis was as good a shipwright as I had been told, he should be able to look at the small model and, by eye, turn it into a full-size ship.

Tom Vosmer, from the Sindbad Voyage, was a genius at making ship models. When I first met Tom he had been working as a professional modeller, restoring damaged antique ship models. Indeed I had never forgotten his wife, Wendy, joking one day that whenever she tried to clean the living room carpet, the vacuum cleaner choked on bits of tiny brass cannon that had fallen into it. At the end of the Sindbad Voyage Tom and Wendy had gone to live in Australia, where he had started a wooden boatbuilding business. Although he was on the other side of the world, I felt that Tom was just the man to take up the challenge of building a Bronze Age ship in miniature.

The result was all that I had hoped for. Three months later a large, drum-like package arrived from Australia at London Airport for me to collect. Opening the package was like solving a Chinese puzzle. After the lid of the drum came off, a series of written instructions told me to unscrew this clamp, twist that latch, remove another layer of wooden baffle, undo this screw, pull on this handle, until finally out of its nest of padding emerged an exquisite model of the galley, perfect in every detail. Even the small tongues of wood which would one day hold the planks of the main ship together were repeated in the model's structure. Each tongue was buried inside the 3mm thickness of the model's planks, and so could not be seen. Yet, with meticulous care, Tom had put them in. All you could detect from the outside were row upon row of neat little dots, each dot no bigger than the tip of a fine needle, yet each was the head of a tiny wooden pin that locked a hidden tongue in place. As always, Tom had been a perfectionist.

I carried the model with me on my next trip to Greece. When I put the model down on his workbench, Vasilis carefully maintained his normal unconcerned expression. 'That's the way the boat should finally look,' I said, also trying to be offhand. For a moment I thought I saw a flicker of approval as Vasilis glanced at the model. 'I've also done some practical experiments since we last met,' I went on. 'I tried bending a large piece of timber to see if I could get the right curve for the keel of the ship, following Colin Mudie's plans.'

Uncle John's nephew, Andy, was acting as my interpreter. Andy was a keen sailor so was able to translate precisely my description of how, back home in Ireland, I had searched the woods for a 16-metre-long tree of the right diameter, felled it, towed it to the village where I lived, cut off the branches with a hand axe, and laboriously trimmed it to the right cross-section. Then I had soaked the timber in seawater to soften it, rigged up a windlass and heaved it up to the correct curve like bending a giant bow. It had all been rather a time-consuming operation, and I hoped that Vasilis would be suitably impressed by the experiment. But at the end of my long dissertation, Vasilis simply replied with one, short phrase.

'What did he say?' I asked.

Andy looked embarrassed.

'Go on, tell me,' I insisted.

'Vasilis just said "So what?"'

Another reason for my trip to Spetses was to learn from Vasilis where he proposed to find the timber for the galley. Broken fragments of early Mediterranean shipwrecks brought up by divers, as well as land excavations by archaeologists, showed that a popular timber for building both boats and houses had been a type of Mediterranean pine, *Pinus brutia*, commonly known as Aleppo pine. I had asked Vasilis to use exactly the same wood in building the galley, and made the happy discovery that Aleppo pine was still the timber that Vasilis and the other Spetses shipwrights preferred for most of their work. This wood came, I was told, from the island of Samos close to the Turkish coast on the far side of the Aegean. So I went to Samos to track down the timber merchant who sent Vasilis his wood. My idea was to ask if he could take special care in selecting the wood for the galley.

High up in the mountains of Samos, in the sort of isolated and unspoilt village beloved of tourist brochures, with a breathtaking view over the Aegean, I found the timber man at his grocery shop in a street so narrow that only mules and pedestrians could pass. Here Vardikos, the timber dealer, explained that the forest had been exploited for hundreds of years, so now the timber cutters were strictly controlled in the amount of timber they could take. Each man had an annual limit. It was fortunate, he said, that I had come to him early enough so that he could set aside Vasilis' special requirements from his quota. He and his son would search the woods, mark the right trees, fell them during the summer months, drag them down to the road with mules, and from there they would be collected by lorries and ferried to mainland Greece.

As I descended the mountain from the village, I left the main road to walk through the straggling forest where Vardikos cut his wood. I could see what he meant by the scarcity of good timber. Most of the pine trees were pitiful specimens, stunted and twisted. Some of the bent trees might suit the curves for the ribs of the boat, but there was scarcely a tree trunk straight enough to provide a decent length of plank. I wondered just how Vasilis could manage with such poor stuff. He was going to have a very difficult task indeed, but there was no choice. I had already seen the bald slopes of Mount Pelion near Volos where Jason's shipwright, Argus, had cut his timber. Now there was not a full-size tree left. The Greek historian Thucydides had complained as early as the fifth century BC that the forests of Greece had been so stripped to build battle fleets that the shipwrights were obliged to travel to Italy and Asia Minor for their timber. A few last stands of Aleppo pine still grew on Samos and the neighbouring island of Mytilene for traditional Greek boat-building. But I was not at all confident that Vardikos would be able to supply Vasilis with what he wanted.

Two months later, Uncle John telephoned me from Athens with shocking news. Even he sounded distressed. 'Tim, I'm afraid we have some trouble. I've just been watching the evening news programme on television, and they report a huge forest fire on Samos. There are pictures of the forest in flames. Fire fighters are being sent there from all over Greece, even special planes are fighting the fire by dropping water and chemicals. It looks very bad. They say that most of the pine forest has been destroyed and I'm afraid that includes the timber for your boat.' Sick at heart, I hung up. There was nowhere else I could obtain the right sort of timber in the time available. It seemed inevitable that the building of the galley would be delayed by at least a year.

A week afterwards Uncle John rang again. He had been trying repeatedly to speak to Vardikos, but without success. The telephone lines on Samos had either been commandeered by the emergency services or had melted. But with characteristic persistence, John had finally managed to get through. 'Tim,' he told me, 'It's almost incredible. Vardikos was not supposed to send your timber to Vasilis until next month. But for some reason he decided to send it early. The wood for Vasilis left Samos by ferry on the day before the fire started. It was the last shipment of timber to get off the island. Everything else, including the cut timber waiting at the roadsides to be picked up and most of the standing trees, is in ashes. But Vasilis will be able to get started on time.'

Samos was not alone in presenting planning worries. I had written a letter to the President of the Turkish Yachting Federation. Could he, I asked, possibly advise me on the correct way to apply for permission to conduct a seaborne expedition around the coast of his country, often coming ashore at night on remote beaches? Would the authorities have any objection? I explained that I was hoping to take a small boat all the distance from the Aegean, through the Dardanelles, the Sea of Marmara and the Bosphorus, and then into the Black Sea as far as the Turkish-Soviet border. Could the Yachting Federation tell me anything about the conditions we could encounter.

Alpay Cin, the Federation President, was courtesy itself. When I arrived in Istanbul to reconnoitre part of the expedition route, he had already been in touch with the Turkish Navy. The commanding officer of the Naval Academy had lent a motor yacht so that I could see for myself the difficulties of rowing up the Bosphorus.

It was a sobering experience. The admiral's motor yacht needed full power to chug up against the swirling water of the Bosphorus, and a pilot of the Bosphorus pilotage service assured me that cargo ships were often the playthings of the currents. Every year at least one luckless vessel was flung ashore, sometimes with its bows crashing through the first-floor windows of houses built on the bank. The broken-backed hulk of a very large tanker lay stranded at the south entrance to the straits; she had come to grief in the currents. Losing control to the eddies, she had collided with another vessel, caught fire, and then blown up in a huge fireball that people living nearby had mistaken for a nuclear explosion.

On the Black Sea coast of Turkey, Alpay's friends in the Yachting Federation had arranged for me to meet the admiral in command of Turkey's Black Sea ships. I was ushered past crisp sentries in white uniforms, white gloves and red-banded helmets to the admiral's office, which was furnished with over-stuffed chairs in almost Ottoman style. He himself was a genial and splendid figure, the very image of the Grand Turk, his ample chest embellished with rows of decorations and ribbons. He offered me tea in fine porcelain cups, and when I explained my schedule for the expedition he gave a throaty chuckle.

'Well, if you manage to get here next summer, at least you'll be visiting us at the right season,' he said. 'The Black Sea has a bad reputation. The locals say that it has only four safe harbours – Samsun, Trebizond, July and August . . . .' And he threw back his head and gave a massive bellowing laugh that made the teacups rattle.

When I got back home, I encountered another of those happy coincidences that seemed to be part of this voyage. I had not intended to start recruiting a crew until the building of the galley was well advanced. But a letter of application from the first, unwitting, crew member was waiting for me. The writer had recently graduated from my old Oxford college, Keble, and was now taking a course in business administration. But he was bored and wanted a change and wondered if, by any chance, I was organizing another expedition. If so, would I consider including him on the team? He apologized that he had virtually no experience of sailing. His main interest was rowing. He had rowed for the Oxford lightweight crew, had been the Captain of Boats at Keble, and was currently coaching the college crew. Then I noticed what he had studied at Oxford: classical languages. My first volunteer was both a classicist and an oarsman. I wondered if Mark Richards, for that was his name, could even guess what he was letting himself in for. He could have had no inkling that I was planning to go in pursuit of Jason and the Argonauts in a twenty-oared galley.

Colin Mudie had by now almost completed his work. Only one element in the galley's design was still undecided – the precise size and shape of the ram. There are no early references to the ram being used as a battle weapon for puncturing the hulls of enemy ships by ramming them at full speed. Colin suspected that it was originally a device to help a galley move better through the water, like the underwater bulge found on the bows of many modern ships. He had arranged for students at the Southampton College of Higher Education to conduct tank tests of a model galley as part of their studies. I was asked to make up a simple tank test model and to provide a selection of three differently shaped noses that could be stuck on the bows and compared during the tests.

One morning I went down to Southampton to see how the students were getting on. I found them hanging upside down from a moving gantry over the testing tank as they took their class notes on the performance of the canary yellow model, which was being towed up and down the tank with much hissing and whirring of the machinery. To my alarm the instructor started up the mechanism that created artificial waves, and on its next run the little boat bounced up and down in demented fashion. Water splashed aboard in such dollops that it was clear that, in real life, it would certainly founder.

'Don't worry,' said the instructor reassuringly. 'The computer that creates the wave mechanism is programmed to make the sort of waves that would be encountered in the North Sea in a gale. I don't suppose your galley will have to face that sort of challenge.'

The tests confirmed what Colin had suspected: the ram made a marked improvement in the galley's behaviour. She slipped through the water more easily, and the ram flattened the bow wave so that the oarsmen would be rowing in smoother water. Obviously the ancient boatbuilders had a very good grasp of boat design, and Colin decided to increase the final length of the ram by 2 feet. The tank tests also underlined a piece of data I thought best not to reveal prematurely to the oarsmen who would eventually have to row the boat from Greece to the Soviet Union: twenty men of average fitness, rowing away at the sort of pace that they could sustain for several hours at a time, would exert, taken all together, only 2 horsepower. Their combined effort, all the muscle-cracking strain, would produce no more power than the size of the tiny outboard motor that propels the very smallest rubber dinghy. How could my crew be expected to move 8 tons of galley, kit and crew up the Bosphorus against the currents that I had recently witnessed? This was a question I preferred not to contemplate.

True to his promise, Vasilis was ready to start work on the galley in early October. He took me to the small sawmill where Vardikos' logs had been delivered from Samos and were to be cut to approximate size. There, for the first time, I saw Vasilis in action with his fellow craftsmen. When we arrived at the sawmill, the place was not ready for us, despite our appointment. There was no one to be seen, and the big bandsaw blade was broken. Vasilis stormed into the mill and let fly: the saw blade must be replaced forthwith and his logs cut immediately. The mill workers took the tirade like lambs. Vasilis stood there muttering under his breath and glaring until the big bandsaw was whirling round and slicing up the wood. Even then he did not relax. From time to time he scowled at the bandsaw operator, picked over the logs, grumbled that Vardikos had not sent precisely what he wanted. But yes, the timber would do. Then the mill owner was bullied into a promise to deliver the cut planks and beams to Spetses in no more than two days' time. Just after dawn on the second day an ancient truck, piled high with our timber, ground its way along the rough track of Spetses Old Harbour. Beside the lorry, bumping along on his scooter and wearing his cone-shaped felt hat, was Vasilis, like a sheepdog snapping at his flock.

Tom and Wendy Vosmer now arrived from Australia; they had agreed to spend the winter on Spetses, helping with the boat. Tom's job was to act as technical adviser, maintaining historical authenticity in the boatbuilding and performing whatever work the fiercely independent Vasilis would let him do. It was a mission which Tom had to handle with the greatest diplomacy. Vasilis, I had been warned time and again, never liked any other shipwright to touch a single splinter of wood on any of the boats he built. He worked alone, or with a single hand-picked assistant whose main job was to fetch and carry, hold the other end of the plank, tidy up the workshop and generally serve in support of the maestro. This assistant, a friendly young man named Mimas, skippered a charter yacht in the summer and only helped Vasilis in the quiet winter months. Five months' work at a stretch with Vasilis was enough for Mimas. He told us, incidentally, why Vasilis never spoke directly to Dino, a shipwright working on a boat on the roadway just above Vasilis' workshop. Dino was also an excellent craftsman, and he even shared the same bandsaw as Vasilis. The two men worked within 10 yards of each other for eight hours a day, six days a week, all the year round. Yet they never spoke. According to Mimas, Dino and Vasilis had trained together as apprentices, and when they started work as fully fledged shipwrights it seemed natural that they should form a partnership. But one day, for a reason never explained, there was such a blazing row that one of them finished up in hospital and the other in the police station. From that day they had not spoken a word to one another.

Tom was very understanding. Traditional boatbuilders, he assured me, were notoriously independent. They liked to work on their own and follow their idiosyncrasies. He had no wish to interfere with Vasilis' way of working. That was all very well, I thought, but the entire project depended utterly on one man – Vasilis. If he lost interest, or went off at a tangent, or – heaven forbid – fell sick, there was not the slightest chance that the galley would be built on time. It was an alarming prospect, but if anyone could get on with Vasilis it was Tom. He too was a perfectionist, supremely patient, and now he was conscientiously learning Greek in order to be able to converse with the maestro.

We rented an out-of-season apartment in a house on the hillside overlooking Vasilis' workshop in the Old Harbour. Every morning from the balcony of the apartment we could see the unmistakable figure of Vasilis wheeling down the steep road on the other side of the harbour on his way to the boatyard. Behind his scooter scurried an extremely tatty bundle of grey-brown fur which was his mongrel dog, and which we had nicknamed Rags. The figure would bump along the track around the back of the harbour, disappear from view, and then re-emerge almost underneath our balcony. The putt-putt of the scooter would stop, and Vasilis, followed by Rags, would march down the path to his workshop while from under planks, scraps of cloth, old upturned boats and empty paint tins appeared a band of half-wild cats, all heading for the plastic bag that dangled from Vasilis' fingers. That bag was a tell-tale. Vasilis, the fierce, scowling Tartar, had a soft spot. Every day he brought food to the waifs and strays who clustered round his workplace. Even on Sunday, his rest day, he would come down from his home at the back of the town to feed them.

Vasilis decided to build the galley on a stretch of foreshore just behind his workshed. Mimas was set to cleaning up the site, and blocks of wood were installed on which to elevate the galley's slender keel. Now came the first head-on collision between Vasilis' traditional habits and the requirements of the new boat. I asked Vasilis to build the keel with a slight upward bow in the middle of it. The theory was that, when the galley was afloat, the weight of men and stores loaded in the centre would press down amidships and flatten out the curve so that the keel lay straight in the water.

As I feared, Vasilis was appalled. No one ever put a curve in the middle of a keel of a new ship, he told me. That was the sign of an old, weary, badly built ship that was coming to the end of its days. He was so vehement that he marched me round to the other side of the harbour to show me just such an ageing vessel on the slipway. 'There!' he said, pointing at the offending curve, 'Look! That ship is on its last legs. You can see she has only a few years left. How can you possibly want a new boat to look like that, sagging at the ends? Never in my life have I heard of a ship being built with a curved keel. It's a crazy idea!'

For the fourth or fifth time Tom and I patiently explained the theory behind the bent keel, and fortunately Vasilis was in a sunny mood. After two hours of argument he suddenly threw up his hands. 'All right. I'll do it. But it's your idea. Not mine.' For comic relief, he pantomimed despair. Putting his head in his arms, he pretended to burst into tears.

A couple of weeks later, when the bowed keel of the future galley was in position on its blocks, with its hump glaringly obvious for all to see, two old men were gazing down on the boat from the roadway and remarked on its bizarre, crooked shape. But by now Vasilis had decided to make a virtue out of the unorthodox structure. 'Can't you tell how excellent it is?' he announced to them with a grand sweep of his arm. 'It's just the way it should be.'

Vardikos had failed to find a piece of wood long enough to make the keel in a single piece, so we had to assemble it from several lengths. The massive centre body of the ram was also made up from smaller pieces pegged to a well-curved section of tree root that gave the basic shape. When all was ready, we gathered round to heave the keel and ram beak onto the building blocks. As soon as the long keel was in place, Vasilis scurried up and down each side, hammering in place a phenomenal number of struts and crossbraces, all intended to stop the timber from warping out of true. This precaution was essential, he explained gruffly, because fresh-cut Aleppo pine twists and bends as it seasons. Unless the keel was trussed up immobile, it would lose its shape, and then it would be impossible to build the boat.

Why didn't he use seasoned timber? I asked. Because seasoned timber was not available at short notice, and fresh-cut pine was better for most jobs because it was more supple. There, I realized, was the practical solution to one of the problems that had bothered historians. They had puzzled over how the Greeks in classical times had managed to replace their damaged fleets so quickly after major battle losses. Some authorities supposed that vast stocks of spare timber were kept in the ancient shipyards, ready to build new ships. If so, how had the ancient shipmasters been able to calculate their future needs? The answer to the problem had been provided by our Spetsiot shipwright: the ancient boatbuilders almost certainly did not use seasoned wood. Like Vasilis, they used fresh green timber, cut as needed and preferred because of its suppleness. The shipwright's skill, whether ancient or modern, was in knowing exactly how each piece of wood was likely to behave as it dried out, how much it would shrink and twist and bend; and then to take this into account as he built his vessel.

Our next step departed from the custom of the ancient shipwrights. They built the hulls of their vessels by attaching planks upward from the keel, like an eggshell, and then dropping in the ribs afterwards. Tom, however, now prepared curved pieces of timber to act as guidelines for Vasilis in shaping the hull. Later, when the hull was at a satisfactory stage, some of these moulds would be thrown away, while others would become ribs for the galley. Tom and I had agreed that this method was sensible. Vasilis was having to cope with producing a shape of boat that was entirely new to him. It was too much to expect him also to learn an entirely fresh work sequence, particularly with planks that warped and twisted so erratically. What mattered was to get the finished hull to the shape that Colin had specified.

In the late afternoon of the day on which we finally put the keel and the first few moulds in position, I stayed behind at the boatyard after the others had left. I wanted to get some feel of the character of the new vessel. For the first time there was enough of the structure in position for me to appreciate what a 3000-year-old galley was going to be like. Standing on the foreshore, looking along the bare bones of the skeleton of the boat, I was struck by how fragile she seemed. The pieces of timber had felt solid enough when we were manhandling them into position. But now, seen in proportion, the backbone of the ship seemed so delicate as to be incapable of supporting its length without snapping in half. I was reminded of the skeleton of a crocodile seen in a natural history museum. The head and massive jaw, like the boat's prow and jutting ram, had seemed too heavy to be sustained by the long, slender backbone.

Vasilis did not seem at all worried, at least not to outward appearances. Every morning he would arrive at work, feed the cats, brew up a tiny cup of coffee on woodshavings, and go to work in his inimitable fashion. Neither Mimas nor Tom nor I nor John Egan, who had arrived to take photographs and serve as a general handyman, had the least inkling of what was included in any day's

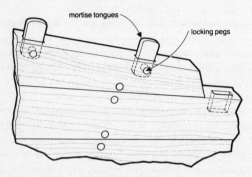

Mortise and tenon joints for hull planks

schedule. There was absolutely no way of knowing what Vasilis would do next; he was totally unpredictable. One moment he would be chopping away with his adze on the shape of the ram; the next moment he would be altering the position or selecting the curve of a plank; or he would suddenly announce that he was going off to the far side of the island to scour the hillside for live oak bushes whose branches he used to make trenails, the wooden pegs for pinning together the structure. Vasilis never gave advance notice of his plans, and he never explained the point of what he was doing. He simply got on with the job to his own rhythm and with his own techniques. Thus Tom and I were utterly baffled when, instead of starting with the first plank near the keel, Vasilis began by putting in what is normally the last plank, right at the top of the hull near the deckline. Then, equally abruptly, he went back down to the keel, and put that plank in place. Tom and I naturally expected that he would next install the matching plank on the opposite side of the boat – not a bit of it. Vasilis put another plank above the first one, on the same side.

'I don't believe it,' Tom said wonderingly. 'I think he's going to plank up one full side of the boat before he even begins the opposite side. He must have terrific confidence that he can get both sides to match. It's the damnedest way I ever saw a boat being made.'

Vasilis promptly turned another theory on its head. Scholars had written at great length about the difficulty of rediscovering the ancient method of joining ships' planks together by the technique known as the mortise-and-tenon method. It was a lost art among boatbuilders, and therefore the experts said it would be exceedingly awkward to recreate. The edge of each plank had to be cut with a series of small pocket-like slots, the mortises. Flat tongues of wood – the tenons – were set in these slots, so that each tongue protruded. When the next plank was put in place, it also had matching slots along its edge, and the projecting tenons fitted into them. Wooden pins then had to be driven at right-angles into the ends of each tongue, locking them in place. It was a very laborious, but extremely strong, way of joining the planks of a ship together to form a single interlocked hull. According to the scholars, hours of experiment would be needed to relearn the technique, calculating the spot where each slot would have to be precut in the edge of each plank, and judging the correct angle and size for the tenon. We were told that it would be such a time-consuming method that it would take two years to build the boat. Vasilis simply scoffed at the idea that it was difficult. Tom made a full-size mock-up of a mortise-and-tenon joint and showed it to him. The shipwright gave his characteristic dismissive shrug. 'That's no problem,' he said. 'I'll prepare the two planks as usual, make the slots and tongues of wood, put the planks together and – tock! tock! tock! –' he gestured like a man swinging a mallet, 'I'll fit them together.'

He was absolutely right. The first plank was joined to the keel with mortises and tenons as quickly and smoothly as if Vasilis had been doing the work all his life. Thereafter each plank was slid into place with equal ease. The only concession was a purely mechanical one. The early shipwrights had worked with large gangs of assistants, often serfs, to cut out the hundreds and hundreds of mortise slots with chisels. But Vasilis was building the hull virtually single-handed, so we found a simple machine to do the same job, and a young English carpentry teacher, Tim Richards, took a break from school to come out to Spetses to help. Tim operated the machine and prepared the tongues of beechwood for Vasilis. Of course the maestro refused to accept any help with the hull. That work, as Vasilis always insisted, was his responsibility alone. He would do it his way and according to his firmly held convictions.

Some of his methods were truly dramatic. He had just finished one side of the hull and it looked splendid – a beautiful, glowing expanse of pale yellow wood dotted with the heads of the wooden pins locking the tenons, a real piece of art. Passers-by would stop to admire the smooth sweep of the timber, the delicate lines of the plank seams, and the sheen of the wood. Then, without warning, Vasilis appeared, dragging behind him a large gas bottle and a blowtorch. With a flourish he lit the torch and turned the roaring tongue of flame on the hull. For a moment it seemed that he had gone mad and was about to burn the boat to cinders. But no – just as the planks began to char and smoulder under the belching flame, Vasilis began waving the blowtorch like a paintbrush. Suddenly it became apparent what he was doing: he was using the flame to dry out a series of holes into which he wanted to drive more wooden pegs. If the wood was dry, the pegs would hold better. This was his drastic method of drying out the timber, and when he was finished the beautiful hull looked as if it had been used for fire-fighting practice.

Then one day Tom and I were in the apartment during our lunch break when we heard shouts and yells from the boatyard. Running to the balcony, we looked down and saw what seemed to have been an accident. The boat was no longer sitting on its keel blocks, but had fallen over on its side and was lying canted on the ground. I imagined all sorts of mishaps – someone crushed beneath the falling hull, the planks cracking on impact. Tom dashed off frantically to the boatyard, then reappeared and ran up the path to the house.

'I've come to collect my camera,' he panted. 'You'd better come and see what Vasilis has done.'

'What's happened?' I asked him. 'Why's the boat lying on its side?'

'That's what I want to take a photo of,' Tom replied. 'Vasilis obviously decided that he's done enough work on the starboard side and it was time to begin planking the port side. Without warning anyone, he removed the props from one side of the boat, called Mimas and Tim, gave a shove and rolled the half-built hull over, leaving them to catch it! He shook his head. 'I just hope nothing's broken!'

I never got used to Vasilis' blithe habit of rolling the galley from side to side like a mahout getting his elephant to turn over while washing it in a river, but this was not my only anxiety. I was very concerned whether the expedition would be given permission to travel all the way to its legendary goal – the ancient land of Colchis where Jason had sought the Golden Fleece, and which is now the Soviet Socialist Republic of Georgia at the far eastern end of the Black Sea. For advice I had gone to Lord Killanin, former President of the International Olympic Committee, in which capacity he had excellent contacts with all manner of world leaders. He immediately put me in touch with the Russian Minister of Sport, who made an intriguing suggestion: the man in the Soviet Union most likely to be interested in my proposed expedition was a well-known medical doctor and television personality, Yuri Senkevich.

The name was familiar to me. Senkevich had sailed as ship's doctor with the Norwegian explorer and anthropologist Thor Heyerdahl aboard his raft replicas *Ra* and *Tigris*. Besides his medical work, Yuri was now the compere of a very popular travel programme on Soviet television. Through the Cultural Department of the Soviet Embassy in London I wrote to him, asking if he could help with my application for the Argonaut expedition to come to Georgia. My letter vanished into the official channels, and for month after month I heard nothing. Time and again I visited the Embassy. The Soviet cultural attaché was charming and polite, but no, he had no reply. I must wait. There was no way in which I could delay the project; I simply had to go ahead, build the boat, select the crew and hope that all would be well. Then I was unexpectedly telephoned by the London correspondent of a leading Soviet newspaper.

'Mr Severin? May I come to interview you?' he asked. 'I want to ask you about your new expedition.' I was puzzled, as I had not yet announced it.

'Yes, of course,' I replied. 'But tell me, how is it that you are interested?'

'My editor in Moscow has been in touch with me to interview you about the voyage in search of the Golden Fleece. Yuri Senkevich spoke about your expedition on his television programme, and said that Soviet TV will be covering your arrival in Georgia.'

Two days later, official confirmation came from the Embassy.

My expedition would be welcome in Soviet Georgia. The Soviet authorities would do all they could to assist, including the provision of extra crew members when we got there. It seemed that the quest for the Golden Fleece had international approval.

By late March Vasilis had almost finished planking up the second, port, side of the galley. Tom was pushing ahead with all the fittings for the boat. He was a first-grade craftsman, and while Vasilis plunged on with the hull – muttering imprecations under his breath which I suspected were directed in equal parts at Colin and at Vardikos – Tom worked on the inside of the boat. He set in thwarts and mast step, shaped the mast and yard from trunks of cypress trees, and carved the blades of the two 12-foot-high steering oars that would guide the boat. He was also an accomplished rigger, and in Athens we had located a supply of hemp rope which Tom spliced, seized and stitched to make the stays, sheets and halyards which now lay ready in tarry-smelling bundles. Whenever fine work was needed, Tom was always on hand to chisel and saw, plane and sand. To top off the sweep of the stern piece he hand-carved a curling tail ornament.

Everything seemed to be perfect. There was only one doubting voice. Up the hill on the roadside, Vasilis' old rival Dino watched the galley take shape and grow. 'That boat's not going to be any good,' he was heard to say. 'It's far too long and too narrow. No wonder the history books are full of stories of the old ships that were wrecked and fell apart. This will be another of them.'

Tim Richards had to return home to take up schoolteaching again, leaving us a legacy of a dozen pulleys for the ship's ropes. He had made them by hand – each pulley a copy of the classical blocks found on Mediterranean shipwrecks, with wooden wheels running on wooden pins. His replacement was a man I had met only once before, and then just for half an hour's conversation. Peter Wheeler had also written to volunteer as a sailor on the expedition, but when he came to see me he was most diffident about his qualifications. Yes, he could sail a bit. What about carpentry or metalwork? His letter had mentioned that he was an engineer. Oh well, he replied cautiously, he could do a few odd jobs around the house – nothing professional, only at handyman's level, mind you. This modesty, I was to learn, was one of Peter's trademarks. He was in fact a very adept carpenter, engineer and designer, the ideal man for looking after the galley's fixtures and fittings while at sea. He could repair a smashed rudder using bits of scrap plank, redesign the tip of the ram, coax any piece of machinery into operating, and always with the minimum of fuss.

Soon after he arrived in Spetses we were all having breakfast in the apartment when someone mentioned that Peter had been out earlier in the morning, at dawn.

Peter Wheeler

'Do you go jogging?' I asked.

'Er, yes,' answered Peter quietly.

'How far did you go?'

'To the other side of the island, I suppose.'

There was a pause, while the rest of us tried to work out how far it was to the opposite side of Spetses. It was perhaps 10 kilometres.

'Do you ever go in for long-distance running, marathons and that sort of thing?'

'Umm . . . yes.'

'When was the last time you ran a marathon?'

'The day before I came to Spetses.'

Silence around the breakfast table.

With the galley nearly completed, the moment had come to register her official existence with the Greek authorities. There was never any doubt what we should name her. From the very first sketch on the drawing board, we had simply referred to her as *Argo*. It seemed obvious to name her in honour of her predecessor, which Apollonius had said was 'the finest vessel to have braved the sea

51

with oars'. Unfortunately, as I soon discovered, it is easier to name a boat in Greece than actually to get permission to sail her in Greek waters. There were a host of government regulations to observe – official measurements, marine surveys, safety requirements and inspections, documents and so forth. In fact I was soon of the opinion that Greek bureaucracy believed in imposing as many and as tortuous regulations as could be devised, just for the sheer pleasure of then inventing even more ingenious ways of getting round the problems they had created. It was like a very clever man playing chess against himself.

The authorities began by treating *Argo* as if she were a small Greek-built cargo ship being launched. She would not be allowed to sail unless she complied with certain government regulations. For example she had to be surveyed by a marine surveyor and declared to meet established construction standards for vessels of her class. In vain I pointed out that there were no established building standards, as far as I was aware, for late Bronze Age galleys. How many watertight bulkheads were there? None – she was an open boat. Then she could not proceed to sea. Did the vessel have reserves of buoyancy, and were the deck and wheelhouse sufficiently strong to withstand a boarding sea? It made no impression to point out that a deck was not historically authentic, and that the helmsman would stand exposed to the elements. Poor *Argo* failed the test on nearly every count – no buoyancy, no structural survey, no crew accommodation, no radio installation, etc. etc. It was even demanded that *Argo* should have a built-in fire-fighting system for suppressing a fire in the engine room. Unfortunately there was not even an engine.

Clearly this was a case for Uncle John to solve, and he contacted his circle of friends. Advice came in from the Hellenic Registry of Shipping, from naval architects, from senior officers in the Port Police, from lawyers and finally from the office of the Minister of Mercantile Marine itself. To general satisfaction a sharp-eyed advocate spotted a special sub-clause in a minor paragraph in the international treaty drawn up by the International Maritime Convention for the safety of ships at sea. The sub-clause made a special exemption from the jungle of rules and regulations for any boat that was an 'experimental vessel'. Obviously *Argo* had to be classified as an 'experimental vessel'. John arranged a meeting with the Minister himself; the Minister scribbled his signature, the magic wand had been waved. *Argo* was now, with official approval, a special case, and we had a unique embossed and hand-written certificate to prove it. She was, according to the parchment, 'an experimental ship of primitive build'. And instead of fire-fighting apparatus, radios, deck officers with sea-going certificates, union-approved crew berths and kitchen space, I was allowed to proceed to sea provided only that I promised to have on board enough lifejackets and liferafts for all my crew, a bosun, a doctor and a rowing master.

A week before the launch of the new *Argo*, an event so odd happened that I was forcibly reminded of something that Apollonius Rhodius had written about Jason's boat. He had said that the first *Argo* carried a very special piece of timber in her prow – a bough cut from a sacred oak at the holy shrine of Dodona. This timber was some sort of lucky talisman, a charm, and according to Apollonius it gave the boat the power of speech. At special moments, for example on the day she set out from Iolcos on her epic voyage to Colchis, the first *Argo* had cried out in a human voice.

On 21 March the new *Argo* lay slantwise on the slope where she had been built. Apart from a few details, she was ready to be launched. Her underbody had been painted with a coat of black pitch mixed with evil-smelling gobbets of rancid mutton fat to make her slip easily down the skids. Vasilis and Mimas had constructed a stout wooden cradle underneath the boat so that she could be manoeuvred into the correct position for launch down the slipway. They had already turned her from her original position lying parallel to the sea, so that she was poised almost at right-angles to the water. It had been a tricky operation, and halfway through it Vasilis called a halt. The four or five people hauling the various lines that controlled the boat moved back and sat down to rest. *Argo* lay on her cradle on the slipway, quite alone. There was no one within 5 yards of her. All was still. And at that moment *Argo* 'spoke'. Quite clearly and distinctly she gave a deep, slow, human-sounding groan. It was utterly eerie.

For a moment I thought I was imagining it. The sound was a long drawn-out mutter, the sort of noise a man might make sighing in his sleep, but in this case it went on far longer, for maybe as much as fifteen seconds. Then it stopped. There was a brief pause, then the long, slow cry began again. I was so startled that I glanced around to see if someone was playing a joke. But the others apparently had heard nothing. Perhaps the sound could only be heard from where I was, about 10 yards away and to one side of the boat. But someone else had heard *Argo* groan – Vasilis. He stiffened bolt upright and cocked his head on one side to listen. Then he walked over to the hull and stalked along it, like a gundog searching out a hidden woodcock. The noise was softly repeated, as if the boat was grumbling to itself. Vasilis whipped out a carpenter's pencil from his pocket and held the tip of it very lightly against *Argo*'s hull. He stepped swiftly to another position and repeated the touch. Then he located the point. *Argo* was shifting ever so slightly in her cradle, and the greased planks were drawing across the supporting timber to produce the human groan. With the palm of his hand Vasilis gently nudged home a wedge. The groan stopped. *Argo* fell silent, but a shiver had run down my spine.

When the first *Argo* was launched, according to Apollonius the Argonauts dug a trench in the beach wide enough to carry the boat down to the sea. They laid wooden rollers in the trench; the oars were swung inboard and fastened so that their handles projected outwards as grips; and the Argonauts stood on each side ready to heave. Tiphys, the helmsman,

> leaped on board to tell the young men when to push. He gave the order with a mighty shout, and they put their backs into it at once. At the first heave they shifted her from where she lay; then strained forward with their feet to keep her on the move. And move she did. Between the two files of hustling, shouting men, Pelion Argo ran swiftly down. The rollers, chafed by the sturdy keel, groaned and reacted to the weight by putting up a pall of smoke Thus she slid into the sea, and would have run still farther, had they not stood by and checked her with hawsers.

The new *Argo*'s launch was scarcely less spectacular. By some special favour the launch took place on the first sunny day of spring. Across on the mainland, just a mile away, lowering thunderclouds were releasing torrential rain, but the Old Harbour of Spetses sparkled in crisp, bright sunshine. Hoists of signal flags fluttered; on *Argo* flew the flags of all the countries she would visit and the nationalities of her crew; a large crowd had gathered, islanders, visitors down for the day from Athens, friends of the project.

Vasilis was in his cleanest, best-pressed jeans, trying to look nonchalant, but he radiated satisfaction. He had said he could build the boat; he had staked his reputation on it. Now *Argo* lay on the slipway, glowing in her new livery – red, blue and white paint copied from the colours found on Mycenaean wall frescoes.

The Greek Orthodox priest of the village had come to bless her. He was a tall, theatrical, handsome figure in his long-skirted black robe, embroidered neckband, luxuriant beard and high black hat. He conducted the blessing with great panache. A table had been erected in front of *Argo*'s ram, for she was being launched stern-first. A cloth was draped over the table to turn it into an altar on which stood a bowl of holy water, an olivewood cross, a censer and a sprig of olive leaves. After the priest had intoned the prayers, he dipped the sprig of olive leaves in the water and advanced majestically on *Argo*. He flicked holy water on the staring 'eyes' above the ram, and then marched firmly up the gangplank to step along the boat from thwart to thwart with his robe hitched up, and spraying holy water over ship and spectators.

When the priest had descended from the boat, Vasilis stepped out from the front rank of the crowd. In his hand he had his *skipani*, the little adze he had used day after day in the building of *Argo*. He walked over to the galley, and with six quick strokes he cut three crosses in a line on the tip of the ram. Then he bent and kissed the marks. It was his personal benediction for the boat. Then he waved to the crowd to stand back, warning them that it was dangerous to remain on the slipway when *Argo* began to move. At that instant, in a remarkable gesture, there suddenly appeared from the crowd the dozen leading shipwrights of Spetses. I found it very touching that these men, who normally worked with such proud independence, should now offer to work directly under Vasilis' orders; it was a tremendous compliment to his achievement. Each shipwright carried a stout wooden stave to help lever the boat along her path in case she faltered. They ranged themselves in two lines, on each side of the slipway. Then they turned towards Vasilis as he stood proudly near the bow of the galley, and awaited his instructions. He crouched down to sight along the line of the keel, waved one man forward and gestured to him to make a minute adjustment with his stave, to inch *Argo* straighter on the slipway by a hairsbreadth.

Then Vasilis gave an order. Four shipwrights swung sledge-hammers and knocked clear the main retaining chocks. When only one chock was left to hold *Argo* back, Vasilis strode forward with a mallet and swung it three times. On the third stroke the chock spun clear and *Argo* began to slide. The two lines of shipwrights encouraged the movement with their staves, and with increasing speed the galley rushed down the slope. The onlookers burst into applause as she plunged into the harbour with a splash, and floated clear of her cradle, pirouetting and bobbing.

Argo looked fabulous, swimming exactly on her painted waterline, the first galley of her type to be launched for perhaps 1500 years. The crowd was cheering. Vasilis stood there, arms akimbo, gazing proudly at his handiwork. Beside me Tom, who had worked so hard to perfect the ship, had tears in his eyes. 'My God,' he said, 'she's beautiful. She's so beautiful she makes me want to cry.'

3
Jason's Kingdom

On the day of *Argo*'s jubilant launch Mark Richards, the rowing master, arrived on Spetses with the first contingent of the volunteer oarsmen he had brought along to test the brand-new galley. Just after the daily ferry from Piraeus docked, a dozen young men appeared, striding purposefully along the quay of the Old Harbour. In the lead was Mark, his shaven head concealed beneath the sort of straw hat worn by English vicars at summer fêtes. He was dressed in a faded tee-shirt, dark blue rowing shorts whose seat was mended with a towelling mat bearing the name of a well-known beer, and broken-down tennis shoes. In each hand he hefted an enormous package. To avoid air freight charges I had asked the trials crew to bring out large quantities of ship's gear, and Mark was bounding forward with great, muscular strides as if on some athletic training mission that involved carrying heavy objects over long distances at top speed. Behind came his rowers, all looking extremely fit, all with packages, and all wearing rowing shorts. A dozen pairs of white, untanned legs betrayed their recent arrival. They looked like a small platoon of soldier ants on the march.

They were all members, or former members, of the Boat Club from Keble College, Oxford, and had offered to come to Greece for their Easter vacation to put *Argo* through her paces. Next day they were joined by a second batch of college rowers, including two girls, and such was the enthusiasm of the Keble Boat Club that the college cox – whose name was Jason – limped in on crutches. He had recently broken his leg in a motorcycle accident, but was determined not to miss the fun. They were wonderful company, full of good humour and energy, and by the time they left Spetses

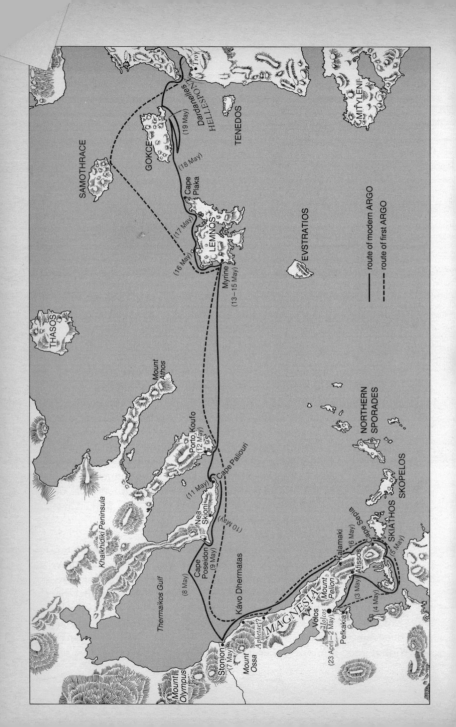

two weeks later they had worked out the best way of rowing the boat, and succeeded in getting *Argo* up to the very respectable speed of 6 knots. On their penultimate day they rowed the galley right around the island before lunch. After they left, I found a tiny copy of the college coat of arms, embroidered by one of the girls, stitched in the corner of *Argo*'s new sail.

During the last few days of rowing trials, a delivery crew had been forming. These were the men who would take *Argo* from Spetses north to the port of Volos, the starting point for her main voyage in the wake of Jason and the Argonauts. Again, the delivery crew was composed of volunteers. Some, like Tim Readman and Peter Moran, would be members of the regular crew; but others were men who had only a couple of weeks' holiday to spare from their regular jobs, and so came to help on *Argo*'s delivery trip. They were to have a gruelling, uncomfortable fortnight because the spring weather was still cold and blustery, but *Argo* had to arrive in Volos right at the opening of the sailing season proper, with time in hand in case we needed to make last-minute adjustments before setting out on the 1500-mile voyage to the Soviet Union.

The Spetsiots gave *Argo* a farewell party. It was held in the main square near the New Harbour, the same place that had looked so bleak and deserted when I first arrived there two years before. Now the square was thronged with islanders. Young men and women from the high school dressed in antique Greek costume took part in traditional dances. The mayor made a speech, and everyone cheered Vasilis, who was looking very uncomfortable in a blue suit, collar and tie, though Evgenia, his young daughter, was clearly delighted that her father was such a hero. As the evening light faded, the young men lined the stone steps of the harbour and held aloft burning red flares while *Argo*, with the flag of Spetses at her bow, rowed out. A dove of peace was released from the crowd. The bird flew out over the heads of the oarsmen, ducked through the smoke from the flares, turned in the air and was gone.

Next morning was our last on the island, and Vasilis made his poignant and personal farewell. He came putt-putting on his scooter down to his boatyard where *Argo* was taking on the last of her stores. As always, the cats of his boatyard ran out to greet him, but this time Vasilis ignored them. He walked straight down to the little wooden jetty where *Argo* lay moored. He was carrying a small bouquet of island flowers that he had gathered that morning, and in his other hand he held his *skipani*, his adze. Clambering aboard *Argo* without a word, he hammered two nails into the curling stern piece, and on them hung his *skipani* and the bouquet of flowers.

'Keep the *skipani* with *Argo*,' he told me. 'It is the tool that built the boat, and will bring her good luck. Remember that she is a boat built in Spetses, and if you ever need help with her, please call on me. She's the best I've built.' With Evgenia holding his hand, Vasilis stood on the jetty waving farewell as we rowed out from the Old Harbour to take *Argo* to Volos, and the start of her quest for the Golden Fleece.

The ruins of Mycenae lie four hours' drive to the northwest of Spetses. The site has given its name to the most spectacular civilization of mainland Greece during the Bronze Age, and its citadel still merits its choice as the symbol of Mycenaean culture. It crowns its hill with an imposing array of massive walls; flights of steps lead up to the great palace; and a ring of standing stones fences the shaft graves where half a dozen of the kings of Mycenae were buried with so much bullion among their grave goods that archaeologists are prepared to accept Homer's epithet of 'Mycenae rich in gold'. Mycenae's glowing reputation is unlikely to fade. The famous Lion Gate, claimed as the first piece of monumental sculpture in Europe, must be one of the most photographed subjects in Greece. Homer's verse has spun a web of immortality around King Agamemnon. The gold mask of an earlier Mycenaean lord, whom the archaeologist Schliemann thought was Agamemnon himself when he retrieved it from a shaft grave, stares through empty eye sockets at every turn – from wall posters, from postcards, from the cover of the National Museum catalogue. Less well known is the tale that Hercules was standing in the market square of Mycenae when he first heard the news that Jason was recruiting men to go on the quest for the Golden Fleece. According to the story, Hercules promptly broke off his series of Labours to volunteer. He had just completed his fourth Labour, the capture of the Erymanthian boar, and was standing with the live animal, foaming at the tusks, draped across his shoulders. As soon as he heard the news, he dumped the enraged beast on the flagstones before the astonished citizenry, and set off for Volos where the Argonauts were assembling.

The Greeks, from Homer onwards, looked back on the

Mycenaean Age as a time for such deeds of high endeavour, and this Camelot quality of the Mycenaean civilization is still its most endearing feature. Indeed life must have been very dashing and agreeable for the kinglets and their ladies who ruled the palaces and citadels that were then scattered across Greece. Wall paintings by their court artists show them hunting for wild game, parading in their chariots with hunting dogs, looking like sleek borzois. Occasionally they are shown going off to the more deadly business of war, while the ladies (or perhaps their priestesses) wave farewell and good fortune. In our museums are Mycenaean gold signet rings by the dozen, exquisite bronze daggers inlaid with scenes of boar hunting, tall-stemmed and elegant drinking goblets, and body jewellery. Of course, somewhere at the base of all this luxury and formality toiled the imponderable mass of slaves or serfs or bondsmen who gave the structure its foundation. But between them and the lordly rulers spread a whole trellis of craftsmen and artisans, who supported the more gorgeous aristocratic blooms. There were excellent potters, gem cutters, tailors and skilled armourers, not counting the whole host of more prosaic occupations that gave employment – stewards, huntsmen, chefs, gardeners, house servants and so forth. And also – we have the Linear B tablets to prove it – each palace had its staff of scribes and clerks, counting in this, checking out that, keeping the ledgers, paying the staff their wages of corn and oil. It was a society on a smaller and less imperial scale than that of Egypt or of the great kings of the Hittites in Anatolia, but it was without doubt cultivated, vibrant and possessed a great sense of style.

In this world Prince Jason grew up. He was, so it is said in every version of the legend, a member of the ruling family of Iolcos, a rich city – now called Volos – to the northeast. Iolcos was not quite as grand as Mycenae, nor as martial as gloomy Tiryns with its immense granite castle brooding over the coastal plain like a suspicious pugilist awaiting a slight. Iolcos seems to have been more mercantile-minded, more prosperous and more subtle. Its closest equivalent would have been Pylos, where King Nestor held his court. Neither city saw the need to build a colossal defensive wall, though both were very rich prizes for any invader.

We know now that the thirteenth century BC, the time of the Argonaut epic, was to end with the swift decline of Mycenaean glory. But it was not a twilight era – quite the opposite. Mycenaean society seems to have been more active, more luxurious, than ever before – even a touch frenetic. Recent discoveries have revealed that Mycenaeans had launched themselves overseas and settled pockets of the Aegean coast of Anatolia, on the western marches of the great Hittite empire. The clay tablets of the Hittite official archives report a strange people who must have been the overseas Mycenaeans. They appear as a flamboyant race given to martial display, driving up and down in chariots and issuing challenges to single combat. Enterprising Mycenaeans with less soldierly tendencies were sending their trade goods to Egypt, Italy and far up the Danube. And finally, of course, the ambitious war leaders of all those petty kingdoms and scattered fiefs were sufficiently imaginative to launch the first major amphibious assault in history – a thousand ships, it was claimed, to fall on Troy.

The tumbled ruins and the artefacts turned up by the archaeologists flesh out the tale – the typical Mycenaean palace had its central courtyard with an audience throne for the lord, and side apartments with baths and plumbing, store rooms and guest chambers. The court ladies enjoyed their trinket boxes, fashionable hairstyles, ivory combs from Africa, cosmetics and perfumes. But what they thought, what they believed in, is much less clear. Their religious notions, so important to the Jason story, have been smothered under the later Greek pantheon. Apollonius writes of

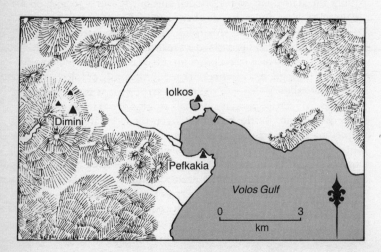

Hera, Poseidon, Apollo, Cupid and the other Olympians who take a hand in Jason's affairs. But, as far as we can tell, these gods did not exist in the thirteenth century BC, or at least not in that form. We can guess that the Mycenaeans believed in an afterlife, for they buried many of their leaders in magnificent beehive tombs. Lords, chiefs and clans probably also had their totems, for we see men grotesquely masked, and women dancing in some holy rite, apparently worshipping the old, mostly animistic, gods. They held sacred the spirits of certain holy places – springs of water and groves of trees in particular – and they seem to have achieved a special reverence for the Great Earth Goddess. Her female shape appears in a number of clay ritual figurines, all-present, all-supreme. Later Greeks were to identify her with Rhea, the mother of Zeus, and she was to reappear in a number of other guises as Dindymene, Demeter and Cybele, all goddesses associated with the earth, with the natural cycle of life, the seasons and nature. She was to have a role, too, in the Jason story.

When we arrived at Volos at the start of our voyage, Vasiliki Adrimi, the curator of the Volos Museum, had something very important to show me. Vasiliki was an archaeologist, and she took me 4 kilometres west of Volos to the top of a low hill surrounded by a crown of cypress trees. The summit of the hill was criss-crossed by low stone walls dating back to the late Stone Age when Dimini, the name of the site, had been one of the first planned towns in European history. But this was not what Vasiliki wanted to show me. Cut into the side of the hill was a passageway, lined with dressed stone, which led straight to a massive stone arch, its lintel a single block of stone 6 feet broad and 4 feet wide. Anyone who had ever seen the Lion Gate of Mycenae would recognize that arch at once: it was the entrance to a Mycenaean burial chamber. Through the arch was the tomb itself, a beehive-shaped hollow scooped out of the heart of the hill, and lined with beautifully engineered blocks of stone. Vasiliki explained that the tomb had been discovered when the roof fell in and a cow had dropped through the hole. Archaeologists had at once recognized it as a Mycenaean tomb, and although the grave inside had been robbed of all but a few meagre pieces of pottery they had no hesitation in pronouncing it to be the burial place of a Mycenaean king who died in the late Bronze Age.

'This was odd,' Vasiliki went on. 'If this was the grave of a king, why wasn't he buried inside the royal city of Iolcos, where we have found other royal graves? Why was he buried out here, at a distance, and inside this hill? Then three years ago a local farmer applied to the archaeological authorities to plough up a field at the foot of this hill. He had to have our permission, because the area surrounding this hill had been declared an archaeologically protected site. So, just to make sure, we excavated the field first, to check that there was nothing important buried there. We had thought that perhaps we might find some more Stone Age remains, connected with the settlement on top of the hill. Imagine our astonishment when we found a small and well-planned Mycenaean town site! No one had expected it. Why should another Mycenaean town have been built so close to the big city of Iolcos? There was no precedent for such a thing. Again, it was difficult to explain.'

Vasiliki walked with me through groves of almond trees to see the walls of this Mycenaean town that she and her colleagues had discovered. They still had not completed their investigations, but one thing was clear: this was a very well thought-out township. You could see where the main street ran, and how the Mycenaean town houses had lined the main thoroughfare. Each house was of typical Mycenaean plan, with three rooms, used for living, sleeping and storage. In the floor of one house the owner had dug a hole to sink a large earthen jar which had been his larder. Vasiliki explained that the town showed all the signs of having been a deliberate foundation, a sort of satellite town to Iolcos, and apparently related to the main city. However it had clearly been a much less prosperous settlement than the metropolis. Everything the archaeologists had found by way of household goods, and that was very little, had been modest and utilitarian.

'And then we noticed two things which were equally strange,' Vasiliki told me. 'First, the town had only been inhabited for a very short period, a century or less. It was built, lived in and then abandoned. And this led to the second puzzle – why did the people leave? They were not driven out by attack or earthquake or fire. We found no trace of these catastrophes. Instead, the people just seem to have cleaned out their homes tidily, and left in an orderly fashion. What made them move out? Where did they go?'

Vasiliki looked at me, and I could sense the fascination of the archaeologist for the detective work of history, seeking to explain past events from a handful of clues.

'You've probably guessed the most obvious explanation. This

site could be connected with the story of Jason and the search for the Golden Fleece. The time when this town was built, occupied and left is the time when the voyage of the Argonauts is said to have taken place. In the legend we are told that Jason's father was dispossessed of the throne of Iolcos by his half-brother King Pelias. Perhaps Aeson, Jason's father, came here with those people still loyal to him, and founded this town outside the city walls. This may be where Jason spent his childhood. The legend says that when Jason returned from the quest for the Fleece, having fulfilled the ordeal, he took back the throne of Iolcos from King Pelias. And that might be when the people of this place evacuated their town, packed up all their belongings, and moved back into Iolcos, following the new king. That is why these Mycenaean houses have been so neatly tidied up by their original owners. And if this is the case, then there is a very good chance that the tomb we visited on the hill was the burial place of King Aeson, Jason's father.'

This was a wonderful boost to the quest for the truth behind the Jason legend. Here, on a hill in his own country, the archaeological data seemed to suggest that the beginning and the end of the ancient legend was true.

According to the legend, Jason had gone on the voyage to win the Fleece, in order to win back the throne of Iolcos, which was his by right, but had been usurped by his step-uncle King Pelias. The latter must have been a terrifying figure. It was said he had been abandoned soon after birth by his mother, a Mycenaean princess who was being victimized by a jealous stepmother. She left the baby in a field, and the infant was found by a group of horse herders after one of their horses stumbled on the baby. Its hoof injured the child's face so that Pelias, who was raised by the horse herders, grew up with a vivid facial scar. After he learned his true parentage, Pelias tracked down the unpleasant stepmother, chased her into the temple of Hera and killed her as she clung to the altar. This crime grossly violated the sanctuary of the temple, and according to Greek notions of divine retribution was to be the reason for his own violent death, which was to be engineered by Jason's wife at the instigation of the vengeful Hera.

Pelias' mother had eventually married the king of Iolcos, and Pelias succeeded in dispossessing Aeson, the rightful heir. He let Aeson live, but as a private citizen. When Jason was born, his parents feared that Pelias would consider the royal child a threat and have him put to death. They announced that the baby had been born dead, and smuggled him out to the countryside where he was brought up, like several of the other ancient heroes, by the wise centaur Cheiron on the slopes of Mount Pelion.

On the day that he was old enough to claim his inheritance, the young man set out to walk to the city of Iolcos. On the way there he came to a ford across the stream called Anavros. There he found an old woman waiting to cross the stream, which was in spate. Though he was in a hurry, Jason stopped to help her. He picked up the old woman, who was the goddess Hera in disguise, and carried her across to the other bank. In doing so, Jason lost one of his sandals, which he left stuck in the mud of the stream bed. Thus, when he appeared in the marketplace of Iolcos he was wearing only one sandal, and this immediately reminded King Pelias, when he first set eyes upon the strange young man, that an oracle had warned him that he would be destroyed by a man who came to him 'with one foot bare'.

Seeking to escape his fate, runs the legend, King Pelias put to Jason the ambushed question: What would he do if he came face to face with the man who, according to a prophecy, would destroy him?

'I would send him to seek the Golden Fleece,' replied the naïve youth.

'So be it,' replied King Pelias.

An alternative version of the tale merely says that Jason revealed his identity to the king and demanded the throne of Iolcos by right, and that, without demur, King Pelias agreed to relinquish the crown provided that Jason proved his worth to Iolcos by bringing back the Golden Fleece. In both versions the task was considered to be suicidal.

The Fleece was of particular significance to Jason's family, the Aeolids, whose clan badge was a ram. Indeed one is left with the strong impression that the Fleece was some sort of sacred cult object which they held in veneration. Its history stemmed back two generations, when there had been a succession of bad harvests in the Boeotian city of Orchomenus, ruled by King Athamas, another Aeolid. Athamas believed that the gods were angry with the city and had to be appeased. The real reason was that Athamas' new wife, Ino, had devised a plot to rid herself of her stepchildren, Prince Phrixus and Princess Helle. Queen Ino had secretly persuaded the woman of Orchomenus to roast the grain seeds before planting them, thereby killing the grain and destroying any prospect of a harvest. Then she arranged that the Delphic Oracle, when consulted for a solution to the famine, should advise King Athamas to sacrifice his two oldest children to allay the curse. Prince Phrixus and Princess Helle had been led to the sacrificial altar when a ram with a golden fleece appeared and told the children to climb on its back. Then the ram flew away eastward. As it passed over the strait dividing Asia and Europe, Princess Helle lost her grip on the wool, slipped off, fell into the strait and was drowned. The strait was thenceforth named the Hellespont in her memory. Phrixus, after a halt on the Black Sea coast of Anatolia, was eventually carried to the far end of the Black Sea, to the kingdom of Colchis, where he was well received by its king, Aeetes. He settled there, married one of the king's daughters, and eventually died in Colchis. At its own request, the ram was sacrificed and its fleece hung in a sacred oak tree.

Possibly the story of the flying ram was a vivid retelling of the escape of the royal children by some other means, perhaps aboard a Mycenaean ship trading eastward, but that is conjecture. As far as the Argonaut legend is concerned, the important point is that the people of Iolcos knew at once what the Golden Fleece was, and where Jason would have to go to fetch it back. All the onlookers, and especially King Pelias, did not expect to see Jason alive again.

Vasiliki, the archaeologist, had another clue to give me. 'When we began to consider the implications of this Mycenaean town,' she told me, 'it was recalled that at the end of the last century, when the first excavations were made on the top of the Dimini hill, the archaeologists – who were interested really in the Stone Age levels – noted in their field books that they cut through some ancient walls resting on top of the Stone Age town. These walls, we now believe, were the remains of a small Mycenaean palace or manor house which stood on top of the hill. That could have been Jason's home. Indeed, now there is this evidence to support the theory, the town council of Volos has been asked to change the name of the stream which runs between Dimini and the town of Volos. This would have been the stream which Jason crossed on his way to meet King Pelias for the first time, the place where he lost his sandal in the mud. It has been suggested that the stream should again be called Anavros.'

From the top of the low hill I could see south to the great sweep of the Bay of Volos, steel-blue in the spring sunshine. To the right a line of hills fell away to a small headland. On the headland a clump of green pine trees gave the place its name – Pefkakia, the place of the pines. Here *Argo* now waited, hauled out on the beach to undergo last-minute adjustments before the start of the voyage to Colchis. Pefkakia, I believed, was the most likely spot for Argos to have built the original *Argo* and it would have been the galley port for Iolcos in Jason's day. The conditions were exactly right: a

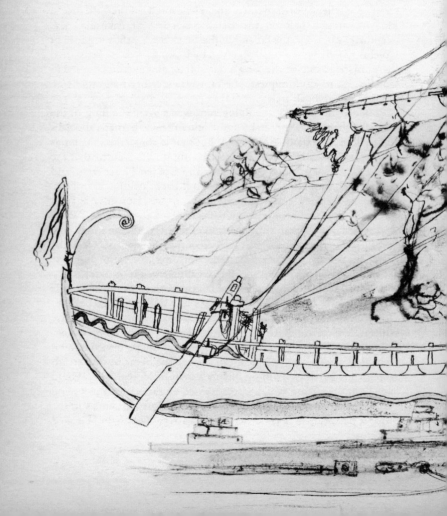

sheltered anchorage, a spring of good drinking water nearby, and a smooth and gentle shelving beach for hauling out the galleys. Just the previous day I had watched a northerly squall rush down on the bay like a dervish off the slopes of Mount Pelion. The squall had struck the shipping in the modern harbour, whipped spray off the surface of the sea, rocked the big ships and sent the smaller fishing

Slipway at Peſkakia

boats scurrying for shelter. The place they all ran for was Pefkakia, with its calm lee and good holding for the anchor. What was suitable for a small boat today would have been equally suitable 3000 years ago. And sure enough, not 50 metres from the modern *Argo* on the beach of Pefkakia rose another mound. Here German archaeologists, digging ten years earlier, had cut away the sandy loam and exposed the walls and foundations of a third Mycenaean settlement.

Peter Wheeler was busy on Pefkakia's beach, adapting the tip of *Argo*'s ram. During her delivery voyage from Spetses we had learned that the ram was an ideal platform for all sorts of functions. If one went for a swim, it was the easiest place to climb back on board. For washing or relieving oneself, it formed a platform with running seawater on both sides. This also explained the strange-looking line of pegs which stuck out of the bow timber on several early Greek boat illustrations. The purpose of these pegs, like tiny horns, had puzzled commentators, but I asked Tom to hammer them in place anyhow, supposing that we would find out their function sooner or later. In fact Vasilis knew what they were the moment he saw them. He called them the *scalita*, the little ladder, and that is just how we used them: as a series of hand- and footholds for someone clambering back aboard the boat from the tip of the ram. However, scrambling from the water onto the tip of the ram itself was still a clumsy business, so Peter had decided to install a convenient handhold which a swimmer could grab at the very tip of the ram and then use to swing himself up. When Peter finished, what he had achieved was immediately obvious. His new handhold had turned up the tip of *Argo*'s nose like a boar's snout, and this was exactly how many of the early Greek artists drew their ships.

Trondur, who had joined during the delivery trip, decided that it was time to improve the 'eyes' of *Argo*. At the moment they looked altogether too innocent and naïve, as well as being slightly crossed. He redesigned them, adding a touch of menace, and gave them the sort of aggressive glare more fitting to a warship about to set out on a voyage to bring back the Golden Fleece from a hostile kingdom.

The new Argonauts were now arriving in Volos. Nick, our doctor, showed up, as imperturbable as ever, and big Peter Dobbs – the two Sindbad veterans. Matching Peter in size was Miles Clark, on leave from the British Army, who soon revealed a well-honed talent as a mimic and humorist, with a vast fund of stories that kept everyone laughing. Peter Moran, the cook, explained to Tom why he needed a set of removable deck planks to provide extra storage room for his baskets and boxes of food. A generous supply of *Argo*-brand wine had been supplied by the city fathers of Volos, and there was scarcely any space to stow the gift.

Modern Volos has honoured the memory of the Argonaut epic. The main street of the town is called the Street of the Argonauts; a fine bronze model of Jason's *Argo* stands near the modern quayside; and several tavernas are named after Iolcos' most famous vessel. Now Volos provided a volunteer for the crew – Elias, a local architect who was very eager to join us, even though it was the first time that he had ever been in a small boat. My idea was that, while *Argo* was in Greek waters, I wanted as many Greeks as possible to join the crew, just as I would try to have Turks aboard when we got to Turkey, and hopefully we would find Soviet crewmen when we got to Georgia. It was, I felt, an important part of the project that each country should have its representatives on board, and participate directly in the adventure.

With Elias were two more of his countrymen – big Theodore, who was an electrical engineer by trade, and stocky, white-haired Costas. In April Costas had telephoned me to ask if I would consider him for the trip. He was, he said, a very experienced sailor and owned his own yacht. He lived in Athens and had done much cruising in the Aegean. He sounded ideal, and his English was superb. I was just about to invite him outright to join the crew, when he paused and tactfully said: 'There's only one thing which may be a problem – that's my age. I'm sixty years old.' I gulped. A sixty-year-old galley oarsman? I didn't want anyone having a heart attack from rowing for hour after hour in the heat, so I suggested to Costas that he should join the crew while we were delivering the boat to Volos from Spetses. If he found the going too tough, he could gracefully retire. As matters turned out, Costas was a gem. He was absolutely determined not to give up. For the first few days he suffered agonies of exhaustion, and in the evenings could be seen trembling with fatigue. But his spirit was indomitable. He was such a cheerful, plucky individual that he was tremendously popular with the rest of the crew.

'I wish my company could see me now,' he told me happily. 'Until last year I was chief pilot for Olympic Airways, and I had to retire because the company has a maximum flying age of sixty!'

Our two film-makers also joined us at Pefkakia. They were to make an onboard documentary film of the voyage, and came half-submerged by the inevitable heap of bright aluminium boxes, film stock, cameras, tripods and all the paraphernalia of their trade. Dick Hill was the cameraman, an urbane figure who had the knack, alone of all the crew, of being able to keep a set of clean clothes even under the thwarts of a cramped Mycenaean galley. Whenever Dick went ashore, he managed to present himself immaculately attired in well-pressed light-coloured trousers without a mark on them, and a silk shirt with the ironing creases still in it. His colleague, Dave Brinicombe, was at the opposite pole. He was the sound recordist, and the space under his thwart was an amazing jumble of electronic gear in which he would rummage like a badger. He never cared how he dressed, and he much preferred to go barefoot. His unkempt, bushy beard adorned a cheerful, snub-nosed face, and as he padded happily up and down the central gangway of the boat, with his feet splayed out and a distinctly prehensile curl to his toes, it was Miles who at once saw the resemblance to Stone Age man and gave him the nickname that was to stick – Dave the Cave, a sobriquet which the sound recordist accepted with a large and cheerful grin.

The day of departure was set as 3 May. By early morning the crowds were beginning to assemble by the boat at Pefkakia. The local schoolchildren had been given a holiday to see the galley set out, and already there was a good throng of them gathered on a viewing point on the hillside above the galley. '*Kalo taxidi! Kalo taxidi!* Good journey!' they chanted in unison, and waved excitedly to the Argonauts who were stuffing kitbags under thwarts, greasing the leather strops that held the oars to their thole pins, and joking about the voyage.

'I've calculated that we may have to do 1.5 million oar strokes per man before the end of the voyage,' announced Mark Richards to the crew, evidently relishing his role as rowing master.

'Oh no, I hope not. Let's pray for a wind,' groaned Tim Readman, the ship's purser. 'I'm so unfit.'

'Don't worry. When we get hungry and run out of food, we'll eat you first,' retorted Peter Dobbs. It was a long-standing tease from the Sindbad Voyage that Tim Readman would be the tastiest meal.

'Ten minutes to go!' I called out, and gave a tap on the brass ship's bell that hung by the tiller bar. Tom and Wendy had come to say goodbye. Tom was looking rather wistful at not being able to stay with *Argo*, but had to get back to work as a boatbuilder. Vasiliki, the archaeologist, was there too; so were Uncle John and his family; Borgne, Trondur's wife, had brought Brandur, their small son, to the jetty to say goodbye, and he was looking distinctly overawed by the press of people.

Then it was time to pour a libation to the gods, a gift of wine to request fair winds and calm seas. I dug out a bottle of Argo wine. Nothing less than an entire bottle would satisfy Poseidon that day. No one seemed to have packed a corkscrew, so I reached for the priest, the wooden club we used for knocking in loose thole pins. Holding the bottle over the stern, I smashed off the neck. The wine shot out in a tremendous spurt and a great cheer of appreciation came back from the crowd. Another double tap on the ship's bell, and someone was casting off the stern line.

'*Kalo taxidi! Kalo taxidi!*' called the children on the bluff. Trondur was in the bows, quickly hauling in the dripping anchor line hand over hand. In a moment the anchor came aboard.

'Anchor clear!'

'Come forward!' I called, and the oarsmen leaned forward to the ready position. 'Medium pressure. Are you ready? Go!' The oar blades dipped in the water and began to move in unison. The oarsmen took up the steady rhythm. *Argo* began to glide across the water.

'One million, four hundred and ninety-nine thousand, nine hundred and ninety-nine strokes to go,' muttered Miles. Gingerly I turned *Argo* on course. The twin steering oars worked in opposite directions. One tiller bar had to be pushed forward, and the other pulled back to make the boat turn. It felt very odd, but *Argo* responded obediently.

It was a good day to start an expedition – no wind and a light veil of high cloud to block the worst of the sun. All around us were dozens of small fishing boats, chugging with their engines at dead slow. Ahead was the Volos pilot boat, ready to clear *Argo*'s path and lead her for the first few hundred yards. Light racing shells of the Volos Rowing Club skimmed around and beside us like water beetles. Dip, pull; recover the blade; swing forward; dip and pull again. The steady repetition of the galley's oar stroke seemed

ponderous beside the modern racing shells. Up ahead I could see the
end of Volos' modern concrete jetty. Standing there were the local
dignitaries – the mayor, the army commander, the senior port
officer and the Greek bishop in his robes. As *Argo* passed, the mayor
raised high an olive branch and tossed it into the water.

'Go in peace! *Kalo taxidi*, good voyage!'

Now we were rounding the tip of the jetty, steering to pass the
main waterfront of the town as close as possible to the land. The
quay was packed with people, mostly children brought by the
coachload to witness the departure of a boat from their country's
distant past. '*Kalo taxidi! Kalo taxidi! Kalo taxidi!*' The children were
roaring the chant in a steady rhythm, like a crowd of football
supporters. The new Argonauts waved back, rowing with one
hand and waving with the other. A racing four came slicing past us.
In the bow position was an oarsman as splendidly shining bald as
Mark. 'You two must go to the same hairdresser,' Miles remarked.

According to Apollonius Rhodius, the departure of the Argonauts 3000 years earlier had been rather more fraught. There had
been rumours that King Pelias had bribed Argos, the boatbuilder,
to sabotage the boat by making her with weak fastenings, so that
she would break up and sink during the voyage. But presumably
Argos had no intention of such treachery, because he himself had
decided to be a member of Jason's crew. On the evening before their
departure, following tearful farewells with their families, Jason's
volunteers gathered on the beach. Jason sent for two oxen to be
driven down to the shore from the family herds. Hercules and the
mighty Ancaeus killed the beasts, one with a single blow from his
legendary club, the other chopping through the animal's neck with
a bronze axe. The sacred morsels from the thighs were wrapped in
fat and burned ceremonially on the flames of an olivewood fire laid
on an altar of shingle. This sacrifice was to Apollo, the God of
Departures. Idmon, one of the two seers on the crew, peered at the
dancing flames and watched the spiral of smoke rising to the sky.
He pronounced the omens good, but added gloomily that he
himself did not expect to return alive from the expedition. His
destiny had been revealed to him, he said. He would die in some
lonely spot on the Asian shore.

The rest of the evening was not much more of a success. Idas, the
braggart member of the crew, got drunk on too much undiluted
wine and began to mock Jason, who was sitting apart from the rest,

having last-minute doubts about the wisdom of the expedition. When rebuked by Idmon, Idas abused him too, and the quarrel would have led to blows but for the tactful intervention of Orpheus the musician, who struck up a tune on his lyre and embarked on a long song about the creation of the gods. That night the crew slept on the beach, and in the morning it was Tiphys, the crack helmsman, who roused them from their sleep and got them started in good time. They already knew their oar bench positions, every man having drawn lots for them the previous day. Only Hercules and Ancaeus were excluded from the lottery. The two biggest and strongest men in the boat, they were automatically allocated the central bench, where their greater strength would be of most effect.

Aboard our modern *Argo* we had made a similar decision: Mark and Miles were our best oarsmen, each man having rowed for his university, and it was natural that they should occupy the stroke position, the sternmost bench, where all the other crew members could watch them and try to copy their style and timing. We did not have a full crew of twenty aboard – there were only fourteen men that day; and what with one man to steer and one to cook it left only twelve oars in action. But it was enough. The trick was to keep the galley moving steadily through the water at all times, nibbling away the miles at about 3–3.5 knots. So sleek was *Argo*'s design that she slid steadily along at this pace even when there were only ten men at the oars. This allowed two of the crew to rest for a five-minute interval, and when their break was over they changed places with two others who could then take their turn to relax. Thus *Argo* did not loose momentum, but kept plodding along, south-southeast across the Bay of Volos towards the little town of Afissos.

Afissos was said, in one tradition, to have been the first stopping point for Jason and his men on their journey. The reason, according to this version of the legend, was that *Argo* herself refused to carry Hercules' massive weight. The ship's magic speaking bough had groaned aloud when the huge Hero first stepped aboard, and she soon insisted that he had to be put ashore as she was not prepared to carry his bulk any farther. As a result, the people of Afissos are still said to be taller than other villagers in the district because they are descended from the mighty Hercules. Certainly there was a Mycenaean settlement at Afissos in the late Bronze Age – pieces of Mycenaean pottery have been picked up near the beach – but the real reason for *Argo*'s halt may be rather more mundane. Bubbling down to the shore at Afissos runs a fine spring of excellent drinking water. Today it has been channelled and captured so that it supplies the taps in the central square, but as we filled two earthen amphorae for the new *Argo* we could hear the water rushing under the paving stones. It was entirely logical that Jason would have put in here to water his ship before going on the first stages of the long voyage. Logically, too, any crew members who might have been rethinking their commitment to the expedition could have taken this chance to jump ship and make for home – including Hercules, though, as we shall see, in most versions of the legend he remained on board until the Argonauts reached the Sea of Marmara.

There were no runaways from modern *Argo*'s crew. The 15 miles from Pefkakia to Afissos was a very convenient first day's run – far enough to stretch the muscles but not too far to exhaust the crew. As we came ashore, we found Uncle John ahead of us. He had driven round the bay to meet us, and naturally he had a friend in the area. This friend had a vineyard, and Uncle John was brandishing a plastic jerry can of home-made wine. Beside him stood the schoolteacher of Afissos with two little girls clutching bouquets of roses – '*Kalo taxidi*,' they intoned solemnly as they handed over the flowers. Our journey had begun.

Mycenaean ram's head ornament

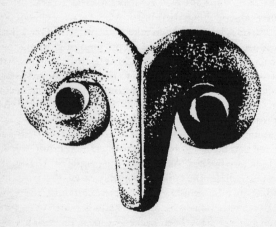

4

Across the Aegean Sea

The Lord of Departures must have heeded the Argonauts' sacrifice, for Jason and his men had the benefit of a heaven-sent wind for the first days of their quest. Scarcely had they left the beach before a fair wind arose and they were able to hoist sail. 'They stepped the tall mast in its box,' wrote Apollonius, 'and fixed it with four stays drawn tight on either bow; then hauled the sail up to the mast head and unfurled it. The shrill wind filled it out; and after making the halyards fast on deck, each round its wooden pin, they sailed on at their ease. . . .'

The twentieth-century Argonauts had no such luck. Our first three days of the voyage were made either in absolute windless calm, or against awkward gusting breezes which scuttled round the headlands and ambushed the labouring galley. Turn and turn about, the crew had to slog on, rowing *Argo* forward across an expanse of unrelenting sea, like men trudging across the desert. The first blisters appeared within an hour, blisters which were not to heal until the voyage ended. The oarsmen had expected the blisters, and each had his own theory about the best remedy or prevention. Some rubbed the palms of their hands with alcohol, others wore cotton gloves or wrapped a protective towel around the oar handle. But it was little use. Nothing cured the problem. Blisters formed, swelled, broke, reformed, broke and hardened. Then, just as the hands seemed toughened, the first exposure to seawater would soften the callouses, and the dead skin peeled away to leave raw patches which were painful to the touch. If, by great care, the blisters were kept dry after they burst, they simply split again under the constant abrasion of rowing, and then another blister swelled beneath the first.

Gradually the crew began to mould together, learning to row as a unit. Mark went up and down the central gangway coaching the novices. He showed them the best way to time their stroke, how to relax the body during the swing forward and how to control the oar blade as it moved through the water. But rowing a twenty-oar galley was very different from rowing a light river-racing shell. The galley's oars were heavier and more unwieldy, and there was no chance to use the leg muscles fully. Rowing *Argo* was largely a question of swinging the weight of the body, pivoting forward and back, forward and back, hour after hour, until repetition dulled the senses. By common agreement, the rowing stroke was kept short. The worst crime of all was to swing too far forward with the oar handle at the beginning of a stroke, and a trifle too late. When that happened, the man in front could be struck in the middle of his back with an oar handle and its 7lb lead counterweight as he leaned into

his next stroke with his full weight. It was like being hit with a sledge hammer, and in those first, less expert, days it was not unusual for oarsmen to come off the benches with telltale black stripes of lead scored between their shoulder blades.

Yet our slow progress had its compensations. On the second evening we found an idyllic mooring on a small island tucked just inside the mouth of the Bay of Volos. The cove where we anchored was enchanting. Rows of olive trees grew on the hillside above us; the ground was covered with wild flowers; a small stone jetty provided easy access to the small beach. A dozen bottles of Argo wine were quickly plunged up to their necks in the water to cool, and Peter Moran prepared a barbecue. As he cooked, a small fishing boat came nosing into the bay, its crew curious to inspect the galley. They presented us with fresh shrimps to add to our supper.

Island mooring at the entrance to the Bay of Volos

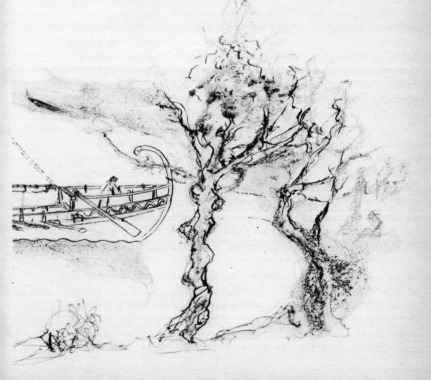

It was the time of the spring festival, and down from the hillside above us came a grandfather, a grizzled veteran leading his two grandchildren by the hand. He had retired to a tiny whitewashed cottage above the point, from where he could look across to the mainland. His grandchildren had seen *Argo* arriving, and had been gathering wild flowers for us. Now they brought their offering – an intricately woven wreath of leaves and bright flowers which we hoisted to *Argo*'s masthead as a symbol of May. The old man searched around inside the cuddy of his own small fishing skiff and handed across a great white ball of mutton fat from his own sheep. He had seen us greasing the leather oar strops on *Argo*, and made this simple and practical gesture. It was one of those small deeds, little acts of kindness, which linger. A thousand miles farther on, along the far north coast of Anatolia, we would still be using smears of that mutton fat, and each time I would recall the old man as he sat with us that evening beside the embers of the camp fire, quietly chatting with the Greek crew members.

Next morning we rowed out of the Gulf of Volos and into the Aegean Sea. Our course lay coastwise, hugging the rim of the fishhook shape of the Magnesian peninsula. Again there was scarcely a breath of wind, and by midday the heat was decidedly oppressive. Sweat poured off the men's bodies, forming damp patches on the oar benches and staining the seats of their trousers. It was easy to understand why the classical Greeks often rowed naked, for this must have reduced the risk of boils and skin rashes which came from sitting in sweat-soaked clothes. Peter Dobbs donned an Arab headcloth, a relic of the Sindbad Voyage, and a variegated assortment of hats and headgear came into use to prevent the sweat from pouring into the rowers' eyes, where it was actually painful.

When the wind did come, it was from the wrong direction, a light breeze out of the east which strengthened in the evening so that the crew had to struggle hard to row *Argo* to a safe anchorage by dusk. That headwind was a sobering experience. Ten men pulling steadily could drive *Argo* forward at 3–4 knots, moving her between 20 and 30 miles a day by muscle power. But it had to be in calm conditions. The merest whisper of a headwind, a scarcely perceptible breeze blowing against the prow of the boat, cut down her speed alarmingly. It was not just like walking uphill, but like walking uphill through shifting sand. Every stroke forward was eroded by the boat trying to slither back. Few occupations are more disheartening than trying to row a boat under such conditions, struggling under oars against a contrary wind, losing half a yard for every yard made good. *Argo*'s rowers had every reason to grow discouraged.

Worse still, if the headwind arose when *Argo* was between anchorages, the helmsman found himself left with only two choices, both of them bad. Either he turned back at once and sought shelter downwind, so losing all the precious ground that the crew had accomplished with such sweat-stained effort, or he had to ask the crew to battle on, watching them grow increasingly weary and hungry, hoping to claw forward those last few miles to the next safe anchorage ahead. There was always a painful balance between the crew's reserves of strength and enthusiasm, and the counterforce of the wind. One never knew how long the ordeal would endure, whether the wind would stealthily increase in proportion to the ebbing strength of the crew, whether the sea state would deteriorate so that the crew could no long row effectively in the rising waves, or – worst of all – whether finally the wind would prove too much, and after a couple of hours of gallant effort you would have to put the helm over and abandon the struggle, throw it all away and run downwind to port.

The truth of the matter was that moving a twenty-oared galley into a headwind by oars was a futile exercise in nine cases out of ten. Galleys were not designed to operate in adverse weather, and this was a caution that I had to bear in mind for the entire voyage. It affected every decision whether to push on or turn back. In two of the three seas we were to sail, the Aegean and the Marmara, the weather is notorious for the speed in which it can change from calm to gale. In the third, the Black Sea, there is more warning from the sky and swell when bad weather is on its way, but the adverse conditions can last longer. And to a wind-driven galley a lee shore is murder.

Cape Sepia, which our *Argo* passed on the fourth day, was vivid proof of such a danger. In 480 BC almost an entire fleet, sent by Xerxes to invade Greece, had been smashed here in a single storm. The armada, galleys and transports, was caught by an unexpected gale after the captains had rashly anchored on the nearby coast. More than 400 ships were lost when their anchors failed to hold and the vessels were blown down onto Cape Sepia, presumably with their crews trying desperately to get out their oars and dig their blades into the water and heave their ships into the channel running past the cliffs. As the raging waves on the base of the cliffs grew closer, the galley captains must have tried again and again to cast anchor and hold their vessels off the land. But the water was too deep. Their anchor stones failed to hold and the ships were shattered, with appalling loss of life. *Argo* must have passed over the bones of those galleys as she too rowed past those deadly cliffs, not 50 metres from the wall of rock, with the swell growling and booming in the sea caves. It was impossible not to invoke the memory of all those early shipwrecks, and to remind oneself that any rock-bound coast was the finish for an early ship caught in an onshore gale. No small galley was strong enough to row herself out of trouble, and if the water was too deep to anchor then your ship was lost, and probably the crew with her.

We had negotiated the Cape and turned north, still hugging the shore, when we ran into the first strong wind of the voyage. It came out of the north, a headwind straight down the coast, and I immediately sought temporary anchorage in a little bay called Paltsi, where the fishermen pulled their small boats well up the beach and even had sets of wooden rails to drag them clear of the worst storms, since by no stretch of the imagination could Paltsi be considered a safe anchorage for a modern boat. For *Argo* under these conditions, however, it was shelter enough. Her draught was so shallow, less than 3 feet, that we could lay out two anchors to seaward, run a long line ashore to keep her stern square to the beach, and warp her into the shallows in the very back of the bay to find a degree of shelter. A deep-keel yacht would have had to abandon the bay and put out to sea, but *Argo* clung on, pitching and swooping within 10 yards of the shore, the waves breaking just under the upsweep of her stern as a gull would settle on the water and ride close to rocks and backwash.

As for the crew, they were learning that for a galley crew patience was just as important as physical strength and stamina. The only safe way to sail a Bronze Age ship is to wait until the weather turns fair. Sooner or later, we all knew, *Argo* was sure to be caught offshore in bad weather; that was a crisis that would be dealt with at the time, and the last thing I wanted during the first week of the voyage was to risk the morale of the crew with a useless battering. For the remainder of that day and well into the night we stayed where we were in Paltsi Bay, just as hundreds of galleys must surely have done in the millennia before us, all waiting for a change in the weather before dashing out along the rock-bound coast of Magnesia. Jason and his Argonauts had known the same delay, and along the same treacherous coast. For two and a half days they had been forced to lay up at a place called Aphetae, waiting for a break in the weather. Aphetae's exact location is impossible to identify, because Apollonius does not give enough details, but probably it lay father north than Paltsi, perhaps near the mouth of the Pinios River.

When the wind does turn, a galley must seize her chance to move. So just after midnight, when the north wind eased, it was time to rouse the crew. They came aboard half-drenched. Nearly everyone had chosen to sleep on the beach, rather than on the pitching, anchored boat, so there was much scurrying and shouting and shaking to wake the shore party. In the darkness they had to wade out through the breaking waves to come aboard, toss their sleeping bags and rucksacks on the stern deck and climb half-naked and shivering to take up their rowing positions. Typically, Peter Dobbs volunteered to stay ashore and cast off the stern line as the galley rowed out, so he came last of all, towed into the bay by the stern warp like a drogue.

For an hour or so it was heavy going. Although there was no wind, there was still a choppy sea, and in the dark it was difficult to row steadily. The boat went lurching this way and that; oars were tossed about like spillikins; the men cursed; and poor Theodore hung over the side, heaving with seasickness. But dawn rewarded the effort. A breeze moved in from the south, with the sun, and we could set sail at last. It was the first time that *Argo* had spread her canvas since leaving Volos.

Her rig was another thing that had not been seen on a Mediterranean ship for many centuries. *Argo*'s sail plan and rigging had been derived from the details shown on sixth- to fourth-century BC painted vases that showed galleys under sail. The sail itself was a rectangle of cotton, hung from the cypresswood yard. On the forward side of the sail were sewn eighty-one bronze rings. Through these rings passed nine light ropes which led from the foot of the sail, up through a line of nine rings, and then over the crossyard and back down to the helmsman standing in the stern of the ship. By pulling on these lines, the helmsman and his assistant could gather up the sail to the yard like hoisting a window blind. It was a straightforward and effective, if somewhat cumbersome, method of handling *Argo*'s cotton sail. At times one felt rather like a charioteer in the stadium trying to cope with nine recalcitrant horses and a mass of reins that threatened to tangle themselves in knots. However, with Notus the south wind astern, *Argo* spent all that day skimming over the waves in Jason's wake like a ship out of a dream. Under full sail she behaved superbly. The hull cleaved through the blue sea, and with the merest touch on the two steering bars *Argo* responded like a well-schooled thoroughbred. She turned as deftly as one could wish, and a second touch on the tillers to bring them level brought her back on course, running sweetly forward. Sitting wedged against the rail in the very stern of the ship, under the curling tail ornament, one could feel the ship quiver as she sped downwind, her keel and planks thrumming as she rolled to the following seas while her ram threw aside a cresting bow wave.

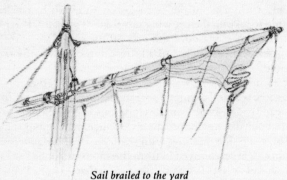

Sail brailed to the yard

That day's run up the wild coast of Magnesia was a delight. For hour after hour *Argo* forged along at 5–6 knots, leaving a clean wake behind her, while the crew relaxed on the benches, their oars hauled inboard out of the way. There was nothing for them to do but sit and relax and enjoy the passing scenery. The mountains marched with the coast, starting with the snow-sprinkled peak of Mount Pelion on whose slopes the centaur Cheiron is said to have educated so many generations of Heroes, including Jason. Then came the massif above Kalamaki with a spectacular waterfall plunging off its flank in a white plume. Finally Mount Ossa rose in view, and behind it the approaches to Mount Olympus, home of the gods.

Along the whole of this rock-bound coast was not a single safe harbour, and in less than eleven hours that blessed wind sped *Argo* 50 miles past all its dangers, while her crew could look up and see high on the mountains the clusters of white-painted houses of the famous Pelion mountain villages, as if a giant had tossed a handful of sugar crystals against the greenery.

On board our spirits soared. The bleary-eyed oarsmen of dawn were now cracking jokes, sunbathing, listening to their portable cassette recorders, relaxing. Tim Readman, puffing on his pipe, judged this the right moment to open his purser's wallet with which he went around the crew, extracting each man's contribution for the week's ration budget which he and Peter Moran would spend ashore buying fresh provisions. Mark, the rowing master, turned out to be a maniac for do-it-yourself handiwork. He was always whittling away on chunks of wood that he had lopped from bushes on the hillsides to make into knife handles or an axe haft, or he would be stitching leather or sewing canvas into bags and holdalls. Now he was embroidering the word 'Argo' in classical Greek script on his sailing smock, below the Union Jack, and he promised he would add the name in Russian script if we ever managed to get to Soviet Georgia. Trondur sat propped against the gunwale, sketching. Dressed in straw hat, baggy trousers and sandals, with a drawing board on his knee and charcoal in hand, he looked, in that brilliant Mediterranean light, like an artist in Provence in the 1920s. Immaculate Dick Hill, true to form, had donned a pair of well-pressed trousers, smart enough to grace the cocktail hour on a millionaire's motor yacht, and had applied suntan lotion to his torso, so that he immediately became known as Sticky Dicky. Miles' trousers, by contrast, already had a seat as baggy and wrinkled as an elephant's backside, a sign of the hard-working stroke oarsman but also good as clown's pantaloons. To round off the general feeling of wellbeing, the day proved to be Costas' birthday. He was sixty-one. From his kitbag he produced a bottle of whisky to celebrate the event, and his health was toasted. He too had collected a nickname. Rowing out of Volos Bay, someone had remarked that the exercise would give everyone tremendous muscles. 'Hey, Costas,' called Peter Dobbs, 'you'll be fit enough to go back to Olympic Airways and kickstart a jumbo jet.' So it was to Kickstart Costas that we raised our glasses.

Jason's route, as described by Apollonius, took the first *Argo* north along the Magnesian coast as far as Mount Olympus. There she turned east and headed out across the open sea towards the headland of Cape Poseidon, the nearest of the remarkable three fingers of the Khalkhidiki peninsula which projects down from the coast of Thrace. Now, as we ourselves approached Mount Olympus along the same route, the reason for the change of course became obvious. Mounts Ossa and Olympus provide excellent landmarks for any ship leaving the coast and striking out to sea. By keeping Mount Ossa directly astern, you can sail across the Thermaikos Gulf and make safe landfall at Cape Poseidon. In the days before compasses good landmarks were vital for early navigators, and they planned their routes accordingly. Their ideal day's run would involve leaving the beach at first light, and being in sight of land and their next anchorage well before dusk. Aboard *Argo* I did not want to use a compass; it was far more interesting to navigate in the old way, by line of sight, by the sun, and by the feel of the waves and wind. There was a compass hidden away for emergencies, but at this stage it proved totally unnecessary. Several crew members were experienced yachtsmen, accustomed to sailing in the tidal waters of the English Channel or the North Sea, where compass, log, echo sounder and radio direction-finder are normal aids. But in the Aegean none of this was required. We could get along very well without any of these modern contrivances. It was enough, most of the time, simply to look where we were going – to the line of the sun, the distant shape of an island as a way marker, and finally to our day's destination itself. Nor did we have a ship's radio – just the two walkie-talkies so that we could communicate between *Argo* and the rubber dinghy when taking photographs, and a waterproof radio beacon that could be switched onto the general distress-and-calling frequency in an emergency. To check our speed we towed a rotor over the side, but this was not accurate enough to help us calculate distances, particularly at low speeds. The only depth-measuring instrument we ever used was an oar counterweight of lead, tied to a long piece of knotted cord.

Only in the matter of charts were we truly anachronistic. It is not known whether in the late Bronze Age anything like a chart existed; perhaps it did, in the form of a stylized diagram. But it is more likely that Jason's expert helmsman, Tiphys, would have worked from a practical experience of the main Aegean routes carried in his head. When he ventured beyond the boundaries of his personal knowledge, he would have inquired of local sailors and fishermen, or even hired the services of a local pilot. However, to take the new *Argo* to the mouth of the Dardanelles, never having sailed those waters before, I had charts to tell me where to go.

Serving breakfast on board, instead of on shore, was the best way to lure modern Argonauts off the beach early enough to make a good start to the day. The prospect of a bowl of porridge or a couple of slices of bread was sufficient to make a hungry oarsman emerge from his sleeping bag on the shingle and come aboard at the first stroke of the ship's bell. So by seven o'clock the next morning, after spending the night in the little harbour of Stonion under Mount Ossa, we were already rowing out to sea, heading away from land and keeping the mountain in direct line with *Argo*'s stern ornament. Our crossing to Cape Poseidon measured 28 nautical miles of open sea, and I hoped to cover the distance in a single long day. But despite a libation to the Sea God – a cup of local wine tossed in the harbour – we failed. First we had a calm, then Boreas the north wind, then calm again, and finally a wind from the southeast which gradually shifted around to *Argo*'s bow and held her back like an unseen hand. When night fell we were still 10 miles offshore, and though we could see the lights of land the oarsmen were too exhaused to row any farther. So we lay down and tried to sleep.

Spending the night aboard *Argo* out at sea was a new experience. Apollonius makes it clear that from time to time Jason and his men also failed to make landfall by dusk, but this was a situation that early Aegean galley sailors mistrusted deeply; they preferred to be ashore on a safe beach by the time the sun went down. Occasionally Jason's helmsman decided to keep travelling at night, usually because he did not wish to waste a fair wind, and once or twice Jason and his oarsmen were obliged to row through the dark because they were becalmed far from land. But there is no mention of them actually sleeping in their open boat at sea, as we did. We had no choice: we were too tired to row on. Each man tried to find enough room to lie down, and this required the greatest personal ingenuity. The entire crew was confined in a space measuring superficially 54 feet by 9 feet at its widest. A third of this was already taken up by the ram, mast, rigging, ship's tackle, cooking area, liferafts and all the other paraphernalia of the ship. The very small spaces under the oar benches were crammed with stores, personal gear and the barrels containing our tools and clothing.

At first calculation it seemed physically impossible for everyone to find enough room to lie down and sleep. Effectively the only area available to each man was his own oar bench, which measured 8½ inches wide by 4 feet long, not a great area to fit a sleeping 6-foot 2-inch oarsman, particularly when shared with several feet of his oar handle which had to be pulled inboard. Yet the new Argonauts somehow managed the impossible. They stretched, crept, wriggled, curled, folded over and draped themselves into whatever gaps they could find. It was like a scene from a yoga class going into its most advanced contortions and postures. Costas lay on his back on his thwart. As his bench was divided by the mast, he had to adopt a right-angle with his legs sticking vertically up the mast. Most of the others took up spoon positions, head to toe on their rowing benches, but Mark achieved a notable first: he excavated a hole in all the dunnage beneath his oar bench and disappeared into the bilge of the boat where, like a corpse in a crowded coffin, he fell

asleep, unable to stretch or move. It showed just how exhausted the crew were, that they slept the night in such cramped conditions, while *Argo* lay motionless on the surface of the sea in such a velvet calm that we might have been tied to a dock.

All around *Argo* moved coloured lights – the navigation lamps of freighters, which steered clear when the night watch flashed a warning torch beam on *Argo*'s limp sail. Occasionally what looked like a whole chain of street lights glided past us as fishing boats set out for their night fishery, towing a string of small rowing boats behind them, each boat equipped with a bright, gas-driven flare to attract the night-feeding fish.

A cloudy sky and a continuing calm brought the dawn, and the cocoons of sleeping bags began to move, disgorging remarkably cheerful men. Mark's bald head emerged from beneath his bench like the body from the mummy's tomb in a horror film. Rolling his eyes in mock frenzy, he leaned over to sink his teeth into Tim

Greek fishing boats

Readman's leg. 'I'm hungry,' the apparition moaned. Thereupon, Pete the Cook, with his inevitable cheroot clenched between his teeth, boiled up eggs and coffee, and the remarkable crew settled down to another three hours of stiff rowing to reach the shore by Cape Poseidon.

The reaction of the Greek fishing communities to *Argo*'s passage of their waters was heart-warming. Some sort of grapevine relayed the message of *Argo*'s presence from one port to the next. After resting on Cape Poseidon's beach, we rowed around its long, sandy spit in strange, unsettled weather. Menacing cloud banks formed; rain dropped from their swollen underbellies; rainbows came, flourished and disappeared. A fickle wind blew now from the land, now from the sea, and *Argo* struggled slowly on, her crew constantly brailing and unbrailing the sail to catch the puffs of wind, or tugging on the oar handles to gain a few more yards. Suddenly a trio of motor fishing boats appeared from the small harbour of Nea Skioni on the mainland. As the boats came closer, we saw that their decks were packed with children gazing at us. With each group of children was a schoolteacher. There were shrieks from the children as the first of the tubby fishing boats cut its engines and turned sharply to pass alongside *Argo*. '*Kalo taxidi! Kalo taxidi!*' Again came the shout we had heard so often.

An unshaven fisherman, villainously scruffy in stained and torn jersey, filthy trousers and sea boots, stepped out from his wheelhouse. Bizarrely, this ruffian figure was holding a delicate bouquet of pink, red and white roses. The flowers were tossed across the gap between the two boats, to be caught in mid-air by the equally piratical figure of Peter Dobbs in his Arab headdress. The second fishing boat chugged past, and lobbed another gift. This time it was a cardboard box of sticky sweets, sent by the ladies of Nea Skioni and caught by Miles. The fishing boats wallowed off, and only one small, battered boat remained. In it stood an old seasoned fisherman. He had stopped his engine and was now rowing in the Greek fishing style, standing upright and facing forward as he pushed on his oar handles. He was a squid and octopus fisherman, for in his worn boat were several tridents, and a large rusty gaslight hung over the stern, wrapped in an old tweed topcoat. At night he would use his lamp to lure his prey to the surface, just as his forbears in Homer's day lit blazing firebrands to attract the fish to the spear. Now he was scrutinizing *Argo* with an air of professional interest, as he shouted across to us in the characteristically laconic style that seamen use as they meet strangers in small craft.

'Welcome,' he called. 'You are at Nea Skioni. How is your voyage?'

'Fine. Just fine,' called back Elias, the architect, leaning over the gunwale.

'There's an old harbour just a little way up the coast – Old Skioni – it's buried beneath the sea, but you can see the columns and blocks of stone if you go there on a calm day and look down into the water. We are descended from the men who returned from Troy!'

It was a curious tale to hear from the mouth of a fisherman, but true. According to the Greek historian Thucydides, Skioni had been founded by Greek troops from the Peloponnese who were returning home from Troy after the fall of the city. One contingent of these soldiers, homeward bound with their boats loaded with booty and captured Trojan women, had come ashore at Skioni to break their journey, and the Trojan women had seized their chance to rebel. They did not wish to become household slaves in Greece, so they burned the boats of the Greeks with the result that the contingent was stranded and the men were obliged to remain on that coast. They married their audacious captives and settled on the spot.

We got a much closer look at Nea Skioni than I had bargained for. Soon afterwards the wind sprang up from the east, a strong breeze from dead ahead. Knowing the futility of trying to row upwind, I turned *Argo* around and we went racing towards Skioni's pier, as if intent on hurtling on to the rocks. At the last minute came the order 'Brail up!' Trondur and Peter Wheeler hauled furiously on the nine bunt lines, whisking the canvas in folds against the yard. 'Oars outboard! Firm pressure! Go!' Ten oars hit the water, and *Argo* shot round the end of the pier with her canvas rattling. She must have looked like a nineteenth-century painting of a fishing boat entering harbour under stress of weather. So Skioni's schoolchildren all got a second holiday, for their afternoon lessons were cancelled in order for them to come down to the little sandy beach at the back of the harbour and stare at the galley.

Argo was giving us invaluable lessons in ancient sailing. Time and again a chance remark or a sudden observation seemed to leap the centuries, and brought us face to face with navigation as it had been practised in a bygone era. At Nea Skioni a local man, Antonis, asked if he could accompany us for the next day's journey. He was an amateur skin diver and knew the local coast well. Soon after we rowed out, I had to duck *Argo* once again into shelter to avoid a headwind. The only possible refuge was a poorly protected open beach with a rocky sea floor on which the anchor slithered and skidded. I was not at all happy about the safety of the anchorage, and remarked on the treacherous combination of rocky coast and sudden shifts in wind in that area.

'Oh yes,' Antonis replied. 'This part of the coast has a very bad reputation. It was a graveyard for ships for centuries. My friends and I in the diving club have found half a dozen ancient Greek and Roman wrecks, lying on the bottom along this short stretch of coast.'

Unwilling to stay longer in that inhospitable spot, I asked the crew to row on. We spent a miserable afternoon thrashing past the jagged rocks of Cape Paliouri, with the sail and yard hauled down to cut the windage, and lashed securely to prevent accidents in the choppy seaway. There were flashes of lightning, peals of thunder, and the sea turned a nasty hostile grey. As soon as we had clawed clear of the rocks of Cape Paliouri I put the helm over, and *Argo* fled for a large and deserted bay, marked on the chart and lying just north of the cape. As we glided into its shelter, Antonis pointed to starboard. 'Just there we found another wreck, a Roman ship. She must have run for the same refuge as *Argo*, but foundered as she came in.'

Roaming the shore that evening, I stumbled across a field of peas, growing wild on the hillside above the anchorage. I called the others, and soon they had gathered enough fresh peas for all of us, while Trondur and Peter Wheeler hunted unsuccessfully for octopus with a trident. After supper we rigged the galley's canvas cover, as the sky was threatening rain, and that night we experienced the most terrific thunderstorm, with strike after strike of lightning spitting from the sky. The wind snatched and rattled at the canvas covers so that we had to cling onto them to prevent them being blown away, and the rain was so heavy that the drops literally smashed onto the sea, spraying the recoil inboard. Yet through it all I heard not a single complaint, only a succession of jokes and laughter as the rain-sodden crew spent a sleepless night.

Jason and his Argonauts had picked up another fair wind off

Mount Olympus. Where the new *Argo* proceeded by fits and starts along the coast, Jason and his men had not had to touch the oars. They sailed straight past Capes Poseidon and Paliouri in a single day and a night; and their second dawn brought them in sight of Mount Athos, the third finger of Khalkhidiki and the next great seamark on their route. Tiphys, the helmsman, decided to push on even farther, to trust to the wind and head direct for the fertile island of Lemnos. It was a good decision. Their weather luck held. 'For the Argonauts, there was a stiff breeze all that day, and through the night,' wrote Apollonius Rhodius. '*Argo*'s sail was stretched. But with the sun's first rays there came a calm and it was by rowing that they reached the rugged island of Lemnos . . . .'

Lemnos was the scene of the first of their adventures during the quest for the Golden Fleece. Unknown to them, the women of Lemnos had recently killed all the men on the island because their husbands had been unfaithful *en masse*. The Lemnian men had been raiding the mainland coast of Thrace, and bringing back Thracian women whom they much preferred to their own wives. Soon the Thracian women had usurped the Lemnian ladies in their own homes, until the moment came when the jealous Lemnian women decided to exact a bloody revenge. They massacred all their men, killed their Thracian concubines, and even slaughtered all the male children on the island. The only male to survive was their aged King Thoas. His daughter, Hypsipyle, smuggled him down to the beach and set him adrift in a wooden chest, in which he was eventually picked up by foreign fishermen, never to return to the island.

For a time after the massacre the Lemnian women managed very well by themselves. They took on all the previous male tasks, the ploughing and the seeding and harvesting, and adapted to their new life. But they also lived in constant fear of a counter-raid from the Thracians. So when they saw *Argo* standing into the harbour of their capital at Myrine, they mistook the newcomers for attacking Thracians, and, dressed in armour, the Lemnian women ran down to the harbour to defend themselves.

Jason reacted cautiously. Seeing the armed host on the beach, he sent ashore his herald, the smooth-tongued Aethalides, a man reputed to have such an all-embracing memory and to be so glib that he could fabricate any apparent truth he wanted without actually telling a lie. Aethalides quickly persuaded the Lemnians that *Argo* should at least be allowed to stay overnight in Myrine's harbour without being molested. This gave the Lemnian women a chance to reflect on their precarious situation. A public meeting was held in the town square, and the royal nurse Polyxo, now a white-haired old woman, pointed out that by killing all their menfolk the Lemnians had condemned themselves to extinction. Either they would be overwhelmed one day by a Thracian war party or, lacking men, they would never bear children and therefore, die out as a race. Accordingly the Lemnian women, led by Hypsipyle who was now their queen, decided next day to invite the Argonauts into their city and encourage them to stay on in Lemnos as their new husbands. The absence of the Lemnian men would be explained away by the fiction that they had been exiled because of their unreasonable liaison with the Thracians.

The stratagem worked very well. Jason, dressed in all his finery, came ashore to be received in the palace by Queen Hypsipyle. There she offered him the throne of Lemnos if he and his men would agree to settle on the island. Jason declined the crown, saying that he and the Argonauts could not abandon the quest for the Golden Fleece. But he did agree that the Argonauts would stay a while as guests.

So pleasant was the visit, with its succession of banquets and

Myrine

celebrations, dancing and feasting, and alluring female company, that the whole high-minded expedition for the Golden Fleece almost ended in the arms of the Lemnian ladies. Day followed day on Lemnos, and still *Argo* did not sail. She stayed moored in harbour, while her crew were equally well placed. Jason settled in with Hypsipyle in the palace, and the other Argonauts with their Lemnian ladies. Only Hercules – for in most versions of the story Hercules stayed with *Argo* for a few days yet – abstained from the general sybaritic life. He guarded *Argo* in harbour until eventually he could stand the delay no longer. In a towering rage he stalked through the streets of Myrine, battering on the doors of the houses with his club and calling on the Argonauts to attend a meeting on the shore, without the women being present. There he rebuked his shipmates hotly. They would lose all prestige, he told them, if they gave up the quest for the Golden Fleece, preferring to live at ease with the women of Lemnos. They would become the laughing stock of all Greece.

Shamed, the Argonauts had to agree, and next day they made their farewells. Their parting with the Lemnian women was amiable and sincere. The woman accepted that the Argonauts had to pursue their quest, and they generously offered to take them back if they returned safely. Queen Hypsipyle, suspecting that she would have a child by Jason, asked what she should do. Jason told her that, if it was a boy, he should be sent to Iolcos to live with his grandparents.

This boy, Hypsipyle's son by Jason, was to become King Euneus of Lemnos. According to Homer, Euneus ruled the island of Lemnos at the time of the Trojan War, and during the siege he supported the Greeks, sending them gifts of Lemnian wine and providing the besiegers with supplies. This corresponds to the facts, because Lemnos was famous for its vines and lies on the natural supply route between Greece and Troy. Much more important, however, this reference to King Euneus enables us to give a date to the quest for the Golden Fleece. If Euneus was king when Troy fell, then his father, Jason, must have visited Lemnos a generation earlier. Archaeologists have dated the fall of Troy variously, mostly between 1250 and 1200 BC, with many authorities preferring *c*.1225 BC. Thus Jason's expedition in search of the Golden Fleece would have taken place some twenty to thirty years earlier, in the mid-thirteenth century BC. This date, as we shall see, agrees not just with the occupation of Dimini – the possible home of Jason's exiled family outside Iolcos – but with circumstances which, sailing in the new *Argo*, we ourselves were to find in far-off Colchis, the land of the Golden Fleece.

When Apollonius describes the Argonauts' voyage from Mount Athos to Lemnos, the crossing we too were about to undertake, he makes the interesting observation that the great mountain threw its shadow on the island, even though it was as far from Lemnos as 'a well-found merchantman can travel by evening'. The distance between Athos and the nearest point of Lemnos is, in fact, 34 nautical miles, and this gives the 'well-found merchantman' a twelve-hour run of 2.8 knots average, rather less than the speed we now expected from *Argo* with a fair breeze behind her. Also, our luck finally changed for the better as we too headed from the Khalkhidiki for Lemnos. We had spent the previous evening on the central finger of the Khalkhidiki in the splendid natural harbour of Porto Koufo, where Antonis the diver left us to return to Nea Skioni, and we put out to sea at one o'clock in the morning, hoping to catch a night breeze from the land. As we rowed out, there was a flat calm and a moon so brilliant that we could hear the birds singing on the mountainside as if it were day. Cape Ambelos was a stark black outline against the starry sky, and in the ink-black shadow of the moonlight I found it was possible to steer by sound, judging the distance of the rocks by the roar of the swell reflecting from the cliff face like a sounding board.

An hour later the wind rose softly from the west, and dawn revealed Mount Athos to port, its summit streaked with snow so that it stood all day above the horizon like a massive beacon, an unmistakable signpost for every sailor in the Thracian Sea. For as long as the sun was in the sky the west wind blew fair, and the helmsman needed only to keep Athos receding over his left shoulder, with the sun arching over to his right, and he was steering *Argo* true for Lemnos. We passed two sperm whales – an unexpected encounter in the Aegean – who were travelling stolidly in the opposite direction, puffing out their characteristic forward-slanting spouts. In a twinkling Trondur was swarming up the mast to sit on the cross trees and admire them. He gazed back in our wake, long after they had passed.

By five o'clock in the afternoon Lemnos was faintly in sight, dead ahead. As the sun set in an orange ball behind the shoulder of Mount

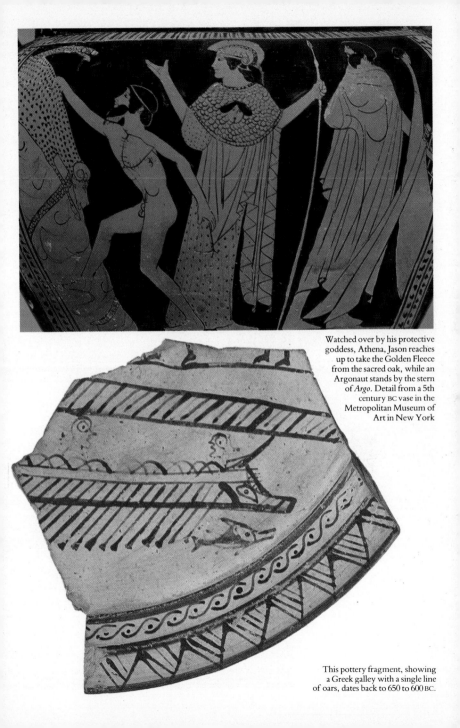

Watched over by his protective goddess, Athena, Jason reaches up to take the Golden Fleece from the sacred oak, while an Argonaut stands by the stern of *Argo*. Detail from a 5th century BC vase in the Metropolitan Museum of Art in New York

This pottery fragment, showing a Greek galley with a single line of oars, dates back to 650 to 600 BC.

(*Right*) 'Tom Vosmer was a genius at making models.' His construction model of *Argo* is held by Tim Severin while Vosmer explains the details

(*Top*) 'On his head was stuck a curious hat, a grubby grey cone of felt . . . I was irresistibly reminded of Rumpelstiltskin.' Vasilis Delimitros, the master shipwright of Spetses, who built *Argo*. (*Above*) Vasilis 'turned the roaring tongue of flame on the hull . . . his drastic method of drying out the timber'

(*Left*) 'The launch took place on the first sunny day of spring . . . The Greek Orthodox priest of the village had come to bless her.' (*Top*) The square sail was painted with the expedition symbol – three Mycenaean warriors with twin spears, boars' tusk helmets, and the ram's head device on their shields. (*Above*) 'It is the tool that built the boat, and will bring her good luck.' The *skipani* (adze) nailed by Vasilis to the stern together with a bouquet of flowers on the day *Argo* sailed from Spetses

The newly excavated Mycenaean town of Dimini where Jason may have spent his childhood (*above*). 'You could see where the main street ran, and how the Mycenaean town houses had lined the main thoroughfare ... Cut into the side of the hill was a passageway (*right*) lined with dressed stone ... it was the entrance to a Mycenaean burial chamber. Through the arch was the tomb itself (*below*), a beehive-shaped hollow scooped out of the heart of the hill, and lined with beautifully engineered blocks of stone' – possibly the royal tomb of Jason's father

SOME MEMBERS OF THE CREW

Top row (left to right): Mark Richards, rowing master; Peter Wheeler, ship's carpenter; Tim Readman, purser

Centre: Dave Brinicombe, sound recordist; Peter Moran, ship's cook. *Foot:* Nick Hollis, ship's doctor; Peter Warren, oarsman

(*Left*) 'It was a good day to start an expedition – no wind and a light veil of high cloud to block the worst of the sun.' The expedition sets out from Volos

(*Below*) Oarsmen at work. In the foreground is Costas Ficardos: 'I wish my company could see me now. Until last year I was Chief Pilot for Olympic Airways, and I had to retire at sixty.' (*Foot*) 'The first blisters appeared within an hour, blisters which were not to heal until the voyage ended'

(*Left*) 'It seemed physically impossible for everyone to find enough room to lie down and sleep . . . Yet the new Argonauts somehow managed the impossible' – each man on his own oar bench measuring 8.5 inches by 4 feet

(*Overleaf*) 'We found an idyllic mooring on a small island tucked just inside the mouth of the Bay of Volos.' Trondur Patursson, ship's artist, on his third voyage with the author, sketches the view

(*Left*) 'The second fishing boat chugged past, and lobbed another gift . . . a cardboard box of sticky sweets, caught by Miles Clark'

(*Previous page*) Tim Readman undergoes the joys of the *hamam* (Turkish bath) at Canakkale at the hands of the masseur, where the author, too, was 'twisted, torn, pummelled, trodden on, and wrenched into every possible contortion'

The Turks entertained the new Argonauts with lavish hospitality (*below*) and with traditional Turkish dancing at Erdek (*far right*). Here Resit Ertuzun, the local historian, showed them the Sacred Harbour (*right*) where Jason's men sought shelter from the gale

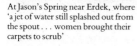

At Jason's Spring near Erdek, where 'a jet of water still splashed out from the spout . . . women brought their carpets to scrub'

(*Right*) *Argo* had 'the best day's sail of the entire voyage' as she sailed up 'the darkly swirling Hellespont', from the Aegean Sea to the Sea of Marmara, with a fresh breeze from the southwest – the same wind that had favoured Jason and his men

The original Argonauts 'rowed up the Bosphorus by sheer muscle power. Now, three thousand years later, we had to show whether that could have been physically possible. We had to do the same.' *Argo* leaves Istanbul, passing the burnt–out hulk of a wrecked tanker

(*Right*) 'The whole scene was pulsating with activity. Ferries were churning in and out of the Golden Horn . . . Merchant vessels of every description were on the move.' (*Below*) Reinforced by members of Istanbul's rowing clubs (Mustafa, with his sunburnt arm), 'the oar blades chopped into the water in a flurry of quick strokes. The crew grunted with the effort'

As Jonathan Cloke was anointed in readiness for the oil wrestling match at Fenerbache when he was matched against the Turkish heavyweight champion, he 'looked distinctly out of place in a pair of red sailor trousers rolled up to his knees instead of buffalo hide breeches'

At the end of the Straits, near the entrance to the Black Sea, 'are the physical remains of the Clashing Rocks of antiquity' (*above*). On the crest of one of them, the author, with Ali Uygun, one of the Turkish volunteers, examines the remains of a Roman pillar which once served as a landmark for sailors

(*Overleaf*) As they rowed through the most difficult narrows of the Bosphorus at Bebek, 'this was all the muscle power they could produce in a short, concentrated burst'

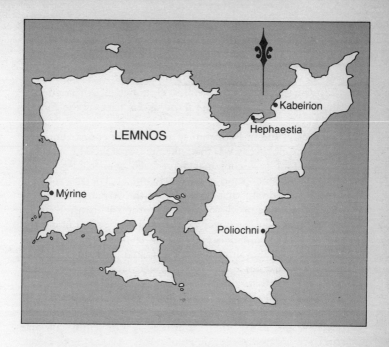

Athos we saw, just as Apollonius had said, how its shadow seemed to fall on the island, and up ahead in the gathering dusk came another armada of welcoming fishing boats to greet us. Watchers on the cliffs of Lemnos had seen *Argo* breast the horizon, and now the fishermen escorted us into the harbour of modern Myrine, their lights bobbing around us and the sound of children's voices singing a welcome. The waterfront itself was jammed with spectators, hundreds upon hundreds of them, craning their necks over the edge of the quay to see *Argo* warp alongside. In the front rank a beaming, robed priest held up a flagon of Lemnian wine.

It was a shock to discover that only a very few Mycenaean remains have been found on Lemnos, although the island figures so strongly in the *Argonautica*. But, as Professor Beschi of the University of Pisa, conducting excavations on Lemnos, explained to me, 'We haven't found any significant Mycenaean remains probably because we haven't been looking for them. There has been so much else to occupy us.' He and his team were busy reassessing the massive archaeological work done on the island in the late 1930s by Italian teams. On the east coast of Lemnos they had uncovered a city, Poliochni, which dates back as early as 3000 BC. Poliochni had been a large and prosperous place, and in the ruins the Italians had discovered exactly the same type and forms of pottery that were in use in Troy on the coast of Asia Minor, clear evidence that trade had flourished between Lemnos and Troy as far back as the middle Bronze Age.

Mysteriously, life in Poliochni seems to have ended about the year 1600 BC. One theory was that, like the fate of the Minoan cities of Crete, that of Poliochni may have been connected with the catastrophic volcanic eruption of the island of Thera. Professor Beschi had little doubt that the story of the Argonauts and the Lemnian women was an echo of some sort of actual historical event. He guessed that Queen Hypsipyle's capital, where Jason and the Argonauts were so enticingly entertained, lay beneath the modern city of Myrine, still waiting to be excavated. For the moment, however, Professor Beschi and his team were far more interested in two sites on the northern rim of Lemnos: the city of Hephaestia, and a cult temple to the mysterious Kabeiri. Both places were linked with the tradition of Jason and the Argonauts.

Hephaestia apparently dated from the seventh century BC and was named in honour of the god Hephaestos. According to Greek mythology Hephaestos was the Smith God, being cunning in all metallurgy and design and serving as the artificer and armourer to the Olympians. It was Hephaestos, by tradition, who had introduced the art of metalworking to the ancient Greeks. He had sided with the goddess Hera when she was quarrelling with her husband Zeus, and the latter had grown so angry that he had picked up Hephaestos and flung him down from Olympus. Hephaestos had fallen on the island of Lemnos, and the impact broke his legs, laming him for life. The original inhabitants of Lemnos, a people known as the Sintians, had been kind to the cripple and given him shelter. In return Hephaestos had taught them the secret of metalworking; and from Lemnos that skill was passed onto the rest of the Greek world.

There is good reason to believe that the transmission of the knowledge of metallurgy was connected with Lemnos' key position astride the sea route to Asia Minor. The archaeological evidence is that one of the earliest centres of metalworking in the

Near East was on the north coast of Anatolia, near the Black Sea. Here have been found some of the earliest smelters and mines in history. If the knowledge of how to work metal was carried by sea from this region towards Greece, it would have come first to the island of Lemnos, and the legend of Hephaestos would have been invented to explain why metallurgy apparently was first taught to the Greeks in this remote island of the northern Aegean. Most scholars are of the opinion that Hephaestos was an imported god of Asian, not Greek, origin, and his significance to the Jason story is that this sea route, between Lemnos and the Black Sea, was exactly the same route that Jason and the Argonauts now proposed to follow, the same track taken by Phrixus, Helle and the flying ram. To emphasize the link, some versions of the Argonaut legend maintain that among Jason's heroes was Palaemon, son of Hephaestos and lame like his father.

Professor Beschi's second site also had a direct connection with the Argonaut tradition and Asia Minor. On the high shoulder of a cliff, looking northwest across the Thracian Sea, the limestone had been cut away to make a platform on which had worshipped a secret cult called the Kabeiri. So secret was this cult that today very little is known about its so-called mysteries, because initiates to the cult swore never to reveal its secrets. However, it is known to have been some sort of fertility cult, and to have been linked with black magic and with the great earth mother in some form. It arrived from Asia Minor and Lemnos and Samothrace became its major cult centres; obviously the position of these islands once again played a role.

What was of special interest to us was that the cult was also connected with seafaring, and specifically with two of the Argonauts – the twins Castor and Pollux. Later pictures of the twins would show them with two stars on their foreheads, the sign used for those initiated into the mysteries of the Kabeiri. It was said that sailors who knew the Kabeiri arts had the power to control the winds and calm storms, and that the twins would appear to them as St Elmo's Fire. Even a glimpse of the two stars, Castor and Pollux, after the twins had been set as a constellation in the sky, meant that the worst of a storm at sea was past. Thus the voyage of the Argonauts entered maritime folklore while, as Isaac Newton observed, other signs of the zodiac were also inextricably mixed with the quest for the Golden Fleece – the water carrier, the fish, the twins and, of course, the ram itself.

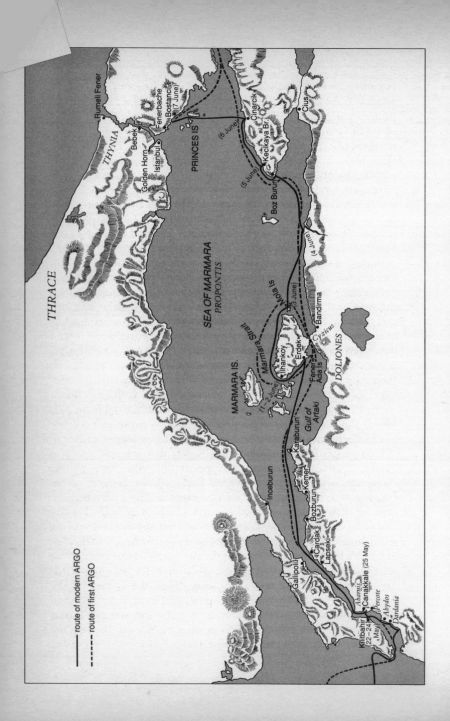

route of modern ARGO
route of first ARGO

THRACE

Rumeli Fener
Fenerbache
Bostancı (7 June)
Bebek
Golden Horn
Istanbul
THYNIA
PRINCES IS
Çınarcık
Kecikaya Br.
Cius
(6 June)
(5 June)
Boz Burun
(4 June)
SEA OF MARMARA
PROPONTIS
Bandirma
(3 June)
Cyzicus
Nola Is
Marmara Strait
Erdek
DOLIONES
İlhankoy
Feneri
Ada Is
MARMARA IS.
Gulf of
Artaki
(1–2 June)
Karaburun
İnceburun
Kemer
Bozburun
Çardak
Lapseki
Gallipoli
Aburnis
Percote
Canakkale (25 May)
Abydos
Dardania
Kilitbahir
22–24
May

5

The Dardanelles and Marmara Sea

Argo was badly short-handed when we left Lemnos on 18 May. Our three Greek volunteers had said goodbye and returned to their own homes, and so we were only fifteen on board. As he left, I asked Elias, the architect from Volos, how he had enjoyed his trip, since it had been his first experience of a small boat journey.

'Were you frightened at any time during the voyage?'

'Yes, I was,' he answered truthfully, 'but not for long. Everyone else seemed so calm. So I just said to myself that there was nothing to be frightened about.'

'So why did you decide to join *Argo*?' I asked.

'It was for the adventure . . . the idea. . . . I wanted to know what people were like who did such a thing.'

The same question must have crossed the mind of the skipper of the Turkish fishing boat which spotted *Argo* at dusk that evening. We had spent the entire day slogging under oars across the strait which divides Lemnos from Gokce, the first island in Turkish waters. With such a small crew our relief periods from rowing had been cut by half, and we were extremely tired. When the Turkish skipper saw a large rowing boat pulling wearily across the sea he thought we were shipwrecked mariners in a lifeboat, so he hauled in his nets, put on full power, and came racing over, thinking to rescue us. When our true situation was explained, with much pantomime, there were smiles and laughter, and he insisted on presenting us with a large box of freshly caught sprats for our supper.

That night I became aware that I had made a navigational blunder. Apollonius said that Jason and his Argonauts had gone from Lemnos to the island of Samothrace, where the Argonauts had visited another Kabeiri shrine. Then they had sailed for the entrance to the Dardanelles, thereby passing along the north of Gokce Island. But on the chart this route seemed wrong. It was a very roundabout way of going from Lemnos to the Dardanelles, adding 40 miles to the journey. I wondered if Apollonius had made a mistake. Perhaps he had introduced the detour to Samothrace because that island, too, was associated with the Kabeiri. In any event I decided that it was more logical to sail a direct course from Lemnos to the Dardanelles, passing south of Gokce.

But logic is not always the best guide to navigating a Bronze Age rowing boat, and this was one case where the use of a modern chart was a disadvantage, instead of a help. A huge volume of water constantly gushes out of the mouth of the Dardanelles, creating head currents for a galley rowing up from the south. I had anticipated some sort of current, but I had no idea that its effect would be so strong off the south coast of Gokce, where it was to delay us badly. In fact I would have done better if I had taken *Argo* around the north of Gokce, following Jason's original route.

So we spent a curious sort of night after the Turkish fishing boat left us, becalmed off the western tip of Gokce. All around us the upwelling water muttered and grumbled like a living mass. In the moonlight the cloud shadows moved and changed on the water. Lines of froth formed and dispersed. *Argo*, her crew dozing uncomfortably, spun in slow, erratic circles, now clockwise, now counter-clockwise. There was barely a breath of wind, yet patches of water suddenly broke into small white-capped wavelets where currents collided, and then as abruptly fell back into treacherous-looking slicks that disturbed *Argo*'s hull and rocked the boat as if a giant fish was nuzzling her keel.

At dawn I saw that we had been carried off course, and were drifting northward. It was vital to anchor and get some rest before we lost any more ground, and gather our strength so that we could tackle the currents with some hope of progress. But now we faced another problem. The only place we could sensibly reach and where we could find anchoring depth was off the western end of Gokce Island, some 5 miles away and rising sheer from the sea. But on the chart was written a strict warning: 'PROHIBITED AREA'. The pilot book said the same. Gokce was a sealed-off military zone, and the Turkish authorities strictly forbade anyone, especially foreigners, from landing there. If *Argo* even came close to the island, I risked getting us all arrested. But there was no alternative; the crew were so tired that they had to get some relief. I hoped that we might not be spotted or, if we were, there would be no objection if we only anchored in the shallows, and did not actually set foot on the forbidden island. Not very optimistically, I aimed *Argo*'s ram nose at the Prohibited Area.

The western end of Gokce is a forbidding-looking scarp which rises steeply from the water and is utterly barren. On the scrub-covered slope there was not a house, a path, or even an animal to be seen. The place seemed totally deserted. We rowed in closer, and soon came upon a small, attractive cove. Again there was not a living creature in sight – not even a track leading from the back of the cove to show that people came here sometimes. I wondered if the Turkish government had forbidden settlement here for so long that all trace of habitation had been expunged. *Argo* crept into the deserted cove and dropped anchor. Everyone shipped their oars, and we lay down gratefully on the benches to get some rest.

Not twenty minutes later a voice said gloomily, 'Oh! Oh! Here comes the military!' I raised my head and peered over the gunwale. Two men in combat uniform were climbing down the hillside, accompanied by a tracker dog. The soldiers had appeared from nowhere, and were obviously heading down to the cove to intercept *Argo*. One man was carrying a submachine gun, and they both looked very serious. I began to regret bringing *Argo* into the anchorage, and imagined all that might now possibly go wrong: the crew being put under military arrest; the boat impounded; having to explain first to a sergeant, then a lieutenant, then a captain, and so on up the military chain of command exactly what we were doing in a forbidden military zone; and then waiting for the reaction from the military authorities in Ankara, who would inevitably have to be consulted as to what should be done. It would be a disastrous start to our visit to Turkey. To make matters worse, *Argo* didn't have any Turkish entry papers. The nearest customs post lay 60 miles farther on, so we did not have Turkish immigration stamps on our passports. I could foresee days and days of delay while we sorted out the mess.

The army patrol clearly meant business. The two soldiers strode out onto the beach, looking very tough in their battledress and combat boots. The man with the submachine gun swung his weapon to point it at us. His companion shouted sternly, and beckoned. With sinking heart, I gathered up my passport and the ship's documents and Peter Dobbs prepared to take me ashore in the rubber dinghy. I told the crew to be patient, and warned them that I might be away for quite some time. The two soldiers looked distinctly unfriendly as we approached in the rubber dinghy. One was a private and the other a corporal, and from the blue berets I supposed they were troops of the special border guards. I scrambled out onto the rocks, and gingerly approached them. The private moved his gun muzzle, which continued pointing at me. How on earth was I going to explain to a corporal of the Turkish Army what a Bronze Age galley of Greek origin was doing trespassing on the western end of a military zone. I could remember only a few courtesy phrases of Turkish, and I doubted that a Turkish-English phrase book would be adequate to explaining the situation.

Putting on my most cheerful expression, I held out my hand. '*Merhaba* – welcome,' I said breezily. The corporal's brown Anatolian eyes gazed back at me stolidly. He was a block of muscle and bone, the very epitome of the hardened non-commissioned officer, determined to carry out his orders precisely, to do everything by the book. I noticed that his hair was cropped bristle-short underneath his beret, and even in the baking heat every button on his tunic was fastened in the correct fashion, right up to the collar. The corporal refused the handshake. Instead he raised his arm and pointed at my ship.

'*Ar-go*?!' he announced slowly. I was flabbergasted. How on earth did a corporal of the Turkish Army, patrolling this godforsaken spot on a remote island, know about *Argo*? It was incomprehensible. But a wave of relief swept over me. If the soldier knew the name *Argo*, then he was not about to arrest us for trespass.

We never learned the corporal's name, because neither he nor his companion spoke a word of any language other than Turkish. But we did persuade the corporal to come out to *Argo*, and he stiffly accepted a cup of coffee for himself and some biscuits for his dog, who loyally swam out behind the rubber boat. Officially, therefore, the corporal did his duty. There was no landing on Gokce. He stood guard over us until we were ready to leave, and then we put him ashore again with another packet of biscuits for the private, who had stood immobile all this time, his gun unwaveringly aimed at *Argo*.

Two hours later, as we rowed along the Gokce coast, a gunboat of the Turkish Coastguard came racing over the horizon. It headed straight for *Argo*, swerved aside, and then came churning past us, its crew mustered on deck and all standing at attention while whistles blew a formal naval salute.

'Welcome to Turkey!' boomed an amplified voice over the ship's loudhailer. It was the gunboat commander on his bridge. 'Do you need any help?'

'No. No, thank you very much. Everything is fine. But it's very nice to see you.'

The gunboat loomed over us, its engines bellowing. 'I've been sent to escort you, and give you any help you need. . . .'

Lieutenant Asaf Gunegren, commander of Patrol Boat No. 33, spoke excellent English and was a very likeable young naval officer. He came aboard *Argo* to meet the new Argonauts and accept our hospitality. Apparently all those letters I had sent with the help of

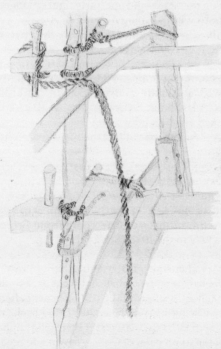

Port steering oar

the Turkish Yachting Federation so long ago had been read in government offices in Turkey, considered and acted upon. Alpay Cin of the Federation and his friends had worked wonders. The Ministry of the Interior, the Sports Ministry, the Ministry of Tourism and the civic authorities had made up their minds to assist *Argo* in every possible way and – for a start – had dispatched Patrol Boat No. 33 to look after us. Asaf had been scouring the coast for the last two days, and alerted the Gokce garrison to look out for us. 'That's how the corporal must have known the name of your boat,' he explained with a boyish grin.

We were sitting on *Argo*'s stern deck. The crew had taken a break from rowing, and *Argo* was anchored close off one of Gokce's sandy beaches. While we were chatting, a group of men in tracksuits appeared on the sand dunes and came jogging down onto the beach. They seemed to be on holiday. Some played volleyball, others went for a walk along the beach; and one burly figure plunged into the sea and swam out to within hailing distance of *Argo*.

'Who are those men?' I asked Asaf. 'Are they part of the island garrison or are they on holiday?'

'I don't know who they are,' he replied, 'but I'll find out for you.'

He shouted to the swimmer, who called back and swam closer. There followed a lengthy conversation in Turkish before the swimmer gave a last shout and swam strongly back to his beach.

'Well?' I asked Asaf. 'Who was he?'

Asaf paused. 'As a matter of fact, he's a prisoner,' he replied.

'A what?'

'He says that good prisoners, of the first category, are sent to live on Gokce. They must stay here.'

'What did you talk to him about?'

'He wanted to know who you were, and what you were all doing. So I told him that you had come from Greece and were rowing all the way to the Black Sea.'

'What did he say to that?'

'He said he'd rather stay on Gokce than have to row your boat!'

The gunboat left *Argo* after lunch and went back to the mainland to refuel. Lieutenant Asaf promised to return next afternoon to see how we were getting on. When he did come back, twenty-four hours later, he must have been very perplexed. He had left *Argo* halfway along the south coast of Gokce, rowing doggedly eastward with her under-strength crew. Yet the next day at much the same time he found us still at the oars, still heaving away, but in exactly the same spot. It was as though *Argo* had been stuck in treacle. What had happened was my second miscalculation of the Dardanelles current. Throughout the first afternoon we had rowed eastward, having a gruelling time against a headwind. At nightfall the wind had eased and, totally exhausted, the crew had lain down to spend the night on the oar benches, as we had done the previous night and off Cape Poseidon. There was a flat calm, and the boat lay motionless on the water. The night watches were peaceful; there were a few lights on Gokce Island, which seemed to be the moving lights of vehicles. Then, to my intense chagrin, as the sun rose I recognized the cove nearly abeam of *Argo*. It was the same cove where we had anchored on reaching Gokce twenty-four hours earlier. During the night the current out of the Dardanelles had silently and inexorably carried us backwards. All the previous day's labour, hour after hour of rowing, had been squandered. Tactfully, no one said anything, but I vowed to myself that never again would I let *Argo* drift at night in an unlit area where there was no way of judging what tricks the current might be playing. It took half the next day to recoup the loss, and now – the fifth day since we had last been able to obtain food – our stock of supplies and water was running low. The only replenishment was a case of beer that Asaf dropped off, a kind deed which subsequently gave rise to a rumour on the mainland that *Argo*'s slow progress was due to the fact that all her crew were drunk.

Indeed I was becoming rather worried. With a crew of only fifteen, there was a real doubt in my mind whether *Argo* would be able to row up against the powerful current once we entered the mouth of the Dardanelles. We simply did not have enough oarsmen on board. Every mile we advanced towards the entrance of the straits, the stronger became the current against us. If we succeeded in rounding the tip of the Gallipoli peninsula and entering the main channel, we could expect to meet the full force of a hostile current which might run up to 3 or 4 knots. Against that obstacle *Argo*'s reduced crew could probably exert only a little over one horsepower.

We were saved by the most extraordinary wind, a changing wind that might have been whistled up specially for us. Starting as we rowed across the final gap between Gokce and the Gallipoli peninsula, it came from the west, directly astern of us. Gratefully we spread the sail and made for land, expecting to anchor when we got there. But when we were no more than 50 metres from the peninsula shore the wind abruptly changed to the north, again exactly the best direction for us to sail around the tip of the peninsula. So I turned *Argo* to run the mile or so down the coast to the lighthouse that marked the end of Gallipoli's spit.

Once again, Turkish soldiers watched us – tiny figures standing on the clifftops by the gun emplacements that guard the straits. As *Argo* circled the point, keeping just beyond the barbed wire entanglements that run down into the sea, the wind again swung round, switching to the opposite direction to the one it had been blowing an hour before. It was uncanny. Once again it was the ideal wind. I turned *Argo* to double the point and entered the Dardanelles strait itself, all sail set, and the crew with nothing to do but sit and watch one of the great maritime spectacles of the world.

To our left was the long whaleback ridge of the Gallipoli peninsula itself, with its succession of monuments to the French, British, Australian and Turkish war dead of the bloody campaigns of the First World War. On the opposite bank the ground ran for about a mile, a flat, featureless shore, and then began to climb up to a distant escarpment. On that hill lay the ruins of Troy, the city which had controlled the trade of the Dardanelles in the Bronze Age. Even today that same commercial and strategic importance is just as evident. As far as the eye could see, commercial shipping was arriving and leaving through the straits – tankers, bulk carriers, general cargo boats, fishing vessels, ferries, cruise ships.

As our twenty-oared warship out of history sailed jauntily up the straits, modern warships came down on us in procession. A Soviet submarine was running on the surface, escorted southward by two Turkish naval destroyers; a squadron of Turkish Navy warships was manoeuvring on the horizon, and no fewer than four patrol boats of the Turkish Coastguard were in sight at one time. Three were engaged on routine patrol duties, but the fourth was our own, Gunboat No. 33, standing over us and warning all this shipping to give little *Argo* a wide berth. By general accord, Asaf and his men were given three cheers and we made Asaf an honorary Argonaut.

The massive arch which is the Turkish War Memorial on Gallipoli was the mark I used to steer *Argo* towards the opposite shore, and slant across the main current. Even with the fine southwest breeze pushing her at more than 5 knots through the water, the galley barely crawled forward in relation to the land. We had scarcely come within a quarter of a mile of the shore and entered slack water there, when our heaven-sent wind finally and abruptly died away. It had done its work. A baking stillness enveloped us, and the crew took up their oars to row to the spot where a little cluster of Turkish officials was waiting on shore to greet us. It seemed that nothing was too much trouble for the Turkish authorities. The officials had come specially from Canakkale, the port of entry, in order to give *Argo* her customs, health and immigration clearance. As the rubber dinghy ferried the officials out, the Argonauts could wait no longer. There were fourteen loud splashes as the oarsmen dived overboard and swam ashore to go racing up the beach and set foot in Asia.

For two more days we waited in the Dardanelles, cleaning up ourselves and *Argo*. It was difficult to decide which was the more travel-worn – the boat or her crews. *Argo* was unloaded of every last item, and we scraped foul-smelling black slime from her bilges. Then the crew themselves were similarly overhauled in the public *hamam*, or Turkish bath, of Canakkale. Nothing could have been better suited to getting rid of a week's grime and unknotting the aching muscles of oarsmen than to immerse themselves in steam and hot water on the marble slabs. By the time I eventually got to the *hamam* the rest of the crew had departed. But Turkish hospitality was vigilant. As I collected my bath towel in the lobby a brawny Turk, wearing only a towel and sitting reading a newspaper by the cash desk, looked up and recognized me. 'Aaah! Captain Tim!' He gave a slow grin that revealed a mouthful of broken teeth. He was the bath masseur, and determined to show his skill, so I was obliged to spend the next half hour on a marble slab, being twisted, torn, pummelled, trodden on and wrenched into every possible contortion until finally the masseur flipped over my limp and tortured body, threw a smart salute, and rapped out, 'Finish, captain!' which indeed I was.

Peter Dobbs' holiday had ended, and another Peter came to replace him, Peter Warren, an ex-Marine from Oxfordshire. He had rowed on *Argo*'s delivery voyage, and so enjoyed the camaraderie that he had decided to rejoin the main expedition. We also took on our first Turkish volunteers. Deniz was a twenty-three-year-old archaeology student with all the energy and enthusiasm of a terrier. Umur, by contrast, arrived looking so glum that I couldn't imagine why he was there. It turned out that he had been sent by his father, a mining engineer, who felt that since his eighteen-year-old son was having to retake his examinations, a spell on a twenty-oared galley might give him a new way of looking at life. As a result Umur started out as a very quiet and retiring young member of the crew. But as time went on, his attitude changed. Originally he said he would come with us only as far as Istanbul, but when we got there he volunteered a second time, and finished up by going on the entire Turkish sector of the voyage, a very gallant effort indeed. Erzin was the third of our new volunteers. He was the captain of a 150,000-ton supertanker operating from Turkey to the Arabian Gulf, so it must have been a great change pulling an oar on an 8-ton galley. But Erzin, a former officer in the Turkish Navy, was one of those people whom everyone likes instantly. He was an excellent seaman and a first-class shipmate. The two remaining Turkish volunteers were old friends. Ali was a marine archaeologist and diver; a serious and scholarly person, he was to be my guide and interpreter throughout the Turkish voyage. At sixteen, Kaan was the youngest of any of the Argonauts during the entire expedition. He was the son of an Istanbul family I had known for twenty-three years. His father, Irgun, had befriended me and my companions when, as college students, we had visited Turkey on motorcycles during my first expedition, to follow the route of Marco Polo. I had never lost touch with the family, and when Irgun learned that I was coming to Turkey with *Argo* he immediately sent his son to join us. Kaan, it transpired, had already done some rowing with one of Istanbul's boat clubs, and thought it all a great adventure.

In theory there should have been two more Turkish volunteers to join the crew, as *Argo* needed maximum oar-power if she was to get the rest of the way up the Dardanelles, where the current ran even more strongly. In fact two extra Turkish oarsmen did turn up in Canakkale, and they helped us move *Argo* from one side of the straits to the other where we were to have an official reception by the governor. It was a short, energetic crossing – only a mile and a half of water, but it took nearly two hours of rowing flat out to get across the racing current. When the two volunteers then failed to show up for the evening meal, the other Turks roared with laughter. 'They took one look at the job, and thought about the 190 miles to Istanbul, and decided that the trip's not for them. They've run away!'

The governor of Canakkale's official reception for *Argo* was the first of a whole series of civic welcomes that had been organized by the local authorities all along our route. A team of dancers performed on the quayside to the drone of pipes and the clatter of a Turkish drum. Boy dancers dressed in baggy shorts with half-gaiters in black embroidered with gold, and waistcoats over matching shirts, leaped and pranced and shouted. The girls dipped and swayed and linked arms, their costume an elegant combination of long flowing pantaloons and soft slippers, aprons and full blouses. On their heads were handkerchiefs sewn with jewellery which tinkled and swayed in time with the music.

The ancient Greeks had called the Dardanelles the Hellespont, for this is where Princess Helle had slipped from the back of the flying ram with the Golden Fleece and drowned in the sea. When the first *Argo* came this way, following the course of the flying ram on its way to Colchis, Jason and his companions had slunk through the straits under cover of darkness, probably to avoid attracting the attention of the Trojans who resented intruders who might bypass their commercial monopoly. 'Just as the sun was setting they reached the foreland of the Chersonese [the tip of the Gallipoli peninsula],' wrote Apollonius.

> There they met a strong wind from the south, set their sail to it and entered the swift current of Hellespont, which takes its name from Athamas' daughter. By dawn they had left the northern sea; by nightfall they were coasting the Rhoetean shore, inside the Straits, with the land of Ida [Mount Ida] on their right. Leaving Dardania behind, they set course for Abydos, and after they had passed in turn Percote, Abarnis with its sandy beach, and sacred Pityeia, before dawn *Argo* by dint of sail and oar was through the darkly swirling Hellespont.

I could scarcely believe the modern *Argo*'s weather luck when she too picked up exactly the same wind – a strong southerly – as we cleared Canakkale harbour and breasted the 'darkly swirling Hellespont'. Normally the wind blows from the north in May and June, but here we had a splendid fresh breeze from the southwest, occasionally rising to just short of gale force, and blowing directly up the Straits in our favour. *Argo* responded by giving us the best day's sail of the entire voyage. She ran like a dolphin with the following sea. Rhythmically she first buried her snout deep in the water, pressed down by the weight of sail so that the sea was rushing past her half-submerged eyes. Then like a sea beast coming up for a breath of air, her snout began to rise towards the surface, boring upward through the rushing water, bubbles streaming, until the tip of the ram broke surface in a fine welter of foam, spurting a foot in the air. A second later followed twin jets of water gushing out to port and starboard from the handhold in the snout, just like an animal clearing its nostrils with a whoosh of air. There *Argo* would hang suspended for a moment, her long hull thrusting out of the body of the wave until the crest passed and she began the cycle once again, the nose starting to dip and bury itself in the rushing sea.

For hour after hour she maintained this motion at a steady 6–7 knots as she scoured her way up the Dardanelles until, just like her predecessor, she had swum the entire length of the straits and entered the Sea of Marmara, the sea the Greeks called Propontis, the vestibule to the Black Sea itself. As Apollonius wrote:

> In Propontis there is an island sloping steeply to the sea, close to the rich mainland of Phrygia, and parted from it only by a low isthmus barely raised above the waves. The isthmus, with its two shores, lies east of the river Aesepus; and the place itself is called Bear Mountain by the people round about. . . . *Argo* pressing on with a stiff breeze from Thrace behind her, reached the coast and ran into a harbour called Fair Haven. Here, on the advice of Tiphys, they [the Argonauts] discarded their small anchor stone and left it at the Spring of Artace, replacing it with a heavier and more suitable rock.

Today, the peninsula which Apollonius called Bear Mountain is known as Kapidag or Door Mountain, and the harbour he knew as Fair Haven has adopted the name of the sacred spring itself – Artace – now written in its Turkish version, Erdek. *Argo* dropped anchor there in the early hours of 27 May, and the next morning I walked just half a mile to the spot where, 3000 years earlier, the first Argonauts had left their anchor stone as a thanks-offering.

By an extraordinary piece of luck – a chance meeting six weeks earlier – I knew exactly where to look for the place which had once been called 'Jason's Spring'. A tipsy crew and a bout of bad weather

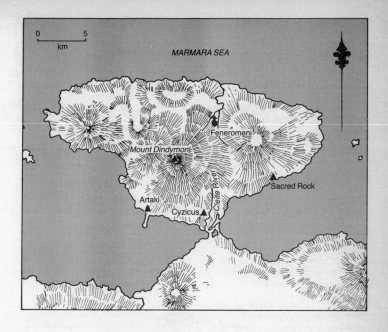

had led me to the discovery. We had been making the delivery voyage of *Argo* from her building place at Spetses northward along the Peloponnese coast to Volos. Our route lay through the channel between the Greek mainland and the large island of Evvia. The weather had been atrocious – cold, rainy and blustery. In fine seagoing tradition several members of the delivery crew had fortified themselves against the elements in a harbourside taverna in the town of Khalkis. They came back aboard in no fit state to row, and shortly after leaving harbour we encountered a gale from the north. For the safety of the vessel and her more incapacitated crew members I ran *Argo* for shelter into the first small harbour in sight. It was certainly not a place I had planned to visit, but with the wind gusting and the rain slashing diagonally across the straits we were glad to moor *Argo* and take refuge in an empty outbuilding, waiting there like wet hens for the weather to improve.

Only then did I notice the name of the little port. It was called Nea Artaki – New Artaki – and I recalled the name of the spring sacred to the goddess Artaki where Jason had left his anchor stone. I went

113

into the town to check whether there was any connection between this modern small port in Evvia and the spring on the peninsula in the Sea of Marmara. At the fishermen's cooperative I was told that New Artaki had been founded by the Greeks who came back from the original Artaki or Erdek during the exchange of population between the Greeks and the Turks in the early 1920s. This information was a complete surprise. Was there, I asked, anyone, by any chance, who still remembered the old life in the days when the Greeks had lived at Erdek, someone who could tell me of the folk tales and traditions of the area? The fishermen, also storm-bound, had plenty of time to consult with one another, and they agreed that there was a sole survivor whom I should talk to – Vasilis Kalatheri.

'Do you think that he would be willing to talk to me about his memories of the old days in Artaki?' I asked. 'Perhaps he is too old now, and does not remember clearly.'

'Oh no, you can judge for yourself,' I was told. 'Vasilis is a remarkable person. Since leaving Artaki he has travelled all over the world. He knows many things, and he remembers his life very clearly.'

Jason's Spring

Mount Dindymun

Later that evening I went to the café where it had been arranged for me to meet Vasilis Kalatheri. He was indeed one of those remarkable people who succeed in living to a great age without losing their faculties. He had been born in 1892, and lived in Erdek until he was in his late twenties, and he remembered every detail of that early life. First I asked him if he knew any place in Erdek that was connected with the story of Jason and the Argonauts. Immediately he knew what I meant. Of course, he replied, there is the spring that everyone had called Artaki Krini or Iason Krini – the spring of Artace or the spring of Jason. It was very well known, though some people had begun to call it Pagatho.

Where was this spring? You had only to follow the main path that led up from the harbour for about a kilometre and a half, and that would bring you directly to Jason's spring. When he was a young man, everybody took it for granted that this was the spring where the Argonauts had left their anchor stone. In fact, said Vasilis, in 1906 a British yacht had visited the port, and in the night sent some men to carry away the stone itself. The stone had been round, and was split open down the middle, and inside there had been some sort of writing that no one was able to read. How would I be able to recognize the spring, I asked. It was quite easy, the old man told me. When I got there, I would find two large fig trees and two chestnut trees growing beside it.

In Erdek, six weeks later and 300 miles away from that conversation with the old man at the café table, I found that only one gnarled fig tree remained of the four trees that Vasilis had last seen sixty years before. The others had been cut down when a local

115

farmer extended his olive grove closer to the fountain. A jet of water still splashed out from the spout and dropped into a trough. Turkish women brought their carpets to scrub, children played in the puddles, and the carters of Erdek stopped here for their horses to drink. Once again it was obvious that favourite watering places had played a vital role in the voyages of the Bronze Age explorers. Knowing where to find good, clean water to replenish a galley with its large and thirsty crew was an essential part of a pilot's job, and, as we had seen at Afissos, such watering places became the fixed points of a coasting tradition. They became fixed points in folk memory, too. The Mycenaeans had believed in springs of water and groves of trees as sacred places, a common feature of animistic belief. A spring sacred to the goddess Artace was a natural place to leave an anchor stone as a thanks-offering for a voyage safely accomplished so far, and the habit of dedicating the anchor stone of a ship was known in ancient Egypt as well as in Greece. Of course it was not Artace who was the goddess of the spring in Jason's time; she was a more recent invention, part of the classical Greek pantheon. In Jason's day the spring would have been sacred to the Great Goddess herself, the Mother Goddess, whose earth-mother role was inherited by Artace. His offering harked back to a far more primeval spirit world.

Nor had that spirit world entirely vanished from Erdek, even in the twentieth century. Just half a mile farther up the path from Jason's Spring was a sacred grove, a place that felt perhaps rather as Jason's Spring would have done when the Argonauts came there. It was a spinney of enormous, venerable chestnut trees, isolated on the side of a low swell in the ground. Another water source broke out from the side of the hill and ran through a natural channel before being led out through a double spout into a basin, and then sliding away down the slope towards some orchards. All around the land was densely cultivated, but this grove of trees had not been touched. It had been left strictly alone, though not shunned. It was a holy place, and felt like it. A great calm seemed to envelop the spot. There was absolutely no sound except the burble of the water and an occasional burst of birdsong. The leaves of the great trees themselves were totally silent. Even the air was cool to the skin. It seemed as if all time was suspended, and here, in the middle of the grove beside the brook, was a great tree so ancient that its heart had rotted away. A tunnel had opened through its great trunk. The sides of the tunnel gleamed, polished slick by the passage of human bodies, over and over again, crawling through the hole in the heart of the tree. It was a wishing tree. At night, I was told, the country people would come secretly to this sacred spot to invoke its magic. They would circle the ancient tree the prescribed number of times and then crawl through the tunnel, making their wish. If they performed the ceremony correctly, the spirits of the place would grant their desire. The supplicants had left tokens on the wishing tree, and its lower branches were hung with strips of cloth torn from their clothes, and little human effigies. The old beliefs, it seemed, still lingered after 3000 years.

Resit Ertezun, the historian of Erdek, was glad to have the identity of Artaki Krini confirmed. He had first come to Erdek in May 1946 as its governor. One day he had noticed pieces of white stone glittering in the surface of a new road that was being built. On inquiry, he was told that some of the new roadstone had been quarried from the ancient ruins of the city of Cyzicus nearby. He went to inspect the ruins, the remains of a Roman city, and that visit changed his life. Forbidding all further robbing of Cyzicus, he began to study the ancient history of the peninsula called Kapidag. He taught himself Latin and Greek in order to be able to read Apollonius and the other authors in the original, and to research the historical background of the Argonaut legend. Now he was the perfect guide to escort the new Argonauts around the sites which he had identified with the early legend.

Soon after Jason and his companions arrived in Kapidag they were met by King Cyzicus, leader of the Doliones, the tribe inhabiting the lowland at the isthmus joining Kapidag to the mainland. King Cyzicus was a young man of about Jason's age, and recently married. His wife, Cleite, had only just arrived from the mainland. Cyzicus invited the Argonauts to shift their boat to the harbour of his city, and to feast with him. During the festivities, according to Apollonius, a wild tribe of aborigines – said to be men with six arms – descended from the interior highlands and attacked *Argo* in her harbour. They were driven off by Hercules (who according to Apollonius was still with the expedition, and would not leave it until the next stage of their journey) and suffered heavy losses.

After the feasting was over, *Argo* put to sea. She sailed out into the Marmara and began rounding the peninsula, only to be hit by a gale which drove her back to land where the crew managed to get a mooring line around a rock at a place they called the Sacred Harbour. What the storm-tossed mariners did not realize was that they had been driven back on to the Kapidag peninsula, and were again in the territory of the Doliones. In the darkness the latter mistook the Argonauts for a band of sea raiders and attacked them. A bloody skirmish followed. Several leading Doliones were cut down and, worse yet, Jason himself killed King Cyzicus without realizing who he was. Dawn revealed the ghastly mistake, and the two sides promptly broke off battle. The shocked Doliones withdrew into their city wall, bearing the corpse of the dead king with them, and the appalled Argonauts set about expiating the terrible crime of killing the man who had been their host only recently.

> For three whole days they and the Doliones wailed for him [King Cyzicus] and tore their hair. Then they marched three times round the dead king in their bronze equipment, laid him in his tomb, and held the customary games out on the grassy plain, where the barrow they raised for him can still be seen by people of a later age.

Cleite, the king's new bride, so Apollonius continues, was unable to face life alone, with her husband in the grave. Capping the evil she had suffered with a worse one of her own devising, she took a rope and hanged herself by the neck. Her death was bewailed even by the woodland nymphs, who caused the many tears they shed to unite in a spring which the people called Cleite in memory of a peerless but unhappy bride.

Resit suggested that King Cyzicus' burial mould could be the large burial tumulus which lies a few miles south of the isthmus, near the town of Bandirma, and which has yet to be excavated. 'Cleite's Spring' is the stream that meanders through the Roman ruins of the city of Cyzicus, named to commemorate the dead Doliones leader. The spring runs through the exact centre of the huge Roman amphitheatre whose jackdaw-infested ruins now dominate cherry orchards and fields of mulberry bushes. In the great days of the ancient city, the spring could be dammed so that it filled the entire floor of the amphitheatre, and mock sea battles were performed by actors in model ships to amuse the audience.

For twelve days after King Cyzicus' funeral, Jason and his

companions were pinned on the Kapidag coast by bad weather, and Resit was confident that he had identified the Sacred Rock around which *Argo*'s hawser had been tied. There was only one offshore rock that would fit the description, and Resit took us to the place that the present inhabitants call Black Rock. Local fishermen still used it as a port of refuge, for it gave good shelter from the northerly wind and waves. The end of the twelve-day period of storms was announced to the seer Mopsus by the arrival of a halcyon or kingfisher which fluttered over Jason's head as he lay asleep on the beach. Mopsus, who understood the language of birds, could interpret the omen. He told the Argonauts that they should now climb to the holy peak of Mount Dindymun in the centre of the island, and make a sacrifice to Rhea, the Great Mother Goddess.

> Leaving a few of their comrades in the ship, they [the Argonauts] climbed the mountain. From the summit they could see the Macrian Heights, and the whole length of the opposite Thracian Coast – it almost seemed that they could touch it. And far away on the one side they saw the misty entrance to the Bosphorus and the Mysian Hills, and on the other the flowing waters of Aesepus and the Nepeian Plain of Adresteia.

Here Argus the shipwright made a sacred image of the Great Goddess, carving it from the trunk of an ancient vine. This statue the Argonauts set up on a rocky point under the shelter of some tall oaks trees, and made an altar of small stones nearby. Then they crowned themselves with oak leaves and made the ritual sacrifices to the goddess Rhea, beseeching her to send the storms elsewhere. Finally, to the music of Orpheus 'the young men in full armour moved around in a high-stepping dance, beating their shields with their swords' to drown the ill-omened wailing and grief that still came up from the city where the Doliones were mourning their king. As a sign of her favour, Apollonius continues, the Great Goddess made the trees shed abundant fruit, and the wild beasts left their lairs and came forward wagging their tails. Moreover, a spring gushed out of the ground where no running water had been seen before.

Resit accompanied us up into the central hills of Kapidag to try to identify the sacred Mount Dindymun, but what had seemed a fairly easy task turned out to be decidedly baffling. The central upland was dotted with various peaks that were much the same height, and we went from one to the other hoping to identify the spot where simultaneously we could see to the Bosphorus, across to Thrace on the other side of the Sea of Marmara, and back down to the Dardanelles whence we had come. The existence of the miraculous spring of water was of little help. We came across at least five small water sources seeping out in the high glens. The most likely peak, we eventually decided, was the point which the Turks called Grandfather Mountain or Dedebayr, the highest summit in Kapidag.

Kapidag coast village

In a pleasant wooded valley to the northeast of the Grandfather Mountain were the ruins of a Greek monastery – the Cherry Monastery, as the Turks now call it, but which was once the monastery of Feneromani. In the early part of this century a Cambridge professor made the interesting observation that the people of the district performed a curious ceremony that may have been a folk memory of the Argonauts' mystic dance around the altar of the goddess Rhea. According to Professor Hazluck, the priests of the monastery would parade every year a sacred icon of the Virgin in the presence of the people of the peninsula. This icon, which was said to have had magic powers, could heal the sick and the lame, and sometimes it would be seized by a man in a religious ecstasy who would run ahead of the crowd with it, crying out and leaping in a frenzy as he ran up into the mountains, while the people all followed him. The professor suggested that perhaps this echoed the ecstatic dance of the Argonauts around the altar to the Earth Mother.

Today the monastery lies in ruins, and the famous icon has vanished. No one in Erdek knew what had become of it – rumour said it was carried away to Istanbul. I, however, knew its real whereabouts, for old Vasilis Kalatheri had also answered that question for me. He told me that the ceremony used to take place every May when he was a young man. Almost the entire population of Erdek would walk across the peninsula to visit the monastery, and the priests would emerge, holding up the icon, and calling 'Hooo! Hooo!' while the crowd followed them. Vasilis had never seen a fanatic snatch the icon and run into the mountains. But he certainly knew where it was now. When the Greeks left Erdek, he told me, they went secretly to the monastery and carried away the icon, and hid it so that they could take it with them when they left. And that evening he showed it to me: it hangs in the raw, new church of Nea Artaki.

Modern *Argo*'s departure from Kapidag was a subdued version of the departure by Jason and his crew. We had been warned that the sea passage around the peninsula was notorious for rough seas and dangerous gusts of wind. Barely had we gone one-third of the way around Kapidag than we were forced to double back and run for shelter, coming so close inshore as we scuttled for harbour that *Argo*'s port steering oar bumped across the rocks with a horrible grating sound. That impact, as it turned out, was to spell trouble for us later on.

After waiting a full day for the gale to cease, we laboured out, rowing through the swell towards the east until we cleared the peninsula and could pick our route along the southern shore of the Sea of Marmara. On 3 June Mark, who had been calculating the number of oar strokes, announced that each oarsman had now completed 100,000 strokes since leaving Volos. A great cheer went up from the crew. This milestone was reached late in the evening, as we were struggling to get to the uninhabited Mola islands for night anchorage. As we rowed, all around us the phosphorescence was stirred into small whirlpools by the oar blades, and below the boat a plume of phosphorescence curled away underwater from the steering oar like a submarine coxcomb. We crept into the anchorage, a deep bay surrounded by cliffs, and our probing torch beams awoke immense numbers of screaming seabirds roosting on the rocks, until they fluttered back and forward in the torchlight like flakes of snow.

Once again we were sharing the experiences of the first Argonauts. This was where, according to Apollonius, the favourable wind had deserted Jason and his men, and they had been forced to row through the hot, long day until everyone was drooping at the oar handles. In the same area we suffered the very same experience. We laboured on, with blistered hands and aching muscles. *Argo* seemed to creep slug-like across the flat, burnished sea. The rhythm of the oars grew slower and slower, as boredom and fatigue set in. I detected a slight counter-current setting against us, and the hazy outline of the land seemed to unroll with agonizing slowness as we clawed along the Marmara shore.

Each day we followed the same grinding routine. We rose at dawn, had a light breakfast, and then took up the oars to begin rowing until noon. Then there was a half-hour break for lunch, before the rowing began once more, on and on, until the sun began to set. Then we headed for the nearest beach, and tried to find a temporary resting place for the night on sand or shingle or perhaps a disused café floor.

Somewhere on this coast, according to Apollonius, Hercules had finally left Jason's team. It was after their most exhausting day of rowing, when the entire crew was so tired that only Hercules and Jason himself had the strength left to row *Argo* to land. At that moment the mighty Hercules had snapped his oar in anger at the weakness of his shipmates. On coming to land he strode off to tear up a small tree and make himself a replacement blade. While he was gone from the Argonaut camp, his squire, Hylas, set off to fetch water. The young man came to a spring called Pegae, and as he leaned over to fill the bronze pitcher, the water nymph of the pool was so entranced by Hylas' beauty that she fell in love with him and determined to keep him. Reaching up, she put her arms around him and drew him down into the water, never to be seen again. Another Argonaut, Polyphemus from Larissa in Thessaly, happened to hear Hylas cry as he was drowning, and went to look for him. He met Hercules on the path, and the two men began to hunt for the missing boy.

Hercules was distraught, and ran here and there calling Hylas' name. Just then a favourable breeze sprang up and Tiphys, the experienced helmsman, decided that it should not be wasted. He ordered the Argonauts to put to sea. Only after *Argo* had made some distance was it noticed that Hercules, Hylas and Polyphemus were not on board. Some of the Argonauts, led by Telamon, a good friend of Hercules, wanted to put back at once and collect them. Another faction, led by Calais and Zetes, the Sons of the North Wind, said no: the gods had sent the favourable breeze as a sign, and it should not be squandered. *Argo* should proceed without the missing men. A quarrel flared up, and soon it was too late to turn back. *Argo* went on without Hercules.

The exact spot where Hylas drowned while going to fetch water is impossible to define. The details about the pool of Pegae are too scanty, and the low ground along the south Marmara shore between Kapidag and the Gulf of Cius is soggy with marshes, springs and even hot mineral waters. According to Greek tradition, Hercules stayed on for some time in the area, continuing his vain hunt for Hylas. When he finally relinquished the search, because he had to go on with his Labours, he forced the people of the area to continue to look. In later years they would hold an annual festival when the young men would go running through the forest calling out 'Hylas! Hylas!' Polyphemus, it is said, founded the city of Cius; and Calais and Zetes, who had advocated leaving Hercules behind on shore, were to suffer the consequences. When the quest for the Golden Fleece was over, and the Argonauts had returned to their homes, Hercules tracked down the Sons of the North Wind and exacted his revenge.

6

Rowing up the Bosphorus

At 6 feet 5 inches Jonathan Cloke was the tallest Argonaut of all. He arrived on 5 June, shortly before *Argo* reached the mouth of the Bosphorus, so he was in time to reinforce the crew for their attempt to row up the straits against the currents and challenge the theory that such a feat was impossible for a late Bronze Age ship. In terms of sheer muscle power, I reckoned that we now stood at least as good a chance of succeeding as anyone. The majority of the new Argonauts were big men, at least 6 feet tall and extremely strong. Of the smaller men, Mark was of course the experienced rowing master and an expert with the oar; Peter Wheeler's stamina as the marathon man was very obvious; and Trondur was a natural sea oarsman, toughened by years of rowing small boats in the rough waters around the Faeroe Islands as well as rock climbing for birds' eggs on the ledges of the Faeroese cliffs.

In addition we were joined at Istanbul by a former curragh-racing champion from Ireland. Curraghs are the small, canvas-covered skiffs peculiar to the west coast of Ireland. They are descended from the original skin-covered native boats which, as early as Roman times, ranged the wild Atlantic coasts, and they are still used by the fishermen as tenders and for netting and lobster fishing. Every summer, at small harbours in the west of Ireland, these fishermen compete in a series of curragh regattas to select the toughest, fastest crew. It is a vividly fought series, conducted with considerable betting and a dash of skullduggery, and the race is started with alarming realism by the umpire firing a shotgun over the heads of the contestants. Two years earlier the winning crew had included Cormac O'Connor, first mate on an Irish trawler. Now he arrived in Istanbul, ready to row for the Argonauts. He was 6 feet 3 inches tall, weighed 216 lb and wore an extra, extra large size in sailing oilskins.

Jonathan's sporting nature was quickly put to the test. He allowed himself to be talked into entering a wrestling match. But this was no ordinary match, nor did he have an ordinary opponent. Jonathan was to compete at Turkish oil wrestling, and he was to wrestle against the Turkish national champion in the heavyweight class.

Jonathan

The reason for this unexpected contest was that a major Turkish newspaper was taking a very keen interest in the progress of *Argo*. Every couple of days an enthusiastic Turkish journalist would show up to check on our condition and interview the crew. Some of his reports were spectacularly wrong. By a mix-up in translations he had understood that our doctor, Nick, who worked as an anaesthetist in hospital life, was a hypnotist. So he informed his readers that Nick's crucial role was to hypnotize the Argonauts into a trance so that they were able to eat the food served aboard. This was a dreadful calumny, both on Nick who was a very conscientious and popular doctor from two expeditions, but above all on Pete the cook, who was having to defend his corner against hungry Argonauts who were highly complimentary of his cooking, and quite undeterred by the regular volley of oaths that greeted them from Pete when meals were ready to be collected from the foredeck.

The Turkish newspaper was determined to make *Argo*'s voyage a success. They had been advertising in their pages for Turkish volunteers to join the crew, acted as our mailbox, and produced a

The Jason Voyage

team of traditional dancers on the quayside when we docked at Istanbul's yacht club in the suburb of Fenerbache on 9 June. It was their idea to hold an oil wrestling match, which was meant to be a substitute for the famous boxing match held between the original Argonauts and the ferocious King Amycus of the Bebryces tribe.

According to the legend, Jason and his companions, after marooning Hercules, had taken advantage of a strong favourable wind to push on briskly towards the Bosphorus. A day and a night's sail duly brought them to a wide bay where they beached at dawn. Immediately they were accosted by Amycus, who had a reputation, according to Apollonius, as 'the world's greatest bully'. It was Amycus' habit to challenge any stranger who entered his territory to fight a boxing match with him. Amycus was a great brute of a man, an expert and deadly fighter, and in the vicious boxing style of the time he was capable of killing his opponent. Already he had killed several of his neighbours and the surrounding tribes lived in dread of him. Backed by his followers, he swaggered down to the Argonauts as they were disembarking on the beach, and announced that they would not be allowed to leave unless they put forward their champion to fight him. Pollux, who was the boxing champion of Greece, took this as a personal affront, and immediately accepted the challenge. The two men, according to the story, were complete opposites – Pollux was young, lithe and skilled; Amycus was older, surly, and like a bull in his tactics. The two were to fight wearing toughened gloves of hardened rawhide which, on the hands of an expert, were lethal weapons. A suitable spot was selected; the gloves bound in place; and, watched by the two groups of supporters, Argonauts and Bebryces, the two champions fought it out to the death.

Amycus, relying on his greater strength and experience, charged at once into the attack, confident of overwhelming and crushing the younger man by sheer power. At first Pollux gave way before the heavyweight onslaught, eluding the tribal chief's furious rushes and relying on his own speed and technique to avoid Amycus' massive blows. But as soon as Pollux had gauged the measure of his opponent's skill and strength, he began to stand up to him, and the two men traded blow for blow, until exhaustion forced them to draw apart and rest, each panting for breath with the sweat pouring off them. Then they rushed together again and took up the fight, battering away to settle the outcome.

Amycus, rising tiptoe like a man felling an ox, stretched
up to his full height and brought his heavy fist down on
the other. But Pollux dodged the blow by a turn of his
head, taking the forearm on the edge of his shoulder.
Then, closing warily, he landed a lightning blow above
the ear, and smashed the bones inside. Amycus collapsed
on his knees in agony; the Minyan lords [the Argonauts]
raised a shout of triumph; and in a moment the man was
dead.

The Bebryces took the defeat of their leader badly. They jumped
up, drew their weapons and rushed at Pollux to cut him down. The
Argonauts ran to the rescue and a pitched battle ensued on the
beach: Castor, defending his twin, split the skull of the first
attacker; and Pollux, still with plenty of fight left in him, took a
running jump at Itymoneus, a huge Bebrycian, and kicked him in
the wind so that he fell to the ground. A right-handed blow put
Mimas, another Bebrycian warrior, out of action, the slashing edge
of the rawhide glove tearing away the man's eyelid and leaving the
eyeball exposed. One Argonaut, Talaus, was wounded in the side
by a spear thrust, but not mortally. And Iphitus, another Argonaut,
was badly shaken by a shrewd blow from a Bebrycian warclub. But
both of the attackers were killed by other Argonauts, and then the
Bebryces broke and ran, leaving the field to the battle-weary
sailors.

Again, there are not enough details in the early text to allow a
positive identification of the spot where the battle took place. The
events read very much as though the Argonauts came up against a
hostile tribe who resented the intrusion of strangers into their
territory, and attacked them on the beach. It is logical that this battle
could have taken place somewhere near the southern entrance to the
Bosphorus or on its banks, where a local tribe either stopped
strangers from passing through, or demanded some sort of toll.
Certainly the Argonauts would have landed near the mouth of the
Bosphorus or during their passage up the straits, simply to gather
strength for the effort of rowing up against the current. A later
tradition places the adventure of the boxing match with King
Amycus on the east bank of the Bosphorus, at about its halfway
point near modern Hisarlik, but does not explain why. The only
clues as to the exact spot are the 'wide bay' where the Argonauts

landed on the beach, and a bay tree around which they tied the hawsers of their ship. The bay tree became, by tradition, a tree which drove men into mad rages, possibly a reference to the berserk fighting style of the barbaric King Amycus.

Oil wrestlers

Fortunately for Jonathan Cloke, his contest with the Turkish wrestling champion was conducted in a rather more good-natured spirit. The spot picked for the oil wrestling match was a grassy field on the east bank of the Bosphorus at Fenerbache, near where *Argo* was a guest of the yacht club. Turkish oil wrestling is said to have originated as a sport for Turkish soldiers celebrating a military victory. After battle the troops would assemble around the parade ground and wrestle with one another simultaneously in a knockout competition. The part played by oil will be described in due course. Today the sport has been revived and is divided into several divisions, like boxing, ranging from heavyweight to juniors and flyweights.

The contest at Fenerbache was more of a light-hearted demonstration match than a championship bout, and an amused crowd of sightseers gathered under the trees. At least fifty oil wrestlers turned up to fight each other. Their costume was a special pair of low-cut breeches made of buffalo hide, tied at the knees. Otherwise the torso and feet were bare. As the wrestlers stood there, thumbs hooked into waistbands and muscles rippling, they looked suitably ferocious, and the most impressive of all, of course, was Jonathan's picked opponent, the heavyweight champion. A man of about forty-five, with close-cropped iron-grey hair, he was built like a locomotive. He had not an ounce of surplus weight, his muscles stood out in sculpted mounds, and he looked like a weathered rock on which the sea had beaten for centuries. His fighting name – Pire Cevat, which means Cevat the Flea – was picked out in brass studs on his breeches. At least, as I pointed out to Jonathan, the Turkish champion had a kindly face. 'Can I go home now?' Jonathan asked mournfully.

A master of ceremonies marshalled the wrestlers. Like a barker at a fairground he was expected to entertain and inform the spectators, as well as judge the contest. He was a short, barrel-shaped man, sporting a large flat hat, a loose white shirt, and an enormous pair of baggy grey pantaloons ornamented with black frogging down the side and girdled with a tasselled white scarf. In this outfit he stalked up and down the grassy ring with tremendous panache, calling out the rules of the contest and bellowing out the name of each wrestler, who stepped forward to take his bow. When he called Jonathan's name, the crowd gave a special cheer. Jonathan looked distinctly out of place in a pair of red sailor trousers rolled up to his knees instead of buffalo hide breeches. I asked my neighbour in the crowd what was the object of the contest. 'To pin your opponent's back to the ground, and offer his belly to the sky!' came the reply.

The master of ceremonies blew on a whistle, and the wrestlers advanced across the grass in the opening ceremony. This was pure theatre. They flexed and rippled their muscles, puffed out their chests, took huge, loping strides and tried to look as ferocious as possible. Every few paces each man would drop to one knee, offer up a short prayer, pick a handful of dust and touch it to his forehead in a formal act of obeisance. Then it was time to begin the contest. The wrestlers divided into pairs. A pipe began to wail, and a drummer started pounding a steady rhythm. The contest would go on as long as the music lasted. As one man emerged victorious from each pair of wrestlers, he could go on to find and tackle another opponent still standing on his feet, until finally only a single victor emerged.

Jonathan eyed his opponent nervously, clearly aware that he was doomed. The two men sparred for a moment to try to find handholds, and suddenly Jonathan found himself snatched up and held upside down, as though his 6-foot 5-inch frame was in the featherweight contest. Gently he was lowered, shoulders first, upon the grass. His second bout lasted slightly longer. This time his opponent dropped into a defensive position and crouched on all fours on the grass. Vainly Jonathan tried to find some way of turning him over. 'It was like trying to pick up a huge, slippery stone, weighing a couple of tons,' he confessed later. 'Absolutely impossible. The man was a solid block of bone and muscle.' A couple of minutes later, Pire Cevat darted out a hand, grabbed Jonathan's leg, and tumbled him head over heels to a roar of appreciation from the crowd who applauded the Englishman's good sportsmanship.

Usually the knockout contest in oil wrestling lasts for several hours, but on this occasion it was speeded up for our benefit. The oil was introduced when the number of wrestlers began to dwindle. Assistants rushed out with tins of olive oil which they poured liberally over the wrestling men, making it even more difficult for them to get a firm grip. The master of ceremonies marched up and down, blowing short blasts on his whistle to denote falls, and acting as referee until finally the field which had been a mass of grunting, grappling contestants was reduced to the winners in each weight division. Cevat the Flea, I was glad to see, had gone on to his usual championship victory in the heavyweights.

A very welcome contingent of Turkish muscle power was also on hand to help us tackle the Bosphorus on 12 June. Eleven Turkish volunteer oarsmen showed up at the yacht club that morning. Six were from the Fenerbache Rowing Club, and five from Galataserai Club. They included the trainer of Turkey's national rowing team, and both clubs' senior coaches.

The day began explosively. The manager of the Sheraton Hotel in Istanbul had generously given free accommodation to the

Argonauts. The crew had already climbed into the minibus that was to take them to *Argo* when Mark came down late to the hotel lobby. Seeing the loaded bus out in the forecourt he ran to catch it, not realizing that the hotel front door, of well-cleaned heavy plate glass, was firmly shut. Mark ran full tilt into it and hurtled straight through in a welter of glass fragments with a tremendous crash that left everyone gasping. Our rowing master tottered for a moment on the pavement, sat down dazedly, and then got back to his feet. Nick checked him for shock and picked out bits of glass from his arms and head, but Mark insisted that he was fit enough to row. As we left the hotel, the magnificently uniformed doorman was still standing there, more stunned than Mark, holding all that was left of his portals – two ornamented door handles that he had collected from the roadway.

There was a certain amount of nervous banter, mostly at Mark's escapade, as the Argonauts took up their familiar places on *Argo*'s

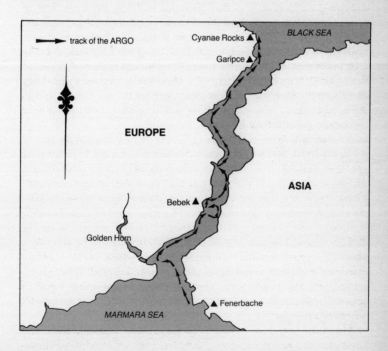

rowing benches and demonstrated the best galley rowing style to our Turkish volunteers. We were well aware that the conditions for rowing up the Bosphorus were far from ideal that day. A breeze was blowing down the channel, a definite headwind. Worse still, a north wind had been blowing strongly all the previous week and this had steadily increased the flow of the current. Before the days of motor power, the normal practice for boats going upstream was to wait until one of the rare southerly winds arose, which at least slowed the current and, if strong enough, could be used under sail; alternatively, the smaller boats were towed up-current by gangs of men on the shore, and a towpath had been provided all along the bank for this purpose. Now, however, the towpath had fallen into disuse. In extreme cases, I was told, the big sailing ships heading for the Crimea had taken more than a month to work their way up the Bosphorus, laboriously heaving themselves up against the current by their windlasses, using cables to the shore as well as patiently dropping anchors in the shallows and kedging forward. But of course none of these options would have been available to Jason and his men. They would have been in potentially hostile territory, with no towpath conveniently at hand, and with the risk of being attacked if they did venture ashore. They would have stayed aboard their galley, which is precisely what Apollonius said they did. They rowed up the Bosphorus, he wrote, by sheer muscle power. Now, 3000 years later, we had to show whether that could have been physically possible: we had to do the same.

We cast off from the yacht club and pulled cautiously out of harbour. Mark and Miles, on the stroke oar position, kept the pace gentle so that the new Turkish oarsmen could get accustomed to the weight and balance of the 14-foot oars. To our starboard side was a low breakwater that gave temporary shelter from the wind and current. Ahead rose one of the world's most evocative and unique skylines – the palaces and minarets of Istanbul, overlooking the Golden Horn. It was a highly emotional moment to be steering a small galley out into this teeming waterway which has been a main artery of trade and seafaring since time immemorial. There is no other place like it on earth. Here is the most important point of contact between Europe and Asia, straddled by a city splendidly worthy of the site.

Ahead of *Argo* sprawled Topkapi Palace with its trees and cupolas, ornate chimneys, steeples, terraces and pavilions dominating the headland which the Ottoman sultans had considered the finest building site in the known world. Behind and alongside Topkapi rose the minarets, domes and semi-domes of truly inspired architecture – the mosques of Suleymanie, Hagia Sophia, Sultan Ahmed and Yeni Cami in a cascade of elegance. Opposite them, across the Golden Horn, Galata Tower stood like a blunt pencil point above the old Genoese quarter of the empress of cities. The whole scene was pulsating with activity. Ferries were churning in and out of the Golden Horn, bustling up-channel towards the northern suburbs or charging recklessly across to Asia, the water foaming around their blunt bows. Downstream we could pick out line upon line of anchored ships in the southern roadstead, where they were waiting to load cargo, receive orders or take on pilots for the straits. Merchant vessels of every description and foreign flag were on the move. A Rumanian bulk carrier was heading north, followed by a Soviet deep sea trawler bound for her home port in the Ukraine. An Israeli freighter was coming south, riding high after discharging cargo in the Black Sea. Behind her a huge oil tanker flying the Liberian flag, deep laden and certainly from a Soviet oil port, glided downstream like a juggernaut with at least 100,000 tons of crude oil aboard. In that treacherous current and shuttling maze of shipping there was no margin for error by anyone. A single false move, and leviathans collided with tremendous force.

Argo rowed past the grim relic of the broken-backed hulk of the crashed tanker that I had seen on my reconnaissance visit to Istanbul eighteen months earlier. The pilot of that doomed ship had headed the blazing vessel out of the main channel and run her aground in the shallows. Teams of men were now cutting up the huge carcass for scrap, like flensing a stranded whale, and *Argo* was utterly dwarfed beneath the huge bow section, looming over us like a rusty cliff. Beyond the tanker wreck was the main current, and I eyed the choppy waves doubtfully.

This part of the Bosphorus, its southern entrance, is some 2½ miles wide, and presented a vast disturbed mass of water spewing south towards the Sea of Marmara at 3–4 knots. That day it was broken into white caps and short maverick waves by the wind and the constant coming and going of ferry boats. *Argo* emerged from the protection of the breakwater, and suddenly we were in the full force of wind and current.

'*Hidi Alla! Hup! Hup! Hup!*' roared the Turkish rowing squad enthusiastically, applying full pressure. The regular Argonauts smiled grimly and heaved on the oar handles in silence. They had already rowed 400 miles, and preferred not to waste a single gasp of breath. There were yells in Turkish of 'Come on! Come on! Pull harder! Pull harder!' as the newcomers realized that rowing 8 tons of galley was not like pulling a featherlight racing craft. *Argo* did not shoot forward like a competition boat; this was going to be a dour, long drawn-out contest against wind and current. 'Hey, is the anchor up?' came a shout, and the Turks laughed.

I set *Argo*'s course at 20 degrees across the current, and tried to slant her towards the opposite bank, just upstream of the Golden Horn. But for every yard we made on that course, we were being swept 2 yards sideways towards the Sea of Marmara. Poor *Argo* was like a floundering beetle fallen into an emptying gutter, in danger of being swallowed down the drain. We were labouring across the surface of the water as fast as we could, but the water itself was washing us away. I began to doubt whether we could actually make it to the opposite shore without being swept helplessly to the southern anchorage. The disturbed surface of the water was our main enemy. Rowing was extremely difficult for the newcomers, unaccustomed to the cumbersome sweeps. *Argo* was bucking and lurching in the waves, and on each forward swing of the oars several blades hit the tops of the waves, breaking up the rhythm of the rowers and reducing our speed. The crew's morale was sky-high, and the oarsmen were laughing and joking. But they could not see – as I could from the helm – that *Argo*'s real progress was barely perceptible.

Then I spotted what I was looking for: the counter-current. The discharge of the Bosphorus is so powerful that, near the banks, the water literally curls round and flows backwards in giant eddies, to fill the vacuum left by the main body of water hurrying south. These counter-currents, which vary in strength and speed and do not form a continuous line along the bank, are the key to a boat getting up the Bosphorus under oars. They exist in patches, particularly in the bays, and there they can assist a boat going upstream. The skill lies in finding the counter-currents and riding them northwards wherever possible. A fisherman had told me that there was an important counter-current just to the north of the Golden Horn on the European side, and now I saw it – a clearly defined line, marked by a grubby streak of foam. On one side the main current was churning and bobbing south; on the other, no more than 5 feet away, the water was virtually flat, moving slowly and calmly in precisely the opposite direction.

'Fifty yards to go and we're out of the worst!' I called out to the crew, and they redoubled their effort, heaving with all their might to gain the last yards of advantage. Suddenly *Argo* slid across the divide. In a single boat's length we passed from chaos to calm, from a hostile environment to a favourable one. It was as if a giant hand had been pulling back on the keel of the boat and shaking it from side to side, and then had abruptly released its grip. In a few seconds the strain was off the oarsmen and they eased their stroke. *Argo* steadied her lurching, and with gentle pressure the crew paddled her northwards. I glanced at my watch. It was 10.30. The crew had been rowing for an hour and a half and all we had yet done was cross from one side of the Bosphorus to the other. Our real northward progress was less than a mile.

Now it was time to keep *Argo* as close as possible to the west bank where the counter-current ran strongest in our favour. It was just like student days when, as cox of a college racing eight, one had to steer the boat as close as possible to the riverbank to gain maximum advantage in a race. But instead of a soft Oxfordshire riverbank of dark loam, the galley's oar blades dipped and rose a yard from the dressed stone river walls of a former Sultan's palace, now a national museum.

I could see that the effort had already taken a lot out of the crew, and they were glad to take the stroke easily for the moment. But the counter-current was fickle. At times we advanced at a brisk walking pace; in the more exposed stretches, where the headwind caught us, we barely crawled along. The palace was followed by another, then by a mosque. Pedestrians using the riverwalk stopped, first to stare and then to wave at us. At 11.40 a shadow passed over us. It was cast by the Bosphorus Bridge, its deck seemingly incredibly high above us as it carried the constant traffic between the two continents while a small Bronze Age galley toiled past below. Guests lunching at a fashionable waterside restaurant, its tablecloths bright yellow, gaped in surprise as we passed, then put down their knives and forks to applaud the labouring oarsmen who grinned and waved back. Next came a line of ships moored against the bank for routine maintenance. Shipyard workers, suspended high above us on bosun's chairs to chip rust from the ships' sides, stopped their hammering and turned to yell encouragement. Their shouts echoed off the towering steel hulls.

Away to our right, out in the main stream, a cluster of small fishing boats rose and fell in the current like a flock of gulls resting on the water. Each fishing boat had its engine running steadily just to hold position in the straits, while they hung their fishing lines into the edge of the deep channel to tempt the shoals of fish which migrate through this single vital artery that joins the Black Sea with the rest of the world's seas and oceans. On the surface the Bosphorus flows steadily south, but deep down another current, which the Turks call the *kanal*, heavier and more salty than the Black Sea's surface water, is seeking to escape in precisely the opposite direction.

At the suburb of Bebek, which was our target for the night, the Bosphorus bends and narrows. This is the choke point of the straits. Here Mehmet II, Ottoman conqueror of Constantinople, built his mighty fortress, Rumeli Hisar, to control the passage. A cannon shot reaches easily to the opposite bank. Through this gap drains all the extra water carried into the Black Sea by the great rivers of eastern Europe and southern Russia, the Danube, the Don, the Dnieper and a host of other rivers and streams rising in an immense arc from the Carpathians in the west to the Caucasus in the east. Some of this water is lost by evaporation, but the bulk of it, 325 cubic kilometres annually, spills out through the Bosphorus. And at Bebek this huge outpouring is constricted to a channel just 800 yards wide.

The result, with a north wind behind it, can be a millrace. The main current ricochets from one bank to the other, from Europe to Asia, twisting and bouncing from one rocky promontory to the next, and in flood times produces tongues of disturbed water that few man-powered vessels could surmount. Certainly *Argo* with her 8 horsepower of human muscle at maximum effort did not have a chance of pulling directly against such an awesome rush of water. Only by using the counter-currents could she proceed. But to reach the counter-currents we had to cross from one shore of the Bosphorus to the next; and in the interval the boat was exposed to the full force of the current.

The little galley crept up the European shore, the crew still rowing easily to save their strength before the next ordeal. I saw the millrace at Bebek point from at least half a mile away. The water was shooting round the corner in a seething mass where a rocky spur thrust out into the current flow. Whirlpools gyrated away from the edges of the race; blobs of foam dipped and spun in the hurrying current. As we drew nearer, I called a warning to the crew: 'Thirty yards to go to the race! . . . Twenty . . . start building up boat speed!' Led by Mark and Miles on the stroke oar bench, the crew increased the rating – the number of strokes per minute – and packed in more effort. *Argo* accelerated. 'Ten metres . . .,' I warned. Just in front of me, Mark began to say, 'Couldn't we stay on this side? Perhaps get round the point, inside the current, and . . .' But before he finished his sentence *Argo*'s bow hit the race, and I heard his startled gasp.

It was like steering failure in a moving car. *Argo* simply went out of control. She skidded sideways as the rushing water flung her off-course, and the current, striking her ram, spun the boat through 90 degrees in an instant. For an awful moment I thought *Argo* was going to be turned right around and projected downstream. She was heeling over from the force of the water, like a small aircraft making a banking turn. The twin steering oars were quite useless, lifeless in my hands as *Argo* lost all forward motion and was swept sideways, her deck at an angle. There was no need to tell the crew what to do. They realized exactly what was happening. At one moment they had been sitting looking down-channel past *Argo*'s stern, and the next instant they were staring at the great curtain wall of Rumeli Hisar with the boat, at right-angles to her previous course, being swept south like a twig.

We had to break out of the millrace. Chunk! Chunk! Chunk! The oar blades chopped into the water in a flurry of quick strokes. The crew grunted with the effort, and rowed at maximum rating. There was no husbanding of effort now. This was all the muscle power they could produce in a short, concentrated burst, twenty men rowing in unison and to the limits of their strength. *Argo* steadied in her crazy swerve; the steering came back to life in my hands, and I could feel the water rushing past the great blades of the steering oars, making the tiller bars quiver. I turned *Argo* to point almost directly up the sweeping current. If only the crew could hold her there, breasting the rushing water, I could inch the galley sideways, across towards the Asian shore. Too much of an angle and *Argo* would be spun once again.

'Come on now! Come on! Maximum pressure! Keep it up! Well done!' *Argo* hung there, poised like a salmon fighting its way upriver. Ever so slowly we began to gain the advantage: it was a barely discernible movement over the ground. I increased the boat's angle of attack to the stream by a hairsbreadth. The gap between us and the European shore began to open up as *Argo* sidled out into the centre of the Bosphorus. On the chart we had just 600 yards to go to reach the area of the counter-current on the opposite bank, but a quarter of a mile against the current meant at least four times that distance through the water. Now, in mid-channel, the wind was much worse. We were exposed to it, and the breeze caught the high prow of the galley and held us back. Even so, I reckoned that *Argo* was making at least 6 knots through the water.

It was a magnificent effort. But was it enough? A quarter of an hour had passed since the first staggering impact of the Bebek current, and the crew were losing their aggressive edge. They were visibly tiring, and a false sense of security was setting in. The shore was too far away for them to judge progress, and we were now out of the most impressive part of the millrace. Only I, as helmsman constantly monitoring the boat's relationship to the shore points, was able to detect that we were no longer advancing. Just perceptibly, *Argo* was being borne downstream. We were no longer in control. The current was now in charge of the galley, dictating her position. If this continued for another five minutes we would become part of the current pattern, swept from one bank to the next, farther and farther south like flotsam as the crew ran out of strength. I realized that the Argonauts had to succeed on this first attempt. If they failed now, the damage to their morale might be irreparable, and the eleven Turkish volunteers might not think it worth coming back for a second attempt. For the first time, as captain of *Argo* I really yelled at the men.

'Come on! Come on!' I bellowed at the top of my lungs, 'You're losing it! We'll be pushed back down to the point we crossed over!' The regular Argonauts looked startled: they had not heard me so vehement before. They went back to full power, and the Turks kept pace with them. Some of the men I could see were at the limit of their stamina. Veins bulged on the forehead of the senior Turkish rowing coach, and he was crimson with effort, gritting his teeth. Chunk! Chunk! Chunk! Thank heaven the rhythm had not been broken. The crew, so many of them new to the boat, were rowing as a real team. The far shore stopped moving in the wrong direction, held still, and then we began to gain ground again.

'They had reached a point', wrote Apollonius of Jason's passage through the Bosphorus,

> where they could see the vast sea opening out on either side, when they were suddenly faced by a tremendous billow arched like an overhanging rock. They bent their heads down at the sight where it seemed about to fall and overwhelm the ship. But Tiphys just in time checked her as she plunged forward, and the great wave slid under her keel . . . . Euphemus ran along, shouting to all his friends to put their backs into their rowing, and with answering shouts they struck the water. Yet for every foot that *Argo* made, they lost two, though the oars bent like curved bows as the men put out their strength . . . .

That is how the first *Argo* struggled through the Bosphorus. And it was exactly how the new Argonauts succeeded. Even as their new burst of energy began to wane, the toiling oarsmen – British, Turkish, Irish and a single Faeroese – heaved *Argo* those last few yards and into the saving counter-current. Gasping with exhaustion, the crew unwound their muscle-cracking stroke, and pulled normally. 'Now that's what I call rowing,' Jonathan grunted.

Once more that day we had to recross the main channel, first creeping up the Asian side to gain a few hundred yards' progress in our friendly counter-current, and then launching out again into the main stream and rowing mightily through the kicking current, back again to an overnight anchorage at Bebek. It was odd, but in those bursts of total effort I noticed that not only were the crew rowing and moving as a single unit, every man swinging in the same motion, but their breathing came in great coordinated gasps as well. It was as if *Argo* in her moment of crisis had acquired a single great set of lungs, pumping with sobs of effort. As we moored *Argo* you could almost taste the feeling of accomplishment. The oarsmen had successfully achieved their day's target: halfway up the Bosphorus against the current and under conditions that were far from favourable. The regular Argonauts burst into a spontaneous round of applause for our Turkish volunteers, who went off proudly comparing their new-won blisters.

'You need forty men today,' Turkey's national rowing coach said next morning as we stood on the quayside at Bebek. A northerly gale was blowing, and the Bosphorus was really showing its teeth. Rowing conditions were totally impossible. Small freighters bound upstream for the Black Sea had their engines at full throttle and the water was piling up around their bows, but they stood almost motionless against the land. In the opposite direction a small rowing boat running downstream was whirling along like a leaf, faster than a man could run, with its canny owner, sitting coolly on the thwart, riding the waves with no need to touch his sculls. I cancelled the day's rowing and went instead to scout the northern entrance to the straits. I got there aboard a sixty-passenger motor launch, and the waves were breaking so steeply that the skipper of the launch refused to venture the last mile; he told me that conditions were too dangerous, and he feared his boat would be swamped.

Twenty-four hours later the gale had eased. The wind was still from the north, and the current was running strongly against us, but with a dozen Turkish volunteers eager to row I decided that *Argo* could still make progress. So we slogged on. This time we had fewer worries. The choke point at Bebek was behind us, and as the straits grew wider so the current speed slackened. To pick up the counter-currents we had to cross to Asia, then back again, but from that point forward we were able to keep along the European side, where the current was weakest and occasionally in our favour. As we approached the Black Sea we began to sense the swell of the open water as the waves came rolling down from the north. Tucking *Argo* as close as I dared to the western shore, we toiled north. The crew had been rowing for more than ten hours when finally we turned into the fishing harbour at Rumeli Fener, the Roman lighthouse. The light marked the end of the Bosphorus. The Black Sea lay before us. The new Argonauts had rowed the entire 18-mile distance from the Marmara to the Black Sea against the current and against the wind. They had shown beyond any doubt that the passage of the Bosphorus could be done in a twenty-oared galley, and the straits had not been an insuperable barrier to Jason and his men in their search for the Golden Fleece.

The experience had also taught me something else: the pattern of currents and counter-currents in the Bosphorus is a clue to the particular shore locations visited by Jason and his companions as described in the *Argonautica*. The currents dictate just where a galley crosses from side to side, either to find helpful eddies or to avoid the worst races. A galley's upstream track is as clearly defined as a footpath that winds through a mountain pass seeking the natural contours of the land. This told me where to look for the home of the blind prophet Phineas who, according to the legend, lived on the banks of the Bosphorus and advised Jason and the Argonauts what would happen to them once they entered the unknown dangers of the Black Sea.

Garipce cliffs

Phineas is the most sympathetic character in the entire Argonaut story. He lived, it was said, within sight of the Black Sea, on the side of the straits. He was a man gifted with the power of seeing into the future, and he had been so accurate in his forecasts and so honest in revealing his predictions to people who came to seek his help that the gods, out of anger at his mortal presumption, had afflicted him with blindness. If he dared see into the future so clearly, then he would not have the power to witness the present. As an additional punishment the Harpies were sent to torment him. These were three winged demons, half-bird, half-woman, and they were reputed to come from a mountain cave in Crete. Whenever blind Phineas was about to eat a meal the Harpies would drop down from the clouds, swoop in with shrieks, snatch away the food from his plate and foul the table with their stench and droppings. As a result, poor Phineas lived in misery and hunger. Local people still came to ask his prophecies and bring gifts of food, but since his blindness Phineas had refused to tell them the entire future, dreading further punishment from the gods.

The figure of Phineas is identical to the same type of wise hermit who, in the Christian era, would choose to live in isolation in a desert cave or on a rocky island at the edge of the ocean. These recluses, too, were credited by local people with special powers, such as healing or prophecy, and were looked after by them. In the same way the people at the north end of the Bosphorus would have left gifts of food for Phineas, who had become their local wise man, and it is hardly surprising that seabirds learned to rob him of food, leaving their droppings on the rocks. Roman commentators reading Apollonius believed they had identified the exact place where Phineas had lived: they called it Gyropolis, the Place of the Vultures, because they believed the Harpies were a local species of vulture that snatched away the blind man's food. The spot they identified, a place on the European shore near the northern end of the Bosphorus, matches Apollonius' description, for he says that Phineas lived near a bay, and from his home he could tell the visiting Argonauts which way they should turn when they emerged from the straits into the Black Sea.

No vultures live today, if they ever did, near Gyropolis; it is now called Garipce, meaning 'strange' or 'weird', because of its curiously shaped rocks and crags which make very suitable sites to be associated with a lonely hermit seer. Moreover the same cliffs are pockmarked and striated with cavities and ledges that make excellent nesting sites for seabirds, and their droppings streak the cliff faces. The seabirds have selected the site not just for its nesting potential, but for the rich fishing grounds nearby. Here the Black Sea forces its way into the narrow funnel of the Bosphorus and the mingling and swirling of the waters produces ideal conditions for fish to feed; and here too pass the huge shoals of fish which migrate annually through the straits. In short, Garipce is the natural location for the species of predatory seabirds that may have preyed on the blind Phineas, and then entered mythology as the Harpies.

But our experience in the new *Argo* offered another reason why Garipce could have been the site of Phineas' home. It is the last sheltered place where one can go ashore in the Bosphorus before embarking on the wide expanse of the Black Sea, and it lies exactly on the galley track dictated by the currents. For the last 6 miles, northward-bound, an oared vessel is obliged by the current to hug the western shore of the Bosphorus. And then, just as the Black Sea opens up before the mariner, he finds the tiny cove of Garipce on his left-hand side, offering a perfect haven. The sailor would go ashore for three reasons: to rest after the exertions of the Bosphorus and before entering the Black Sea; to seek sailing directions in the unknown waters ahead; and, most important of all, to take on his essential need – fresh water.

That, surely, is what Jason would have done. Garipce is still the last natural harbour before the Black Sea. Today both sides of the northern approaches to the Bosphorus are military zones, forbidden to civilians. But tucked away inside this military enclave survives the village of Garipce. Where the curious, black, contorted cliffs are pierced by the small gap of the tiny cove a handful of fishing boats are pulled up on the beach, completely safe from the massive swells of the Black Sea which heave down on the entrance to the Bosphorus, driven by gales sweeping out of Russia. Garipce is just a hamlet of traditional wooden Turkish houses with a simple mosque, a charming, traditional place, untouched by modern life because of its military isolation. And above it lie the ruins of a fort.

In days gone by, no boat bound for the Black Sea would have passed by this haven without stopping. At the foot of the cliff at the back of the village I found what I half-knew would be there – a spring of superb fresh water bursting out of the rock. A splendidly worked brass spigot closed off the waterpipe which tapped a water source emerging from the base of the cliffs. Irgun, whose father, when I first met him, made his living as a water seller in Istanbul, tasted the Garipce spring water and pronounced it delicious. It was, he said, as good as any water imported to the city. Even if they had not needed to visit Phineas to ask his advice about navigating the Black Sea, Jason and his men would have stopped here to take on fresh water for the next stage of their long journey.

The legend says that Jason did much more than resupply *Argo*. When they heard of Phineas' troubles with the Harpies, two of the heroes, Zetes and Calais, offered to deal with the three bird-women. For this task they were particularly well qualified: as Sons of the North Wind, they had the power of flight. A banquet was spread as a bait for the Harpies, and Zetes and Calais hid in ambush with drawn swords. Sure enough, they soon heard the rushing sound of the Harpies' approach and the creatures' dreadful screeches as they swooped down and began to tear at the food. At that moment Zetes and Calais leaped out of ambush and chased off the intruders; the Harpies took wing and flew away, and the Sons of the

North Wind followed them. After a long chase Zetes and Calais caught up with their quarry, some say near the rocks called Strophades off the west coast of Greece. There the two heroes would have cut down the Harpies with their swords if the Olympian gods had not intervened. They sent the goddess Iris as their messenger to warn the sons of Boreas that they were not to harm the Harpies, but let them go free, and in future the bird–women would no longer torment the blind seer. So Zetes and Calais gave up the chase, and turned back to bring the good news to Phineas and the Argonauts, waiting at the northern end of the Bosphorus.

In gratitude Phineas now gave the Argonauts all the directions they needed for the next part of their quest. He told them to turn east as they emerged from the Bosphorus and row far along the north coast of Asia Minor, hugging the shoreline. He listed the tribes they would encounter, the harbours they would find and the adventures they would have. But what would happen to them when they finally reached Colchis, the Land of the Golden Fleece, he refused to divulge. That, he said, would be to reveal too much; the Argonauts would have to learn for themselves.

Phineas' greatest service was more immediate. He revealed to the Argonauts the secret by which they could escape the greatest physical danger of their entire voyage, the danger which had destroyed every ship that had previously attempted to pass through the straits. This was the menace notorious throughout the ancient world as the Clashing Rocks.

Garipce village

7

The Black Sea

'When you leave me,' said Phineas,

> the first thing you will see will be the two Cyanean Rocks, at the end of the straits. To the best of my knowledge, no one has ever made his way between them, for not being fixed to the bottom of the sea they frequently collide, flinging up the water in a seething mass which falls on the rocky flanks of the straits with a resounding roar. Now if, as I take it, you are god-fearing travellers and men of sense, you will be advised by me. You will not brashly throw away your lives or rush into danger with the recklessness of youth. Make an experiment first. Send out a dove from *Argo* to explore the way. If she succeeds in flying between the rocks and out across the sea, do not hesitate to follow in her path, but get a firm grip on your oars and cleave the water of the straits.

The stratagem with the dove worked beautifully. As Jason's crew rounded the last corner of the straits they saw the Cyanean or Clashing Rocks ahead of them. The rocks were two great moving masses of stone which floated about the mouth of the straits, colliding repeatedly with tremendous shocks. Whenever a ship tried to pass between them the rocks closed together like a giant trap, pulverizing the intruder. Even now, the Argonauts saw, the rocks had just snapped shut, and were beginning to move apart again. As *Argo* rowed up to the gap Euphemus, the runner, released the dove, which flew low and straight between the rocks.

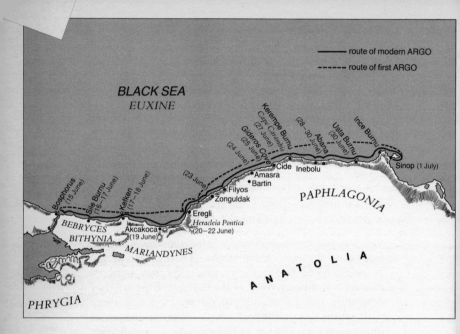

Immediately they collided again, but too late. The Argonauts saw that the dove had dashed through the gap, and the rocks only succeeded in nipping off her tail feathers.

This was the signal for Jason and his men to forge ahead. As the rocks sprang apart, the rowers made a terrific spurt, and *Argo* sped into the gap. For a dreadful moment the boat hung there, caught in the swirling backwash and unable to move either forwards or back. It seemed certain that the rocks would crush her. At that moment, according to the *Argonautica*, the goddess Athena intervened to save them. With one hand she held back the rocks, and with the other she pushed *Argo* through the gap. It was in the nick of time. The Clashing Rocks banged shut, sheering off the galley's stern ornament. From that time forward, wrote Apollonius, 'the Rocks were now rooted for ever in one spot close to one another. It had been decided by the happy Gods that this should be their fate when a human being had seen them and sailed through.'

For hundreds of years attempt after attempt has been made to attribute the phenomenon of the Clashing Rocks to natural causes.

146

They have been explained as a shallow reef which, it is said, was sometimes exposed and sometimes covered by the tide on the Asian side, where many coast-hugging ships had come to grief. Another idea was that the Clashing Rocks were huge ice floes, brought south from the Crimea in the spring break-up, which damaged ships in the approaches to the straits. But sea ice has very rarely been recorded so far south in the Black Sea; nor are there really dangerous reefs on either side of the Bosphorus' northern entrance, only a few offshore rocks which are easily spotted and just as easily avoided in waters that have very little tidal rise and fall.

Yet much of Apollonius' description does ring true to anyone who navigates the straits in a rowed boat. His description of the swirling back eddies between the rocks, the manner in which *Argo* lay helpless in the current, how it seemed that at the last moment Athena literally seized the boat and pushed her forward at the critical instant when the oarsmen no longer had the strength to drive her on against the current – these are dramatized versions of very real difficulties. Farther down-channel, when struggling up through the Bebek section of the Bosphorus, any galley would encounter the millraces, the uncontrollable behaviour of a small boat whirled suddenly around in the current, the odd sensation when a counter-current picks up the boat and lifts her forward, just as the goddess Athena was supposed to have saved *Argo*. Then, 11 miles farther north at the entrance to the Black Sea, comes the rest of his description: the spray being flung high by the storm-driven swells surging into the constricting funnel of the Bosphorus' northern mouth, and the booming crash of the waves as they strike the headlands on either side and rebound in a tossing backwash.

Here, too, are the physical remains of the Clashing Rocks of antiquity. The ancients did not hesitate to identify them as the two large chunks of rock which lie 80 yards off the northern headland at Rumeli Fener. Their other name was the Cyanean, or Dark Blue, Rocks because as Mark, our classicist aboard the new *Argo*, told me when we had clambered up to the top of them, dark blue was the colour of menace and danger in classical times. In reality the rocks are a charcoal colour with tones of green; they are formed of huge lumps of conglomerate that appear to have broken away from the nearby cliffs. A narrow cleft cuts them in two, so that by a stretch of the imagination one could suppose that they had once been apart and floating like vast lumps of pumice stone on the surface of the sea. Their evil reputation as the Clashing Rocks was pure myth, an invented symbol to explain the real difficulties of passing through the straits of the Bosphorus. Once Jason and his Argonauts had succeeded in making the passage and entered the Black Sea, the rocks symbolically lost their power; never again did they menace any ship passing that way.

Ironically, the dreaded rocks have now been converted into a shelter, not a threat, for shipping. A very recent concrete mole joins the rocks to the mainland, and in its lee nestles a large fleet of fishing craft. The fishermen say that in the winter gales the spray still bursts right over the rocks, some 40 feet high, and the accompanying roar can be heard far inland. And the rocks, they claim, are still the true boundary of the Bosphorus' dangers. In bad weather no ship, however large, can be considered to be in safe water until she has passed north of the rocks, clearing the turbulence of the shallowing mouth to the straits.

On the flat crest of the innermost rock Mark and I found the

Mustafa

remains of a Roman pillar, a fluted block of marble some 4 feet high and about 3½ feet in diameter. It was a segment of a stone column which had once served as a landmark for ships entering and leaving the straits. Before that, the Greeks had built their own altar on the same spot, for here they made sacrifices and sought the favour of the gods before they dared venture upon the northern sea. This was a crucial moment in a voyage, the place when a man embarked upon the sea the ancients feared so much that they called it 'The Inhospitable Sea'.

The Black Sea still keeps its notoriety. Time and again we had been warned – by Turkish fishermen in the Bosphorus and the Sea of Marmara, and by Greeks in the Aegean – that the Black Sea was no place for an open boat. There were sudden gales, they said, which struck without warning. Even the wave pattern, according to some of the Turks, was different from anything else they knew. In some areas off the coast we would encounter a peculiar repetition of three waves, larger than the others, which came one after another close together. No boat was entirely safe or comfortable among the triple waves, they said. She could be swamped or damaged, and would ride the seas unhappily, shaking herself to pieces. So notorious was the triple wave that no fishing boat would operate off certain sections of the coast: the sailors just refused to work there.

So it was with a certain amount of trepidation that on 15 June *Argo* steered out from the harbour behind the Clashing Rocks, and we began the long haul eastward along Turkey's north coast. A fresh batch of Turkish volunteers had replaced the men who had helped us from Canakkale to Istanbul. Mustafa was black-bearded and serious; Ziya normally worked as a translator in an import-export company; his great friend Yigit was a twenty-six- year-old economics student who turned out to be a natural seaman; and Husnu was a friend of Ali's, an architect by training and with a similarly excellent command of English. Young Umur, who had seemed so glum when he first joined, now announced that, far from ending his trip aboard *Argo* in Istanbul as had been the original plan, he would like to stay with the Argonauts as long as possible. Finally there was a twelve-year-old supernumerary aboard – my daughter Ida, who had been promised a few days on *Argo* to make up for the long absences of her father while the expedition was preparing and the galley was being built.

Ida was delivered to *Argo*, while at sea, by Kaan's family, my Istanbul friends of long standing. There was nothing the family would not do to help the expedition. Irgun, the eldest son, was now a businessman on his own account, running an office that arranged driving licences and car registration with the traffic police. His energy and optimism were boundless. 'When other people give up,' he told me with his characteristic confidence, 'that is when I begin. There is no such word as impossible.' Indeed Irgun seemed to be some sort of genie appearing out of the Turkish lamp. At Istanbul the Turkish Coastguard had decided that *Argo* was not going to sink forthwith, and so we no longer needed a constant patrol boat escort. Instead the Coastguard would keep an eye on us from time to time when they had a vessel in the area. Now it was Irgun who kept on popping up in unexpected places. Like Uncle John back in Greece, he seemed to know everyone connected with harbour life – captains of ferry boats, skippers of fishing trawlers, yachtsmen, customs officials, coastguard controllers, Bosphorus pilots. If they glimpsed *Argo* rowing past their stretch of coast, they contacted Irgun and he would suddenly appear on the quay of some obscure port or his voice would surprisingly answer back from the little walkie-talkie radio which I used to contact the rubber dinghy when it went on shopping trips to collect supplies.

But Irgun had a rival. Mukaddes, his youngest sister, was determined to outdo him. I had last seen her as a shy thirteen-year-old with enormous fawn-like eyes, the seventh in her family of eight, all happily clustered round the dining table in their two-room apartment. Since that time, however, Mukaddes had flourished extraordinarily. She was now a highly successful Istanbul businesswoman, just as energetic and enthusiastic as her brother. She struck up an alliance with an older sister, Ikun, who was a supervisor in a telephone exchange, and together, by telephone, they put together a watching system which was the equal of Irgun's. Not a lighthouse keeper or a harbour master was left undisturbed by telephone calls from Ikun and Mukaddes, checking whether *Argo* had been sighted.

Mukaddes picked up Ida at Istanbul's airport, whisking her away under Irgun's nose, for he too had gone to meet her, and the next morning Mukaddes had persuaded a fishing boat skipper to set out in chase of the galley which was by then in the Black Sea. Mukaddes, Ikun and several other members of the family were waving from the bridge of the trawler when it caught up with us and Ida scrambled aboard. At the same time Irgun's voice could be heard calling us faintly on the walkie-talkie, and by the time we got into the next little harbour there he was, having driven four hours to get to us. Searching the sea with binoculars, he had spotted us from a clifftop and was on hand to greet us with the words: 'Is there anything you need? Just let me know.' He had already advised the harbourmaster, the local mayor and the corporal in charge of port security that *Argo* was on her way. Then he left us for another four-hour drive back to Istanbul – in the wake of a major operation, after which he had emerged from hospital only two weeks before.

Such meetings were bright interludes in our long, gruelling haul eastward. It was no holiday. The day's routine normally began at 6 a.m. when the crew roused themselves and left the beach where they had been sleeping on the sand. They climbed back aboard to join the three or four men who had spent the night asleep on the foredeck and central gangway to provide an emergency team in case the wind increased in the night and *Argo* began to shift her moorings. We weighed anchor and rowing began immediately. The men would row for an hour, keeping to the standard rota of ten men at the oars, while their companions rested. Every five minutes one bench of two oarsmen was replaced by a fresh pair of rowers. Then, after an hour's hard work, the system changed. The entire crew divided into two equal groups, and one group rowed for a quarter of an hour while the other group took breakfast. Then the two groups switched places until, breakfast completed, the normal rota was resumed, and *Argo* went grinding forward at 3–3½ knots for another five hours, with just a mug of tea for sustenance.

Newcomers found the regime crippling. Even the fittest of them were sagging with exhaustion after three hours of such toil. The regular Argonauts kept rowing on and on until midday, when there was a break for lunch. We would anchor *Argo* in the shallows, and the crew wolfed down their meal before going for a swim. Then at about 1.30 in the afternoon the cry went up again: 'Oar bench positions! Time to get going! Oars outboard. Are you ready? Row!' and the aching routine would continue until we reached our evening's halting place. On the very worst days the crew rowed for eleven blistering hours before *Argo* put ashore for the night.

Understandably, everyone loathed the actual rowing. It was mindless, repetitive and boring, and almost any diversion was welcome. Some tried reading as they rowed, propping up a book on the bench beside them. Others put on headphones and listened to music on cassette players until the tapes themselves became tedious. Word games were played and joke lists were instituted. Each man in turn had to tell a joke, the longer the better, but if the joke was too awful a time ban was placed on it and it could not be repeated for at least two weeks; truly painful jokes were forbidden for two years. By far the most successful activity was singing, whether solo or in chorus. Songs gave a rhythm to the oars and coordinated the efforts of the rowers. Modern pop songs rarely fitted. The best tunes were either beer-drinking songs or rousing Church of England hymns, whose rhythm was particularly suited to a galley stroke. So the Turks listened in puzzled wonder as the regular Argonauts, led usually by Tim Readman, roared out *Hymns Ancient and Modern*, interspersed at random with bar-room ballads. Our champion singer proved to be Cormac, who had a fine singing voice and a wide repertoire of sea shanties and traditional Irish songs; with the crew taking up the chorus behind him, Cormac sang our way along the Anatolian coast.

Steadily the expedition crept eastwards. On good days the breeze might come to our aid and the crew would take a break, resting their rowing while *Argo* glided forwards under sail. At such times there was no question of halting to pick up food supplies. Even ten minutes of the favourable breeze was far too precious to be wasted. Pete the cook and Tim the purser would set off in the rubber dinghy with its little outboard engine, from which we also took photographs, and make their way ashore to find a town and buy food, while *Argo* continued down the coast. Later the supply party would rejoin us whenever they were ready, and in the meantime *Argo* made use of every whisper of breeze.

Food was becoming increasingly difficult to obtain in the smaller settlements: the demands of a large, very hungry crew of oarsmen were sometimes more than a village grocer or butcher could meet. Peter the cook had to work hard to satisfy everyone's appetites – we ate tubs of yoghurt, sacks of fruit and bread, and whatever meat was available. Fish was virtually unobtainable – the only time we ate fish was when Cormac caught it for us. Peter Warren, Peter Wheeler and Trondur were fanatical fishermen, and the areas around their benches were booby trapped with a repellent-looking selection of lines, rusty hooks, lead weights and rotting pieces of meat and fancy lures. But they only ever caught tiddlers. Cormac, on the other hand, had the magic touch. If there were fish, they came to his hook, and he successfully pulled in several dogfish, 3 feet long, that made good eating.

Trondur, however, harvested the sea in other ways. At the port of Kefken, and again near Zonguldak, he went hunting in the sea caves for nesting seabirds. Over his tennis shoes he pulled thick socks of grey Faeroese wool so that he would not slip on the weed-covered rocks, and he disappeared with the rubber dinghy into the gaping mouths of the caves where cormorants and seagulls could be seen coming and going. At the back of the cave Trondur would jump ashore and begin clambering towards the upper ledges.

'It was a great sight,' Tim Readman told me after returning from one hunt. 'Trondur went straight up the rock face, with the young cormorants peering out from their nests above him, clucking and gobbling with curiosity and alarm. Then, suddenly, Trondur's shaggy head appeared over the edge, and the next thing there was a frantic squawking and squalling, and feathers flying out in all directions and a terrific scuffling. By then all you could see of Trondur were his woolly socks sticking out from the ledge while he grabbed his prey. Then he reappeared and came back down dangling a young cormorant in each hand, by the neck.'

'A cormorant's neck is long enough,' said Cormac, looking at the catch, 'but when Trondur's finished with the creature it looks more like a giraffe.'

Skinned and boiled in sauce, cormorant casserole *à la* Trondur Patursson was a great success. The flesh had the colour and taste of jugged hare, and the best meals started with an appetizer of mussels gathered off the cave walls and baked over a driftwood fire on the shingle.

On 19 June, at 2.30 in the afternoon, the 200,000th oar stroke of the voyage was announced by rowing master Mark, and the crew were still exuberant enough to speed up the rating, churning the water with exaggerated power and roaring out the countdown. It didn't seem to matter that they had been rowing since 7.15 in the morning, without a proper break for either breakfast or lunch. That evening a thunderstorm brewing out to sea gave us a helping breeze, and we sighted the headland of Eregli, behind which, according to Apollonius, lay the Mouth of Hell and the next identifiable point on the track of the original *Argo*.

An armada of fishing boats was waiting to greet us. They came churning out of Eregli and formed up in a jostling phalanx all around, their decks crowded with spectators. To my alarm, one large trawler cut across directly ahead of *Argo* and a burly Turk, stripped to his underpants, climbed on the rail of the flying bridge and flung himself into the sea, a 25-foot drop, landing directly in our path. He disappeared from sight, and I was terrified that he would be chopped to mincement by the propellors of the fishing boats crowding in behind us. By a miracle, he grabbed the handhold which Peter Wheeler had made for *Argo*'s ram – and came

climbing up the bow, dripping, moustachioed and as furry as a seal.
He was drunk, and determined to give a huge hug of greeting to the
first Argonaut he met. That Argonaut happened to be Trondur, in
full beard and bushy hairdo, and the tipsy Turk was slightly
disconcerted.

'This lofty headland,' wrote Apollonius of Eregli,

> with its sheer cliffs, looks out across the Bithynian Sea.
> Beneath it at sea level lies a solid platform of smooth rock
> on which the rollers break and roar, while high up on the
> landward side it falls away in a hollow glen. Here is the
> Cave of Hades with its overhanging trees and rocks,
> from the chill depths of which an icy breath comes up and
> covers everything with sparkling rime that melts under
> the midday sun. The frowning sea mingles for ever with
> the rustling of the leaves as they are shaken by the wind
> from Hades Cave. Here, too, is the mouth of the River
> Acheron, which issues from the mountainside and falls
> by way of a deep ravine, into the eastern sea . . . . The
> Argonauts brought their ship to the same spot. Shortly
> after the wind dropped, they beached her in the shelter of
> the Acherusian Cape.

The Mouth of Hell is the second in a row of three caves which pierce
the limestone hillside on the left bank of what is now called Frog
River, Der Bagh, by the inhabitants of modern Eregli. The river, as
Apollonius said, runs out into the Black Sea just beside the
Acherusian Cape, which is now a military zone, for Eregli is a
strategic harbour on the north coast of Turkey and the headquarters
of the Turkish naval commander. The development of the modern
town of Eregli has covered over the classical Greek harbour and
altered the shoreline, but it is still possible to follow the road that
leads up the winding course of Frog River where, until the
beginning of this century, small boats used to moor beside the first
of the caves, which contains the remains of a mosaic floor and a very
early Christian chapel.

The second cave is far larger. Its entrance is only a narrow cleft in
the rock, and it was easy to see why it was considered to be the
Mouth of Hell. Apollonius wrote that an 'icy breath' came out of it.
In spring and winter, said our guide, who was the local apothecary's
son, a dense mist fills the thickly overgrown valley and shrouds the

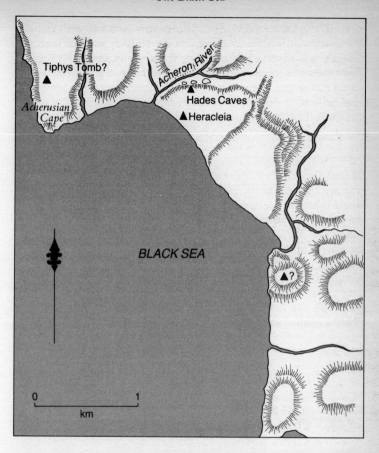

bushes and trees and the surrounding slopes with a clammy white
fog that seems to emanate from the cleft. The narrow cave entrance,
just big enough to squeeze through, plunges downwards and turns
a tight spiral, so the visitor must hold onto the clammy rock, which
glistens with condensation and Apollonius' 'sparkling rime', the
limestone surface sheen. Inside, the temperature drops still further,
and the passageway leads out onto the floor of an underground
cavern which once penetrated 1½ kilometres into the heart of the
mountain, though in 1960 a massive rock fall closed off the back of
the great cave. In the centre of the underground chamber lies a pool

155

of deep, clear water; the sides of the grotto shimmer with runnels and gutters of limestone glaze; and the chill air is filled with the constant sound of water dripping from the ceiling, or trickling down the walls to embalm everything with lime. To a Bronze Age visitor, standing there with only a firebrand or oil lamp for illumination, it must indeed have seemed like an entrance to the Underworld. Scraps of pottery, broken Greek and Roman statuary and the soot marks of lamps have been found where the ancients practised their cult worship.

Hercules was said to have come here on his Labours, to drag out the guardian of the Underworld, the hideous dog Cerberus. The creature slavered at the indignity of his capture, and it is said that where the deadly drops of his spittle flecked the ground, there grew the poisonous plant aconite, which is still gathered around Eregli and used as a folk medicine. Whether this was Hercules' only visit to the place is not known, but legend has it that he also passed this way when he went to capture the jewelled girdle of the Queen of the Amazons, another of the Labours, and assisted the local people in their tribal wars. In any event, the modern town commemorates the Hero, for Eregli is the modern version of ancient Heracleia Pontica, named in his honour.

The Acherusian Cape

When Jason and his Argonauts arrived, they were particularly well received. The local tribe, the Mariandyni, were bitter enemies of the Bebryces, whose bullying King Amycus had recently been killed by Pollux in the boxing match. The Mariandyni and the Bebryces had been fighting a border war, and King Lycus of the Mariandyni was delighted that the Argonauts had inflicted such a punishing defeat on the Bebryces. Pollux, of course, was lionized as the man who had slain the bully himself, and he and the other Argonauts were invited to stay at Lycus' palace and share in a feast of celebration. King Lycus also announced that in honour of the great Castor and Pollux he would build a monument on the headland, where it would serve as a sea mark to all future sailors who passed that way. Moreover he would send his own son, Dascylus, with the Argonauts to serve as their guide and to act as their envoy to friendly tribes living farther along the coast of Asia Minor.

Sadly, though, the visit to Lycus ended in a double tragedy. From the start of the venture Idmon, the soothsayer, had known that he would never return alive from Jason's voyage; he was doomed to die on a foreign shore. At dawn, as the travellers were returning to *Argo* from Lycus' feast, loaded with presents from the king, they disturbed a sour old wild boar lying in the reed beds of the river. The brute charged out and gored Idmon, gashing his leg. Idmon fell, mortally wounded, and though his companions killed the boar with javelins, they could do nothing to save Idmon's life. They carried him back to *Argo* where he died in his friends' arms. His death demanded three days of formal mourning, and on the fourth day the Argonauts buried their shipmate on the slopes of the headland, raising a barrow over the grave and planting it with a wild olive tree as a memorial.

The delay caused by the funeral rites was fatal for another Argonaut, this time their crack helmsman, Tiphys. He sickened and died after a short, unexplained illness which may have been fever contracted in the marshy swamps of the Acheron. Tiphys, too, was buried on the headland, close to his companion, and for a total of twelve days the quest for the Golden Fleece came to a gloomy halt. Jason was downcast by the loss of his two companions and lost all will to continue with the voyage. The other Argonauts were equally despondent, and it was left to Ancaeus to take the initiative. He offered to replace Tiphys as helmsman, pointing out that he also was a very experienced sailor, and he managed to rouse the others from their glum mood and cajole them into continuing with the quest.

By a fortunate chance the most likely site for the graves of Tiphys and Idmon has escaped the expansion of modern Eregli. The 'Acherusian Height', where they were buried, according to the

Argonautica, lies within the present military zone and is still unspoilt countryside covered by turf and small trees. As we rowed out aboard *Argo* we could look up from the sea, as the early sailors had done, and there on the very peak of the hill noted the ruins of an ancient building, almost certainly the base of a former lighthouse or watchtower. The ruins stand on a low mound which appears to be artificial, and could be an ancient barrow grave. When the military zone is open to the archaeologists, this must be the first place to be searched for the last remains of two of the men who sailed with Jason aboard *Argo*.

Beyond Eregli, where my daughter Ida left us, we came to the coal town of Zonguldak, and the mayor sent out two tugs to divert the galley into harbour. Another dance troupe was waiting for us on the jetty, this time to perform a true Black Sea dance. They were clothed in tight tunics of jet black and performed the Fish Dance, quivering and shaking in imitation of a shoal of anchovies taken by the fishermen's nets and spilled flapping on the deck. Flashing silver chains, shimmering tassels and leather straps, all trimmed in silver, glistened and glittered as the dancers mimicked the capture and the death throes of the struggling fish.

Akcakoca, Eregli, Zonguldak – every town we passed on this coast wanted to make us welcome with gifts, flowers, folk dances and food for the new Argonauts. The delay in Zonguldak had put us behind schedule, so dusk found us rowing tiredly off a bleak and exposed beach. A few local fishing boats were moored in the shallows, but the rest of the fleet was drawn far up the beach, well out of harm's way. It did not look a very safe spot to stay for the night, but we were too exhausted to continue. The anchor went down, we ran out a stern line to the shore and had our supper. Then most of the crew bedded down as usual on the sand dunes, while with the members of night watch I remained on board. At about midnight, the stars were blotted out by great black clouds that swept in from the north. Suddenly there was frantic activity on the beach. Lights began to bob up and down as the local boat owners appeared and began to run back and forth. There was much shouting.

'The black wind is coming!' Ali called to me from the beach. 'They say it is dangerous, and we must be careful!'

The local fishermen were wading out into the sea to reach their moored boats and manhandle them to the sand with tow lines.

Others were turning home-made beach windlasses to haul the craft high out of the water.

'They say it will be better if you take *Argo* from the sea,' Ali shouted again. 'They say there is a big windlass to pull her, and they will help.'

I decided that it would be wiser to trust to *Argo*'s anchors, and leave her where she was. Fiddling around on an open shore, in a rising wind and in the dark, was not likely to be effective, and *Argo* ran more risk of being damaged in the manoeuvre if she was caught half-in and half-out of the water when bad weather hit us. The onboard emergency watch was stirring – I could see the three sleeping bags on the foredeck change shape. Their occupants had been awakened by the pandemonium and were obviously peeping out, reluctant to crawl out into the rain which was beginning to spit down in the darkness. They soon realized that there was nothing of it but to pull on oilskins, tend to the anchor warps and start rigging the wet-weather canvas cover.

We were still lashing down the last corners of the canvas when the squall struck. It was not as fierce as the fishermen had feared; nevertheless the onboard crew were kept busy, casting off the rope that held *Argo*'s stern to the beach, pulling in on the main anchor so that the boat floated out into deeper water, and heaving out a storm anchor to hold her from being driven ashore by the rapidly increasing waves. By then the rain was really coming down hard, and the first flashes of lightning illuminated the scurrying black shapes of the shore-based Argonauts running pell-mell for shelter from the downpour. They could crawl under upturned boats to keep dry, while the onboard watch got soaked.

'So they call this the luck of the Irish!' muttered one of the drenched figures beside me on board as we struggled to heave in a soggy mooring warp. It was Cormac, and I realized that, by chance, the onboard night watch was composed entirely of the Irish Argonauts. From that day forth the foredeck where the three of them had decided to sleep that damp night was known to the rest of the crew as the 'Irish Embassy'.

The thunderstorm was a portent of a change in the weather. For another three days, as we rowed and sailed eastwards, the rain showers became more and more frequent. Beyond the ancient and beautiful port of Amasra, where we spent one night moored in the oval of the old galley harbour, the coastline of Turkey began to change. Steep hills now came right down to the sea, and the land had a much wilder and more desolate air. We rowed past magnificent precipices where the seagulls wheeled against the rocks like white specks of foam. The mountains behind them were covered with forests of chestnut and mile upon mile of hazelnut bushes which were harvested by the local farmers. From time to time we passed an isolated cove, joined to the interior only by a narrow earth track. At the back of each cove was often a small flat area of meadow land where we could see a wooden farmhouse, one or two barns, and several small fields divided by wooden rails. There were horses or cows in the fields, and seen from afar the tiny figures of the animals and buildings looked just like a child's model farm taken from a toy box and spread out on the carpet.

On 26 June we reached the nastiest-looking stretch of coast we had encountered so far. Cliffs and rocks, more cliffs and more rocks, were all that we saw as we laboured forwards, a few hundred yards offshore. The weather was foul – that morning the sun had come up behind banks of rain clouds so thick that by 9 a.m. the light was already so poor that it felt like dusk. In the grey gloom the mountains to our right were merely black shapes behind the cloud wrack. Strands of mist dragged against the cliff faces, and patches of cloud oozed in the high valleys. For the previous twenty-four hours the wind had been blowing steadily from the northern quarter, and somewhere out in the Black Sea a storm must have been brewing, because the swell was rolling in heavily and breaking sullenly on the rocks, the spume floating out in the backwash. It began to rain. The first few minutes of heavy downpour made the crew's skin glisten, for the oarsmen were still naked from the waist up. Then the rain settled down to a relentless, pattering insistence and the coast vanished into a grey blur. The hands of the rowers turned white and clammy, and their hard-won blisters looked like dead flesh.

Life on board should have been miserable but – astonishingly – the crew actually revelled in the conditions. The heavy rain made a change, and any break in the monotony of rowing was welcome. They began to sing – song after song, mostly scurrilous, as well as some childhood favourites, ballads and drinking songs. Tim Readman jumped up on the central gangway and performed a cabaret turn on the slippery catwalk. He was joined by Adam, a doctor colleague of Nick's who had joined us near Zonguldak, and then by Mark, who for his act produced a Turkish fez from his

Argo sails past the Clashing Rocks and into the Black Sea.

Turkish fishing boats greet *Argo* into port

(*Above*) 'Pete the Cook and Tim the Purser would . . . make their way ashore to find a town and buy food'

(*Right*) Dr Adam Mackie, a medical colleague of Nick Hollis, finds himself in cramped conditions

(*Left*) Off the Black Sea coast of Turkey. 'On the very worst days the crew rowed for eleven blistering hours'

(*Below*) Cormac O'Connor 'had the magic touch. If there were fish, they came to his hook'

(*Foot*) Sheltering from bad weather in Gideros Cove on the north coast of Turkey. 'It was a refuge as perfect as nature could devise'

(*Top left*) 'There was a horrendous, rending crack. The port steering oar had snapped . . . It was important to get into shelter as quickly as possible.' (*Top right*) Tim Readman and Peter Wheeler 'grabbed the ropes that hauled the sail up to the spar.' (*Above*) Pete the Cook held on to one corner of a makeshift headsail, made from a rain cover, to help steer *Argo* off the rocks

(*Left*) Peter Wheeler inspects the broken steering oar. The shaft had snapped where it joined the blade. (*Centre*) Jonathan Cloke helps Peter Wheeler (in red) to repair it and (*above*) Cormac O'Connor and Mark Richards put on a temporary lashing under Peter's supervision

'This was the moment of truth for . . . the sea-keeping qualities of a Bronze Age vessel.' (*Below*) Prelude to heavy weather – the sky off Sinop. (*Left*) 'We lowered the mainyard a few feet on the mast, and set the sail loosely so that the wind spilled out most of

its strength.' (*Foot*) 'The crew were beginning to show increased signs of physical exhaustion. They looked haggard and drawn.' Mark Richards (*left*) and Peter Moran

The land of the Chalybes. 'This black sand is so rich in iron that the grains can be picked up with a magnet' (*below*). Peter Wheeler (*left*) on the iron-bearing beach

'You have very special clearance,' Turkish customs officers told the author (in red cap) as *Argo* left for Soviet waters. 'No ship has been cleared from Hopa since the Second World War'

(*Overleaf*) *Argo* enters Soviet waters

'*Tovarisch* . . . the three-masted square-rigged barquentine of the Soviet training fleet was looking her best, the morning sun reflecting off her pyramids of canvas, and her white hull set off against the grey clouds and the pale green sea . . . It was quite obvious that she was coming to greet us'

(*Top*) *Tovarisch* escorting *Argo* off the coast of Georgia

(*Above*) 'Officialdom arrived in the uniformed shape of a senior officer of the Soviet Frontier Guards'

(*Right*) 'Suddenly blue track-suited figures were tumbling aboard, big, powerfully built men in running shoes (*top*). All . . . were physical training instructors, trained athletes. Every one was rated a Master of Sport of the Soviet Union. (*Below*) They could not wait to get started on the rowing'

ARRIVAL AT POTI

(*Top*) 'The far side of the harbour was black with people, thousand upon thousand. They crammed the quay wall, overflowed into the public square, clustered on the balconies'

(*Left*) 'We set foot for the first time in Georgia.' The author receives a bouquet from one of the 'horde of children . . . Each carried a bunch of flowers which was thrust eagerly into the hands of an Argonaut'

(*Above*) 'The astonishingly complicated, intricate, emotional art of choral song has been brought to its finest pitch with the traditional singers of Georgia'

After two and half months at sea, *Argo* is rowed up the River Rhioni, on whose banks stood the sacred oak where the Golden Fleece hung. (*Top*) 'Lush watermeadows lined both banks, and the Georgian farmers and their families came down to watch us toiling upcurrent.' (*Foot*) 'We were sufficiently composed to dig out three red rocket flares, and we fired them into the sky to symbolize the end of our journey'

Determined to get to the reception ceremony at Vani, the Georgian volunteers manhaul *Argo* up the river. (*Foot*)
'Everyone would leap overboard, push and shove and haul, waist deep in the river'

Gala at Vani on the banks of the Rhioni, site of a classical Greek colonial town now being excavated. (*Left*) 'The entire surface of the wooden stage was crammed with forty or fifty boy dancers . . . who leapt and stamped their way through their number with great gusto.' (*Below*) 'A flautist gave a virtuoso performance.' (*Foot*) 'My companion for the evening was 'Princess Medea', a stunningly beautiful Georgian actress, dressed in a pure white Grecian costume.' (*Far left*) The author and Yuri Senkevich, the doctor-traveller who had sailed with Thor Heyerdahl, sign a column to commemorate *Argo*'s arrival

Greek writers called Colchis 'rich in gold.' The epithet and the Jason legend are supported at Vani by (*below left*) solid gold bangles with ram's head decoration dating back to the 4th century BC. (*Foot*) 'Into these streams the Svans placed sheepskins, with the fleece side uppermost . . . As the water ran across the fleeces, the flecks of gold were trapped in the wool.' (*Below right*) A Svan gold-gatherer in the Caucasus mountains uses 'a simple wooden trough to pan out the silt in a final search for gold.' This, wrote Strabo, the Greek geographer in the 5th century BC, may be 'the origin of the myth of the golden fleece'

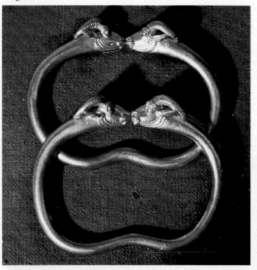

kitbag. The crew sang and laughed, and kept on rowing. During the cabaret, the wind freshened and turned more to the east. Now *Argo* was barely making a knot through the water, and ahead, over the crew's cheerful faces, I could see that the little galley was being driven towards the rocks. The prospect was distinctly uncomfortable. The water was much too deep to anchor off this grim iron-bound coast, and our only chance was to find a cove, marked on the Turkish charts, which cut a notch in the forbidding line of cliffs. As *Argo* was pushed closer and closer to the coast, I grew increasingly concerned. We were getting dangerously near the rocks, and the crew were falling quieter as the constant slog began to sap their energy.

Then I saw a white mark at the foot of a cliff, a small dot which turned out to be a short stone pillar. It stood on a shelf of rock to one side of a narrow cut in the cliffs. Without the pillar to mark it, one would not have spotted the entrance to the cove until too late. The cove was a freak of geology. Some time in the distant past, the sea had weakened a fault in the line of cliffs, gnawing a hole about 30 yards wide. Breaking through this gap, the water had rushed in and submerged a small glen behind the cliffs, to form a nearly land-locked basin. Its only entrance was the almost indistinguishable cleft in the cliff wall.

'Watch out! There's a rock in the middle of the entrance,' suddenly called Ziya in alarm as a great, round-shouldered wave rolled into the narrow entrance and erupted in a welter of foam. But the leap of water had been caused by the wash of the sea rebounding from the cliffs on each side, when it met and clashed in the middle of the narrow channel, kicking up as if it had broken on rock. I turned *Argo* at right-angles to the entrance and drove her hard at the gap. She rose on the back of a wave, heaved forward, fell back and was picked up a second time. The crew rowed flat out to keep her moving through the water so that I had enough speed to steer her and to keep the boat from wavering off-course or broaching to the waves. In a spectacular roller-coaster ride the galley went tearing through the gap, her fierce eyes staring straight ahead, and we entered the haven.

The cove was a world apart. In 50 feet, *Argo* passed from the outside waves and swell to a flat calm. All that remained of the angry sea outside was an arc of foam which fanned out into the cove from its entrance, and undulated gently. The water of the cove was scarcely disturbed. It was like being inside a great glass jar. On all sides the ground around the haven rose so steeply that the cove was completely walled in and protected from the elements. Outside the Black Sea grumbled, and overhead the north wind swept a veil of grey scud to swirl about the mountain slope. But inside the drowned glen, the merest breeze ruffled the leaves of the bushes growing on the hillside. It was a refuge as perfect as nature could devise. At one end of the cove stood a hamlet of three or four buildings; at the opposite end a single, one-storey house with a porch, a small boatshed, a tiny strip of beach and a neat jetty that had been cunningly constructed to join together a line of half-submerged rocks. The owner of the little house must have seen *Argo* bursting out of the gloom, for he was already climbing into a small rowing boat to come and meet us.

Entering Gideros Cove

Argo glided across to his corner of the haven, dropped anchor, and the stranger greeted us courteously, taking a mooring line ashore for us and looping it around a boulder. The galley would be completely safe inside Gideros Cove, he assured us. In the worst winter storms no wave or swell ever penetrated the secret haven.

He had lived there for twenty-five years, and had never once been disturbed by bad weather. Gales might rage not 400 yards away, but the vines on his porch scarcely rustled in the wind. In summer, by a quirk of nature, not even mosquitoes disturbed his life. When the weather was right, he made his living by fishing the waters outside the cove. For the rest of the year he tended his garden, grew vegetables in the tiny fields on the steep slope above his house, and looked after his cherry trees. There was no road to his house, only a steep track gluey with mud. But it was only a short climb to the main road, and there he could catch the bus into town 5 miles away. His life, like the cove, seemed an idyll.

Paphlagonia was the name the Greeks gave to this section of the coast, and the natives had a reputation as tough warriors who resented foreigners and were fully capable of throwing them back into the sea. Even today this remains the most inaccessible and remote region of Turkey's Black Sea coast. The broken terrain, and the high mountains so close to the coast, have isolated the region from the rest of Turkey. The first coast road is still under construction, and the small towns have no natural hinterland. Their people depend on forestry and fishing, and the indifferent farming of the foothills. Cide, the town closest to Gideros Cove, was a run-down, sad place. Most of its young people had left to find work in Ankara or Istanbul or abroad. Only the older generation were left, many of them living on money sent home by their children. Yet even here, in this obvious poverty, the town council of Cide was not going to let the Argonauts pass by without offering hospitality. The mayor sent a bus to collect us from the cove, and we went scrambling up the slippery footpath in the mud and drizzle to be ferried into town where we were given a meal, a bath at the *hamam* and beds for the night.

By dawn we were already back on the sodden oar benches. *Argo*'s sail had not had a chance to dry out in the last damp days and black stains of mildew were spreading across it, giving her a somewhat bedraggled appearance. Her crew were equally mottled. Even debonair Dick Hill's immaculate wardrobe was showing the first signs of decay, while for the rest of us the damp and the lack of space for stowage gave a very sea-stained appearance to our gear. All our clothing was smeared with mutton fat from the oar strops, our shirts were torn and dirty, our grubby trousers misshapen by hour after hour of rowing. Our eating utensils were battered and none too clean, either. The metal army-style canteens, which had looked so trim and neat when we began the voyage, were now dented and scratched. We drank from an assortment of grimy plastic cups or squalid metal mugs. Anything which accidentally slipped down into the bilge had to be condemned and thrown overboard, for it was impossible to wash out the stench from the slimy, black bilge water. Books and magazines were carefully hoarded and passed around, but their pages were swollen with damp. Jonathan had stepped on his reading glasses, and now cut a strange figure: one lens was totally starred and opaque with a fracture right across it, so that he looked like a man with one blind eye.

For another four days we laboured on past a long, dark coast which was periodically slashed with river gorges. Headlands succeeded one another, and moved astern with wearying slowness. At Cape Carambis, according to Apollonius, the north wind split, deflected on one side westward and on the other to the east. The modern Argonauts hoped sincerely that this was true, for at least we would then have a following breeze beyond the Cape. The crew were beginning to show the strain. Peter Wheeler and Peter Warren were unstoppable – apparently they had the stamina to row on for ever. Mark, the rowing master, was so game that he never gave anything less than maximum effort, but although he was growing muscles on his muscles he often finished the day in a state of physical collapse, totally drained by the effort of pulling an oar for six or seven hours with only short breaks. The really big men – Jonathan and Cormac – had the sheer weight and power to help them keep up the pressure. But in varying degrees everyone began to show fatigue – there were drawn faces, sunken eyes, aching backs, sore elbows and buttocks, skin peeling off in strips.

There was not a man aboard who could not lead the team, rowing in the stroke position and adjusting the rowing style to suit the changing conditions. In calm water a long stroke was fine, but when the sea grew choppy a shorter and more exhausting stroke was essential to control *Argo* as she heaved and rolled. Every oar had taken on its individual character. We all knew which oar was stiff, or too heavy, or slightly warped. Others were too light and whippy, while the best had just the right amount of spring in them, so that one found oneself, in the long turn and turnabout of crew reliefs, looking forward to the moment when the crew change brought you to a good blade.

Keeping the boat level became an obsession. After almost two months at the rowing benches the crew were as sensitive as any spirit level to the change in trim. If *Argo* heeled by only half a degree the oarsmen on the upper side found it twice as hard to reach the water with their blades. Then the cry came down the boat: 'Trim ship!', which sent the men on relief watch scrambling from one side of the boat to the other to balance *Argo* with their weight. Occasionally the water-soaked stitching of an oar strop would break in mid-stroke, and the luckless rower would be catapulted backwards off his bench into the bilges. When that happened, no one laughed. The crew were too tired, and it had happened too often. Apollonius had described it all:

> They laboured at the indefatigable oar. They worked like oxen ploughing the moist earth. The sweat pours down from the flank and neck; their rolling eyes glare out askance from under the yoke; hot blasts of air come rumbling from their mouths; and all day long they labour, digging their hooves into the soil. Thus the crew of *Argo* all through the night ploughed the salt water with their oars.

Off Cape Carambis the wind did begin to show signs of shifting in our favour, as Apollonius had said it would, but the weather had a treacherous feel to it. As we sped past the Cape, sails spread to a strong breeze from a lowering, rain-spattering sky, we were swept by a couple of squalls that whipped the spray over the boat and made me decide that discretion was still the better part of valour. The new Argonauts were excellent oarsmen, but their skill as heavy-weather sailors was untried. Until now, perhaps 70 per cent of the voyage's duration had been spent under oars, rowing and not sailing. Half the crew – all the Turks and several of the regular Argonauts – had virtually no experience of handling open boats in heavy weather, and *Argo* was, after all, very vulnerable in bad conditions.

In the hands of an inexperienced or tired crew she could rapidly get into trouble. A breaking sea could swamp her. She had no deck to throw off a boarding wave, and loose water slopping up and down the bilge would make her dangerously unstable. And if she was taken aback, so that her sail filled with wind on the wrong side and pressed against the mast, only quick thinking and smart action would save her from being rolled over if the mast did not snap quickly enough to reduce the leverage. In a stiff breeze a rogue wave could throw her off-balance, and then the crew would have to move their body weight very quickly to bring her back to trim. After ten or twelve hours of rowing, a crew was far too tired to react with the necessary speed. All in all, I felt it better to sail defensively and still try to put ashore each night. The last thing that I wanted was for *Argo* to be hit by a vicious squall or a sudden gale in the dark with an exhausted crew, several of whom were likely to be seasick.

My caution increased when, on 29 June, Trondur, the most experienced sailor on board, had to leave us to go home to the Faeroes. It was sad to see him go, particularly as he would be missing the last and potentially most exciting sector of the voyage. But he had been called home, and filled every last possible hour with preparing his sketches of the voyage, working both on board and from the rubber dinghy. The day of his departure was made even more depressing by the total opposition of the wind. We set out from the little port of Abana at 5 a.m. and rowed and tacked, rowed and tacked, for more than six hours to try to make headway, before I finally had to admit defeat and put back into the little harbour. It all seemed a terrible waste.

Then, as is so often the case on a long voyage, the worst day was followed by one of the best. Again we rose in the half-light and by sunrise were rowing out of Abana harbour. This time the calm held all morning, and in the afternoon came a gentle breeze from the west so that we were able to make sail. Cormac put out a fishing line and caught several meaty dogfish which were enough to make supper for the entire crew. When the sun went down the breeze was still in the west, and the weather looked so settled that I decided to take the risk of sailing on through the night. The crew were well rested and totally relaxed. Two of the Turks, Mustafa and Umur, were playing chess; the cassette player was sending out gentle classical music; and the rest of the crew were reading or chatting among themselves. We had passed the last safe harbour, and it seemed a shame to turn back. To reward us, that heaven-sent wind blew all through the night, with a sky full of stars to steer by, and *Argo* ran forward at 3–4 knots while the watches changed. Each sailing watch consisted of four men: two of them, the watch leader and his deputy, had sailing experience; the other two were novices, but they too had their turn at taking the helm and learning to sail a square-rigged galley. It was not easy, and a mistake usually meant that the wind got on the wrong side of the sail and then the other members of the watch had to pull out the oars and row *Argo*'s head round so that she was pointing in the right direction and could begin sailing again.

By dawn we were passing Ince Burnu, the most northerly cape on Turkey's shore, where the Black Sea narrows to a waist. Here we were only 160 miles from the coast of the Crimea, and had come farther east than Suez. With the waves rolling in from the north, we scudded past cave-riddled limestone cliffs, uninhabited except for the solitary lighthouse on the cape which marked this crucial turning point in our voyage. Pete the cook served up a breakfast of scrambled eggs, water melon and bread, and at last the distant tabletop hill of Sinop, our destination for the day, came in sight. We had made splendid progress: *Argo* was clipping off the miles in fine style. The wind was gusting now, and the waves growing steeper as they heaped up out of the deeps, expending the energy they had gathered on their long fetch from the Ukraine. With considerable caution I set course to avoid Sinop's headland by a wide margin, and aimed well clear of the area where waves were bursting against the rocks. It was a defensive decision and one for which I was to be very thankful over the next few hours.

A large wave picked up *Argo*. She skidded across the crest, slipped down the far side, and there was a horrendous, rending crack. Her port steering oar had snapped. The shaft of the oar, 3 inches by 7 inches of prime, hand-picked timber, had broken where it joined the blade, which flapped uselessly to one side, joined only by a few twisted splinters of wood. Perhaps the steering oar had been weakened when we scraped over the rocks back in the Sea of Marmara; perhaps it was just a freak wave. Whatever the reason for the break, half of *Argo*'s steering capability was now gone.

At first the situation did not seem to be too serious. *Argo* was still running with the wind on her quarter, and the remaining steering oar, on the starboard side, seemed to be holding her on course to clear the wave-lashed headland. There seemed to be a very good chance of slanting the galley's course gently so that she skimmed past the menacing rocks. The horrified looks on the faces of some of the crew members, when they heard the crack of the rudder, were replaced by expressions of interest to see what would happen next. Peter Wheeler, the ship's carpenter, came aft and stoically examined the broken fragments of the steering gear. Calm as always, Peter merely shook his head over the damage, hauled the broken bits aboard, and tied them safely with cord.

'I'll have a go at repairing the damage when we get into Sinop,' he said reassuringly.

Argo sailed on. She cleared the first headland. Then I eased back on the starboard steering oar to turn her right-handed to run past the cliff face, picking a channel between the rocks and a small jagged offshore islet. My plan was to shoot through the gap and then duck round the back of the headland to find shelter from the wind, which was ricocheting off the cliffs. The manoeuvre seemed simple enough. It only needed a steady nerve and good timing, for I knew it was important to get into shelter as quickly as possible. If we were blown past Sinop's headland with only a single steering oar, we would be in trouble. Our Bronze Age galley could not turn back in a strong following wind if we overshot the mark, and if we failed to duck into Sinop we would be blown onwards into the 50-mile-wide bight of Bafra Bay. On the far side of that bay was the Bafra foreland, a low, flat delta pushed seawards by the outflow of the Kizilirmak River. It was a bleak coast, without a single harbour, and constantly changing shoals and banks. The pilot book warned shipping to give it at least 5 miles' clearance for safety, as even the charts were unreliable. The next port beyond that was Samsun, nearly 100 miles by sea from Sinop, and much too far to attempt with a half-crippled ship.

But as I pulled back on the starboard steering oar I had a sharp, frightening lesson in the way a galley steers. For a few seconds everything went well: *Argo* turned smoothly. Then, as she swung past a certain critical angle, the tautly filled square sail suddenly took control of the boat: *Argo* simply went maverick. The sail had more turning power than the single steering oar, and the smooth turn abruptly became a violent right-handed swerve. Instead of pointing at the gap between the cliffs and the islet, *Argo* rushed straight at the cliff wall. The single steering oar flopped weakly in my hand. With a will of her own *Argo* settled on a natural course, tucked down her shoulder and began to accelerate fast, heading fatally for the rocks. I felt exactly like a novice skier who, turning gently on a slope, finds his skis taking control and rushing him towards the lip of a precipice.

'Starboard brace, let go! Hard in, port brace! Ease out starboard sheet! Haul in port mainsheet!' With a rapid-fire sequence of orders I tried to swing the sail round and get *Argo* to straighten up. But it was no use. The ram was now behaving as a forward rudder, biting into the water and steering the galley on a suicidal track. The bulging sail was a menace. Without two steering oars to control her, *Argo* was as wild as a bolting horse.

'Brail up!'

Tim Readman had the knack of always being at hand in a shipboard emergency, and with Peter Wheeler he scrambled to the aft position and grabbed the ropes that hauled the sail up to the spar.

'Hands to oar bench positions! Blades outboard! Starboard side row on! Port side back her down hard!' The oarsmen on the starboard side began to row frantically ahead, while on the port side their companions plunged the blades of their oars into the water and pushed backwards to serve as a brake. The idea was to turn the boat about its axis, but the combined strength of fourteen oarsmen was not enough. *Argo* continued to drive forwards at the rocks, gripped by the wind. Now there was only 50 yards to go before we hit the cliff. Somehow the head of the boat had to be turned downwind, and quickly. On a modern yacht the foresail or jib would do this work. But *Argo* had just a single square sail. A jib, temporary jib. . . .

'Quick! Get the forward rain cover and rig it to the forestay as a sail.'

Tim Readman and Pete the cook hurried to where the rain covers were stowed in a sail bag, wrenched open the draw cord and pulled out the small triangle of canvas that normally sheltered the foredeck from the rain. 'Quick!' Crippled *Argo* was still blundering onwards to the rocks, despite the best efforts of the oarsmen. The men trying to brake the vessel were flattened by the pressure of their oar handles, leaning back and hanging on with one hand to the gunwale to stop themselves being pushed down below the oar benches.

Tim and Pete ran back down the central catwalk with the canvas. Big Cormac flung down his oar and went to join them. He hoisted Tim on his shoulders so that Tim could reach up high enough to attach one corner of canvas well up the forestay. There was no time to rig control ropes, so Pete the cook held another corner of the sail and Peter Warren hung onto the third. The small scrap of canvas clattered in the wind, and then bellied out. Distinctly I felt the tug of the mini-sail in the bow, urging *Argo* to straighten up. Slowly the galley's ram turned to the correct course, and *Argo* was heading in the right direction again.

Five minutes later I decided to try using the mainsail again, but as soon as it filled with wind *Argo* again spun round and streaked off towards the cliffs. This time we were well prepared – up went the makeshift jib-cum-awning, and *Argo* curtsied out of the danger sector. In this lopsided fashion the stricken galley zigzagged crazily along the foot of the cliffs. Now the port-side rowers dug in and held their blades rigid to act as rudders; now the starboard side rowed to give us propulsion. On the foredeck the three Peters and Tim Readman twisted and turned the awning to catch the wind and control the bows of the galley, while the single remaining steering oar hung uselessly. We were coming up to the rocky islet. All being well, we should sidle through the gap. I looked at the chart. With half a gale behind her, *Argo* was on the verge of being shot out into the great sweep of Bafra Bay.

'There's a chance we'll find a patch of shelter just around the point,' I told the labouring crew. 'But the moment we come to the end of the cliffs, we'll have to row like hell to try to duck into it and escape the wind. Get ready, and when I give the word go for it!' I sidled *Argo* gently towards the cliffs, getting as close as I dared to the rocks. As we swirled past the last point, I yelled: 'Pull away! Pull away!' and turned *Argo*'s nose to starboard. We shot round the corner, the crew rowing as desperately as on the worst of the Bosphorus. We had just enough speed to overcome the drag of the wind buffeting off the cliffs.

To my intense relief there was indeed a tiny patch of undisturbed water, no more than 30 yards wide and 20 yards deep; a small fishing boat was already anchored in it, riding out the squalls. *Argo* skittered into the refuge and Cormac threw the anchor overboard. For a moment the anchor refused to hold, and *Argo* began to slide back towards the sheer cliff face, so close that Peter Wheeler stood by with a boat hook to fend off. The oarsmen got the boat underway just in time, and Cormac smeared butter on a lead oar weight, then lowered it to the sea floor to check for sand or rocks. When the lead came up with grains of sand sticking to the butter down went the anchor again, and this time it held.

Peter Wheeler began attending to the broken steering oar. He prised up two of the cook's planks to use as wooden splints, drilled a line of holes in the broken rudder shaft, and began hammering in some wooden pins to hold the splints in place. The whole assembly was then reinforced with lashings of cord. He was still busy on this temporary repair, enough to let us limp into Sinop, when around the headland came a large fishing boat crowded with cheering and clapping Turks. Sinop was celebrating the end of the Ramadan religious festival with a regatta. *Argo* could not have come at a better moment. Please would we row into harbour when the wind eased, they shouted. And then they unfurled a large, slightly misspelled, banner. It read: 'SINOP WELLCOMES THE ARGONAUTS'.

Husnu

8
The Last Lap

If Jason and the Argonauts made their voyage into the Black Sea some time in the thirteenth century BC, as the evidence suggests, what sort of people would they have encountered living along the coast? The curator of Sinop's museum took me to see the remains of the kind of settlement which would have been flourishing on the coast when the Argonauts sailed by. The site was on the crest of a steep hill some 5 kilometres from Sinop, and it commanded a wide sweep of the bay as well as the rolling, hilly country that extended inland towards the mountains that effectively severed the coast from the interior of Anatolia. The late Bronze Age houses had all been built of timber, the natural building material of this heavily wooded area, and the people had made a plain pottery and tools of bronze and bone. The general impression, said the curator, was of a culture that was simple, robust, and had close links with the other tribes living along the coast in both directions. The inhabitants, a people known as the Kaskas, occupied a section of what was in effect a coastal corridor, running from the Bosphorus in the west to the Caucasus in the east, and had contacts with one another along the coast rather than inland to the plateau. Once the Argonauts emerged from the Clashing Rocks and entered on that corridor it would have carried them naturally to Colchis, the land of the Golden Fleece.

The Kaskas are something of a mystery people. They appear about 1600 BC in the Hittite records, and there is reason to suppose that the Hittite rulers established some sort of trade route from their capital at Bogazkoy in north central Anatolia to the Black Sea coast in Kaska territory. The importance of this trade route is only just beginning to be appreciated by historians who traditionally have been much more interested in Hittite contacts southwards to the Mediterranean. But a glance at the map shows that the Hittites' nearest access to the sea was north – to the Black Sea. And this may have some relevance to the Argonaut story. Recently a dozen Mycenaean pottery jars were discovered in the ruins of a small Hittite palace at Masat in north–central Anatolia. This caused great excitement among the archaeologists, for these jars, humdrum containers for oil, were the first indisputably Mycenaean articles to be found in the Hittite heartland. Paradoxically the jars date from a time when the Hittite kingdom was breaking up and the overland routes were in disarray. On the other hand, the jars do coincide with the time ascribed to the Jason legend, and it may well be that they are evidence that contact had at last been established by sea, via the

phorus, between the Mycenaeans on the one hand and the
tites, the Kaskas and the other peoples along the coast on the
other. If this is so, then the Jason story would symbolize the first
Greek penetration of the Black Sea.

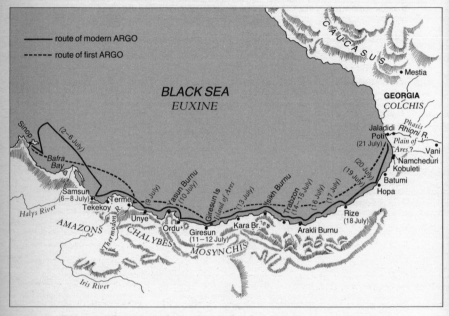

Boom! Boom! Tacca! Tacca! Boom! Every beat of the drum could
be heard clearly across the water. The drummer himself was a
bizarre figure – naked except for a pair of white undershorts – as he
came striding down the harbour pier at Sinop, staring rigidly ahead
and pounding on his drum. He did not give a single glance in our
direction, even though it was obvious that he had come to see us off.
The man was in his sixties, tanned mahogany by months of near-
nudity, and at his heels trotted a small terrier, black and white, with
a large black patch over one eye like a dog in a newspaper cartoon.
The dog, too, glanced neither left nor right, but trotted with its
nose a few inches from its master's naked heels. No one else was on
the jetty, just this eccentric fakir beating a mad cadence to our oar
strokes as we rowed back out into the Black Sea.

For some reason the stiffly marching figure, the insistent thump

174

of the drum and the brisk little terrier trotting along like a warlock's familiar made me uneasy. Peter Wheeler had done a first-class job on mending the steering oar. He had located a woodworking shop and repaired and strengthened the splintered shaft, which now felt solidly comfortable as it rotated in its notch in the crosspiece. The crew had visited Sinop's *hamam,* courtesy of the mayor, and we had tidied up *Argo.* Why, then, should I feel a sense of foreboding? There was a clear sky, a gentle following breeze, and to our left the rearing bulk of Sinop's tabletop headland gave us a placid lee in which to sail. The only slight irritation was that the evening breeze, which was carrying us out into the bay seemed fitful. My plan was to cut across the bay and clear the dangers of Bafra Point by late next evening when we would still have daylight to check our course. I hoped that the wind would hold, so that the crew would not have to begin rowing at dawn to get around the point. If we had known what would happen over the next five days none of us would have raised any objections to rowing, because we were now to have our baptism of heavy weather in a Bronze Age galley.

At midnight the wind shifted into the east, the worst possible direction. To avoid being blown back down onto the cliffs of Sinop in the darkness, I headed *Argo* north towards the open sea to find sea room. The wind began to increase. It was not a dramatic, swift change, but a steady gain in strength as the hours went by. With the stronger wind, the sea began to tumble and break. Now the triple wave described by the fishermen showed itself: occasional groups of three short, steep waves larger than the others came rolling down on *Argo* and sent the galley lurching violently. For a while the crew tried to row as we struggled to claw off the dangerous lee shore, but soon it was completely impossible to handle the oars. The boat was far too unstable. No one could get a grip on the surface of the sea with their blades. Men slipped on the spray-splashed oar benches, cursed, fumbled their strokes and eventually abandoned the attempt. The crew pulled their blades as far inboard as possible and wedged the oar handles under the benches so that the blades angled upward as far as possible clear of the waves. This was not just a question of convenience. There was always the danger that a bank of oars could be caught by a breaking wave, act as levers and trip the boat.

By 2 a.m. the sliver of a new moon illuminated the extent of *Argo*'s distress. She was wallowing from side to side with a sick-making motion. Sometimes the roll was so violent that the oar blades, despite their angle, plunged underwater and emerged again with great gouts of water and an alarming rattle of the oar handles that shook the whole length of the boat. Occasionally a larger wave thrust the boat farther over, and the sea slopped over the gunwale. Then we were obliged to pump out the loose water from the bilge.

It was time to increase our defensive tactics against the sea, and try to ride out the heavy weather as safely as possible. This was the moment of truth for Colin Mudie's design and the seakeeping qualities of a Bronze Age vessel. We did not know how well *Argo* would hold up, or if the weather would deteriorate even further. The early Greek texts were full of tales of galleys which sank in storms, and the greatest losses were always when the fleets were driven on the rocks by gales: that was when men had died by the thousand. I decided that, so long as *Argo* could carry sail, we should

continue to head out to open water. We lowered the mainyard a few feet on the mast, and set the sail loosely so that the wind spilled out most of its strength. After a few experiments we found *Argo*'s natural position, lying aslant to the waves, rising and falling to their advance and giving a lurching sideways heave as each crest passed under her keel which, being only 2 feet in draught, gave very little grip on the water. In essence *Argo* was just a long, slim rowing boat far out to sea in heavy weather, and it was up to her crew to give her the best chance of survival. To try to keep the boat from tipping too much, the crew now lay down on their oar benches and wriggled themselves into position, so that their heads – the heaviest part of the body – were close to the windward rail. It made the cramped conditions even more uncomfortable, because now, whenever the waves lapped aboard, the slop of water drenched the men's heads and trickled down their necks.

Argo *in heavy weather*

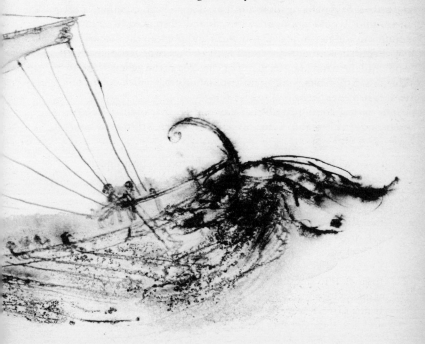

At dawn the faint outline of Sinop headland was only just visible, very low on the horizon, and disappearing from sight as we drifted farther out into the open sea. There was a radio station on the cape, and I tried calling up on the walkie-talkie to ask for a weather forecast and to report our position. But the little handset, no bigger than a camera, was not powerful enough; there was no response. I groped under the central gangplank where the emergency lifeboat-style radio was secured, extended its aerial and tried again; once more there was no reply. In the Black Sea there were few listening watches on ships or shore stations. I folded up the aerial and put the set away. We would just have to look after ourselves.

As the morning dragged by, *Argo* was pushed farther and farther out to sea. The headland disappeared, and we were surrounded by an endless vista of dull, breaking waves under a sullen sky. We saw no ships, for *Argo* was now outside the track used by the handful of coasters that rounded the cape. We were finally on our own, trapped in the classic situation that all galley sailors have feared since the earliest days of navigation: adrift in an open boat, crammed with men who would soon grow tired and dispirited if weather conditions did not improve; too weak and puny in the face of bad weather to dictate our course; and with no chance of getting back to land until the wind blew itself out or changed in the galley's favour. The new Argonauts were as close to the original galley conditions as they had ever been.

The ordeal continued all that day and all that night. 'Another pretty miserable night,' reads my journal, written thirty-six hours later,

> spent with the sea continuing rough, and the boat under reduced sail, flinching over the white-crested waves. We are being steadily driven northward. All the Turks are now down with seasickness, unable to eat and huddled in their blankets on the benches like dead men. Ali tries to eat dried bread to stop his retching, but Umur and Yuksel are totally prostrate and refuse all food. Occasionally a wave comes aboard, or a shorter wave thumps into the side of the boat and shatters into spray which whips across the sleeping men on the oar benches. If it's a larger wave, solid water goes down their necks and into their sleeping bags. . . . The tinned hot dogs we

ate last night tasted foul, enough to make even Peter Wheeler throw up. I think they must have gone sour in their tins, but it is difficult to cook anything more substantial in these conditions. The only bright spot was when Pete the cook handed out a single slice of water melon to each man – delicious. We are having to be careful about water consumption. I have sixteen men aboard, and our water supplies are limited.

The reactions of the crew varied. A few, like poor Yuksel and Umur, were laid so totally low by their seasickness that they couldn't have cared less what happened. They were dead to the world for almost two days, sodden blankets drawn over their heads as the galley lurched and heaved, and they lay limply amongst the kit. If *Argo* had capsized, they would have had little chance. The majority of the other crew members were phlegmatic. They lay in their sleeping bags or curled up in their oilskins, and occasionally a rogue wave dumped water on them. The only diversion was to wriggle right up to the edge of the gunwale and peer over it to watch the steady succession of waves rushing down on *Argo*, and to wonder just how far each wave, depending on its size and angle, would come up the side of the vessel towards one's nose.

Nine times out of ten *Argo* had a critical point of stability, tipping over on her side as the crest of the wave rushed up the gunwale, closer and closer to the edge of the planking until, just 3 or 4 inches short, she gave a little jerk, levelled out, and the wave top hissed by underneath us. Again and again she wriggled in this manner over the waves, and only occasionally did she take water aboard.

One or two of the crew were beginning to look genuinely distressed. It was the waiting which sapped their morale. As the hours dragged by and *Argo* just went on wallowing and lurching, threatened by wave after wave, it was difficult for newcomers to accept that we should continue to lie so passively to the seas and trust to the design of the boat. In fact, our best plan was to conserve energy and wait for the bad weather to cease. Only then could we try to find our way back to land. In the meantime our safest place was to be as far away from shore as possible, and to help *Argo* ride the seas. We still had the option of turning and running with the waves and wind, relying on the galley's fine upswept stern to rise over the breakers, but there was no way of knowing how much trouble the ram might give in this situation. It might possibly dig into the water, wrench the bow sideways and broach the galley. *Argo*'s heavy-weather behaviour was a venture into the unknown. None of us knew how well the galley would stand up to the conditions, and each member of the crew had his own limits of experience by which to judge. Those witnessing their first heavy weather in an open boat were naturally the first to worry; those with more experience had a higher threshold of concern.

At about 3 a.m. on the second morning the wind at last began to ease, and by sunrise *Argo* was no longer being menaced by the rollers. 'Thirty-six hours of heavy weather in an open boat with a large crew are enough,' my notes go on. 'I hope that it doesn't continue. The best thing about these conditions is that the sun shines even during a Force Seven wind, so that the waves are sparkling and fresh as they bear down on *Argo*. Enthusiastic aggression rather than surly menace. . . .'

One thing the gale did do for us was to put an end to our practice of navigating without a compass. When the wind eased and we could begin sailing again, a small pocket compass mysteriously appeared, placed where the steersman of the watch could see it. We had come 800 miles without the help of a compass, and proved the point that sailing from Greece to the Black Sea was perfectly possible without one. Some members of the crew evidently thought that enough was enough; historical experiment should only be carried so far, and they were more interested in getting back to land as soon as possible. Of course the sun and stars still made it quite clear which direction was south, where the land lay, but the compass was reassuring, though strictly speaking it was more of a psychological prop than a precise navigational aid. Its usefulness was severely curtailed by the fact that we did not know our starting position after a day and a half of heavy weather which had driven us well clear of all land.

My guess was that we were about 30 miles north-northeast of Sinop. Without knowing our starting point or accurately checking our speed through the water, or being aware of the effects of the local currents, we still had no way of calculating when we would come back to land, or where we would strike the coast. Looking up at the night sky as *Argo* turned back for the coast, I found it just as reassuring to see the two stars, Castor and Pollux, shining in the constellation of Gemini in honour of the original Argonauts. By keeping the twins at the end of the starboard yardarm during the first night watch, *Argo* was on course for the Turkish coast.

Food was beginning to run short. There was simply not enough space aboard *Argo* to carry sufficient supplies to feed sixteen men for any length of time, and already we had consumed the normal two days' allowance of bread and vegetables. The reserve supply of food included the tinned hot dogs which were suspected of being tainted, so it was safer to dump them overboard and not risk food poisoning. We were therefore on short rations, and a single egg with a handful of rice was our supper, while breakfast and lunch together consisted of two small biscuits per man and a cup of coffee or tea. But, more important, we did have plenty of fresh water. We could get along without food for several days – and the seasick crew members had no appetite anyhow – but to run short of water would have been disastrous. We had made a point of never leaving harbour without our water containers being at least 80 per cent full, and they had been topped up in Sinop. Now the crew rationed themselves to 2–3 pints per man per day, and even then we had enough fresh water for at least a week.

My main concern now was the wind, which had to stay in our favour for at least two days. If it changed back into an offshore breeze we would be certain to be pushed still farther out into the Black Sea; on the other hand, if it died away we were too far from land to get there by rowing unless we had an absolutely flat calm, and in the Black Sea this was unlikely. There was too much open sea to the north, and the swell built up much more than among the islands of the Aegean. As it was, the troubled sea showed no immediate signs of abating as we swooped and spiralled our way southeast. Then at 8 a.m. on the morning of 5 July, we again heard the unmistakable crack of a steering oar breaking.

This time it was the shaft of the starboard steering oar which had sheared. Exactly as before, *Argo* had been sliding down the face of a wave; the weight of the boat proved too much for the steering oar and the solid timber shaft had snapped in half, leaving the rudder blade flapping. Tim Readman quickly rigged up an emergency auxiliary steering system with an oar stuck over the stern, and for an hour he helped the helmsman keep *Argo* running downwind while Peter Wheeler carried out the repairs with which he was becoming all too familiar. Once again the cook lost his two floorboards, which were snatched up and cannibalized to make splints for the broken steering oar. Then Peter supervised Mark and Cormac in putting a thick lashing around the temporary joint. When the steering oar was lowered back in its notch, it looked far from secure. The blade wobbled from side to side as the emergency joint moved, and the bandage of lashings and wedges stopped it from turning fully so that the steering oar could no longer be rotated in its groove. It now projected down into the water like a very shaky fin keel, but at least it was sound enough to keep *Argo* on course, provided no harsh rudder movements were needed.

The accident did not affect either morale or progress. *Argo* was bowling along merrily at 3–4 knots and in exactly the right direction. The old hands from the Sindbad Voyage had seen similar crises before. On the way to China our Arab ship had suffered chronic problems with her rudder and yet she had brought us all the way to Canton. All that was needed was the ingenuity to make running repairs at sea, coupled with a steady nerve. The fact that this was the second steering oar to break on *Argo* also helped. We had seen it all before, and we knew we could make and mend. It would be much the same if we hit another batch of heavy weather. Now the crew had been through a heavy sea and survived the experience, their confidence would be immeasurably enhanced.

It was just biscuits again for supper, and then during the fourth night at sea we saw the loom of lights on the horizon, which we calculated had to be the major town of Samsun, and began to row towards them. At 8 a.m. we passed the head of the breakwater of Samsun harbour, and soon afterwards tied up to a quay. It was the fifth day since we had set out from Sinop, and the Argonauts were exhausted. What we all wanted now was a good, unbroken sleep and a hot meal. We had been living aboard the galley for far longer than had been the original design. Ali, scouting ashore to find a café for our breakfast, came back with a copy of the morning newspaper. He was grinning. 'Look at the headline on the front page,' he said. 'It's about the Argonauts. It says "Twenty-five British sailors lost in the Black Sea!"'

Samsun is one of the best harbours of Turkey's north coast, and in the late Bronze Age there was already an important settlement at a place now called Tekekoy, 14 miles to the east. Preliminary excavations at Tekekoy have brought to light late Bronze Age graves containing bronze knives, earrings and two ceremonial bronze spearheads. These finds suggest to archaeologists that Tekekoy was one outlet of the land route joining the Black Sea with the major Hittite cities of the interior. The coastline in this area has been drastically altered by the masses of silt, stones and sand brought down by rivers such as the Izilirmak, and deposited as deltas pushing out to seaward. Apollonius had noted how this stretch of coast was a land of changing deltas – the outfalls of the Rivers Halys, Iris and Thermodon, the latter famous as the home of the warrior Amazons, and the Iris renowned for its ninety-six branches and tributaries which meandered back and forth over the Amazonian plain, many of them vanishing underground never to reappear, while the surviving handful joined up to discharge into the Black Sea near Themiscyra. There, said Apollonius, the Argonauts beached *Argo* overnight, intending to challenge the fierce Amazons, but a fine northwest wind sent by Zeus persuaded them to push on again with all speed, heading towards Colchis, so the anticipated battle was avoided.

Something of the same spirit of impatience was starting to take hold of the new Argonauts. We spent two days in Samsun, recuperating from the offshore escapade, while a kindly ex-officer of the Turkish Navy, invalided from active service, expertly repaired the broken steering oar for us. He refused any payment, asking only for a set of *Argo*'s plans so that he could later make a model of the galley. In his repair he used sidepieces of mulberry wood, pins of Turkish oak and fillets of beech. 'We could now award a prize,' Peter Wheeler remarked, 'to anyone who can guess correctly just how many different types of timber have now gone into this boat.'

The moment the steering oar was back in place we set out, skirting the delta of the Yesil Irmak which continues to spew out its gravel and sand northeast of Samsun. 'CAUTION: shoaling having occurred, vessels should not approach within 5 miles of the shore in the vicinity of Iris Point,' warns the Admiralty chart, nervous of the constantly changing depths. We, as befits a galley, were less than 200 metres from the strandline as we approached the large stain of milky-looking water which filters out through the shingle fan marking the outfall of the river.

'We ought to be in sturgeon country now,' said Peter Wheeler, hopefully baiting up an outsize fish hook. 'It would be very pleasant to have caviar for breakfast.'

'Aren't sturgeon caught in nets?' some non-fisherman came back pessimistically.

Conversation was rather subdued as *Argo* plodded forward. Several members of the crew were suffering from monumental hangovers, acquired at a late-night party in Samsun; one or two were too ill to stir. Once again *Argo* was adopting her bad habit of sidling down towards the coast even though we had set the sail as taut as possible, hoping to nudge her upwind.

Then Nick said quietly: 'Why not try moving everyone astern? It might help *Argo*'s sailing.' Two months earlier, soon after leaving Volos in Greece, we had made a similar experiment, moving as much of *Argo*'s stores as possible aft to see if we could make the galley sail closer to the wind. Then it had seemed to produce little difference. Now, however, anything seemed worth trying if it would make *Argo* more of a sailing, and less a rowing, craft. The entire crew, fit or hungover, clambered aft and crowded onto the tiny stern deck. There was not room for everyone to stand. They perched on the stern rail or sat on top of one another in a heap, more than a ton of human flesh abruptly transferred aft. The effect was wonderful. *Argo*'s nose lifted a trifle, and suddenly she was pointing 15 degrees closer to the wind.

'Terrific!' exclaimed Seth. 'No more rowing! We can sail to Georgia!'

In fact Nick's suggestion did more than any other single item to improve the conditions for the rest of the voyage. Obviously our previous experiment near Greece had not been drastic enough. If we were to move ballast, we had to do it massively. Now we altered the stowage of the boat permanently by hauling out the anchors and stowing them under the aft deck, sorting out the heavier barrels and moving all of them aft, then lashing the water containers as far aft as possible, even though it meant carrying water for cooking all the way down the length of *Argo*. And we made a point of being careful where the crew sat, resisting the temptation to drift forward and gather on the tiny foredeck. The temptation was understandable: in the bows there was better shelter from the wind and – above all – this was Peter the cook's domain. The lure of the occasional snack and a cup of tea or coffee was strong.

'At nightfall on the following day,' wrote Apollonius,

> they reached the land of the Chalybes. These people do
> not use the ploughing ox. They not only grow no corn,

plant no vines or trees for their delicious fruits, and graze
no flocks in dewy pastures. Their task is to dig for iron in
the stubborn ground, and they live by selling the metal
they produce. To them no morning ever brings a
holiday. In a black atmosphere of soot and smoke they
live a life of unremitting toil.

Anatolia is, in fact, one of the earliest places on earth where
mankind is known to have forged iron, and the reason can be seen
on the beaches east of Samsun. The sand is black or a very dark grey
where the waves have sorted out the grains of iron-bearing soil
washed down by the rivers. This black sand is so rich in iron that the
grains can be picked up with a magnet, and the blackest sand can be
smelted into crude iron simply by heating it up in the embers of a
fire. Iron was so valuable to Bronze Age people that the metal was
given as tribute to rulers, as prizes in contests or as the most
generous of gifts. The Greeks, as we had seen on Lemnos, believed
that the knowledge of metalworking had been brought to them by
the god Hephaestos when he came to the island. If, as is likely, the
knowledge actually came from the regions along the Black Sea
coast of Anatolia, then the most likely route for its transmission was
the same sea corridor which Jason and his companions travelled.

Indeed there is evidence in the *Argonautica* that some sort of trade
connection existed even before *Argo* passed that way. Jason's great
galley may have been the first Greek ship to travel the whole
distance along the Anatolian coast, but the Greeks themselves may
have penetrated to parts of the area even earlier, either overland or,
more probably, by coasting voyages in local craft. Not only had
Phrixus with the flying ram gone before the Argonauts to Colchis,
but at Sinop, the legend recounts, Jason and the Argonauts found
three Greeks, Delieon, Autolycus and Phlogius. These three had
been left behind from Hercules' overland expedition against the
Amazons, and were glad to be picked up by their countrymen. The
possibility that there might have been a well-established coastwise
sea route is strengthened by the extraordinarily fortunate encounter
which now took place between Jason and four of his cousins, who
had been coming by ship in the opposite direction, from Colchis
itself. The four young men – Cytissorus, Phrontis, Melas and
Argus – were the sons of Phrixus. Their mother was Princess
Chalciope, the daughter of fierce King Aeetes of Colchis whom
Phrixus had married in the land of the Golden Fleece. After the

death of their father, the four young men had decided to visit his country in Greece to claim whatever inheritance was due to them. Setting out from Colchis in a local ship, they got as far as Giresun when a storm blew up in the night. Running for shelter before a howling north gale, and presumably heading for the safe anchorage of Giresun, the Colchian vessel struck a rock and broke in pieces. The young men managed to cling to the wreckage and were cast up on an island sacred to Ares, the God of War. There, very soon afterwards, they were rescued by the arrival of *Argo*.

There is no difficulty in identifying the island of Ares. Only four islands worthy of the name are found along the entire north coast of Anatolia. An exploring vessel which follows the coast would naturally make these islands its stopping places, for the very good reason that the islands provide secure camp sites at a safe distance

Giresun Island

from any hostile natives on the mainland. By the time *Argo* came to the Amazon country she had already passed three of these islands, and the fourth and last island, said Apollonius, was actually used by the Amazons as a place of worship on which they would sacrifice horses, using a sacred black stone as an altar to their war god.

Giresun Island, 1½ miles northwest of the present town, fits the location exactly, while nearby Palamut Rock, an isolated danger, is an excellent candidate for the place where the Colchian ship came to grief. On a coast that is remarkably free from offshore reefs for hundreds of miles, Palamut Rock is an exceptional hazard in just about the worst place. It lies in the northern approach to Giresun harbour and lurks just beneath the surface; only the occasional white break of swell washing over it gives any warning of its presence. The Colchian boat, running for shelter in Giresun during the confused darkness of a northerly gale, would not have had a chance even of seeing the danger before she struck this isolated fang and was split open by the impact. Her crew would have been thrown into the water, and the luckier ones would have swum for Giresun Island half a mile away.

Phineas, the blind seer back at the entrance to the Bosphorus, had warned the Argonauts that they would find the island of Ares infested with hostile birds. 'You must beach your ship on a low-lying island,' he had told them, 'though not before you find some means of driving off the innumerable birds that haunt the lonely shore.' The birds would attack humans. As the Argonauts rowed towards the island, the legend recounts that a bird flew out and shot a feather at them, wounding Oileus in the left shoulder. Eribotes, who sat next to Oileus on the same oar bench, pulled out the feather and bandaged the wound, while Clytus succeeded in shooting down the next bird with an arrow. Half the Argonauts then locked shields over their heads to form a protective canopy over *Argo*, while the others continued to row for the island. As they came ashore they raised a great din, clattering their weapons on their shields and giving a loud shout, so that 'the birds in their thousands rose into the air and, after fluttering about in panic, discharged a heavy shower of feathery darts at the ship as they beat a hasty retreat over the sea towards the mainland hills'. This is clearly an account of the Argonauts landing on an island which was the habitat of large numbers of birds. Giresun Island is exactly that. Rank upon rank of cormorants and gulls could be seen sitting on the rocky flanks of the island as we approached, launching themselves out in squadrons as they took fright at the arrival of the new *Argo*, while others circled ceaselessly in the updraught that was deflected from the humpbacked island.

Landing on Giresun Island still needs caution. There is no harbour, just a rough quay cut into the solid rock on the landward face. No one lives on the island, which is only some 250 metres in breadth, though it was fortified in Byzantine times. Now the island is visited every 20 May by people from the mainland who come to invoke its magic. For here, once again, we found that an Argonaut site has retained a very strong tradition of magical powers. The custom is to go first to a riverbank on the mainland and throw in seven double handfuls of pebbles, followed by a single handful. This symbolizes a release, the act of casting off care and misfortune. Then the supplicant hires a boatman to row him out to Giresun Island and circle it three times, always from east to west. Going ashore, the visitor approaches a solitary black boulder, which stands exposed on the eastern shore of the island. This black rock, some 10 feet in diameter like a huge billiard ball, is made of very much the same conglomerate material as the Clashing Rocks and is pockmarked with small holes. In these holes the believer places tokens of his wish: a pair of small pebbles nestling together comes from sweethearts who hope to marry, a single stone is from a childless couple who want to have a baby. A strip of cloth may be nailed to the rock simply as a token. If he is young and fit, a man can strengthen the magic by climbing around the rock itself, spreadeagled against its rough surface, again three times.

The old boatman who made a living ferrying these visitors out to the island spoke of men who had dug for buried treasure on the island, the centre of which is now covered with thick undergrowth, groves of trees and tumbledown Byzantine ruins. No treasure has ever been found, as far as he knew, but the black rock was famous among all the country folk for its magic. Could the massive black boulder be the same ancient 'black stone' where Apollonius said the Amazons slaughtered sacrificial horses? It is possible. The alternatives would be the low boulders now buried among the ferns and brambles in the centre of the island, where the seabirds constantly wheel overhead as the wind sweeps over Ares Island.

The four sons of Phrixus, half-Greek, half-Colchian, were aghast when they heard that the Argonauts intended to take the Golden Fleece. Did they not know, they asked the Argonauts, that their father King Aeetes was suspicious of all foreigners, and usually put them to death for trespassing in his realm? As for the Fleece, it was held in great reverence by the Colchians, and had been hung in the sacred oak in a sacred precinct. There it was guarded by a huge serpent which never slept. To continue with their mission was an act of madness. Yet, because the sons of Phrixus were blood relations to Jason and owed their rescue to the Argonauts, they agreed to accompany them to Colchis. When the galley got there, they would at least intercede with their father on behalf of the travellers.

From Giresun eastwards the harbours on the Black Sea coast are spaced more closely and a new road wriggles along the shoreline where the mountains run close the sea. In Apollonius' time the forests of this region had been famous as the home of a bizarre people, the Mosynchis, named after the *mossynes* or wooden houses in which they lived. These aborigines had strange, reversed notions of decency. Acts which other races performed in public the Mosynchis coyly did in private, but all normal private acts the Mosynchis did in public, coupling with one another quite unperturbed in the presence of their neighbours. But they were not a cruel people, and when their tribal leader made a mistake they punished him only by imprisoning him in a room for a day with nothing to eat.

Today the slopes of the Mosynchis mountains are remarkable for being covered either with teabushes or with hazelnut groves, acre after acre of them, and everywhere we went we were given hazelnuts to eat – raw, roasted, in sweets or in a paste.

'If we eat any more hazelnuts, we'll all be growing bushy tails, scurrying up trees and hiding them for the winter,' Mark groaned, after yet another shopping trip brought back several kilos of nuts.

Where teabushes grow it rains, heavily and often, and as *Argo* advanced past the terraced hillsides of Turkey's tea-growing country we were constantly saturated with steamy rain showers that watered the tea gardens. By now each member of the crew knew all the others' foibles: John Egan's bursts of ebullience; Seth's cockney bounce and chaotic kitbag, which periodically had to be made to disgorge its extra items; and big Jonathan's habit of wandering up and down the boat at dusk, trying to find space to fit his 6-foot 5-inch frame and tripping over those who had already settled down for the night. 'That's my head you're standing on,' Mark remonstrated quietly one evening from beneath the bench where Jonathan had been standing for two minutes looking around for a sleeping place, blissfully unaware that he was poised on the rowing master's bald cranium. Tim Readman had also taken to sleeping in the bilges as the ideal nest, and in the mornings he would re-emerge, round-faced, blinking his blue eyes, with snub nose and beard and a battered hat pulled down low so that he looked somewhat like Paddington Bear in a good humour.

As the beards of the crew grew thicker and thicker, so their haircuts were growing shorter and shorter. At every harbour we visited someone always seemed to be inclined to have a close crop from the Turkish barber, and came back aboard even more bristle-haired than before. Giresun, Tirebolu and Akcacale all saw the crew's hair grow shorter and shorter. At Trebizond the harbourmaster gave us a splendid meal in the park overlooking the sea, and in the evening a ballad singer, renowned in the region, serenaded us with a newly minted saga about the Argonauts, Turkish, British and Irish, who were so obsessed as to want to row along the Black Sea coast.

Various extra Turkish volunteers came and went: a businessman who ran a car wash and could spare a couple of days; a medical student; a high school pupil. They came, Mustafa told me on the day he signed off the crew to go and get himself a summer job, out of curiosity or on impulse or because of an ideal. Mustafa himself had joined because he sought adventure, wanted to meet new people and to find himself. He had failed his dentistry exams and hoped on *Argo* to win back his self-confidence. He told me that he had learned a great deal more about himself in the twenty-five days he had spent aboard the galley. Now he knew that he could withstand physical hardship, the wet, the hours of rowing, the cramped conditions, the misery of having to stand watch on a damp, cold night or, worse still, having to row in the darkness to hold *Argo* off a lee shore or to pull her head through the eye of the wind. Mustafa went off happily, regretting only the times he had suffered from seasickness and the worst stretches of rowing. As he put it succinctly, 'Sometimes it was really torturing.'

By the time that Mustafa left, the crew were beginning to show increased signs of physical exhaustion. In the final week of rowing along the Turkish coast a lethargy set in. The reason was partly psychological – the oarsmen were husbanding their strength for the last push across the border to the Soviet Union and into Georgia, the modern land of the Golden Fleece. But in part, too, they were genuinely worn out by day after day of cramped living space and physical effort, interspersed with nights that were never comfortable and often broken by sudden demands to row or handle sail. They looked haggard and drawn, and three or four hours of rowing in a morning, which they had once accomplished with such verve, now became a deadening chore which left them tired and lacklustre. After a quarter of a million oar strokes, the thought of even another hundred miles under oars was stupefying. Every man aboard preferred to wait for the wind, however fickle or however late it came. Night or day, rain or shine, *Argo* was on the move just so long as there was wind to fill her sail and rest the oarsmen.

As it turned out, the favourable breezes mostly came after dark, so the crew got even less sleep as *Argo* groped her way forwards, keeping parallel to the string of shore lights and occasionally surrounded in the darkness by the snuffling sounds of schools of small Black Sea dolphins. Our voyage had begun in the lands of the olive, grown everywhere to supply cooking oil. Now we were beyond the zone of the olive, and instead the people of Trebizond had once used dolphin blubber as their only source of oil. When we left Greece in late spring the landscapes had been stark and clear, and on sunny days the air was crisp. Now, in midsummer, the eastern Black Sea was warm and steamy, visibility was poor, and the clouds constantly rolled over the mountains. For ten consecutive days we never glimpsed the sun.

On 18 July the crew went overboard to clean the hull, and we scraped off ten weeks' accumulation of weeds and barnacles, using the sharp edges of our much-abused eating canteens as scrapers. As the muck peeled off the hull, we saw how it drifted in a cloud in the water behind us, a sure sign that even here *Argo* was still nudging a slight adverse current. The scraped-down hull added a quarter of a knot to our speed, and even that fractional gain was deeply welcomed. *Argo* tacked in and out from shore, laboriously clawing up to the wind. When the breeze failed, we heaved out the oars and rowed back towards land until we could anchor, for we hated the thought of being sent backwards by the current or being blown offshore for another bout with the gales. The entire night of 18–19 July we moved in a futile zigzag, going out to sea as far as we dared, then turning back towards the land only to find ourselves at virtually the same place we had left the previous evening.

At first light on 20 July I awoke to find the dawn watch of Peter Warren, Peter Wheeler and Seth, reinforced by Cormac, gallantly rowing the last mile towards a harbour pier. They were bringing *Argo* to Hopa, the last port in Turkey, just 4 kilometres from the Soviet frontier. We had looked forward so much to reaching Hopa that it was a disappointment to land in such a down-at-heel and drab place. It was a shame, I felt, to be leaving from a point that was thoroughly depressing a country that had been so warm and helpful. Hopa's main street was potholed and broken from convoy after convoy of heavy trucks that came to load freight for hauling overland to Iran and Iraq, Hopa being the nearest port on the Black Sea to these countries. The reinforced concrete houses were ugly and neglected and the port, which had been greatly enlarged to meet the Middle East trade, was suffering from a sudden slump in commerce. The vast harbour held only two or three freighters. Hopa had a dead and defeated air; it felt like the end of the world.

Nevertheless the Turks at Hopa were as eager as everywhere else to help us. Previously any boat intending to sail from Turkey to the USSR had been obliged to clear customs and immigration formalities at Trebizond, farther back down the coast. Very few cargo boats made the crossing, and it was unheard of that a boat should sail direct from Hopa to Soviet Georgia. I said I was entirely prepared to take all the crew's passports by road to Trebizond, get them and the ship's papers stamped and come back to Hopa. The officials looked appalled. It was a five-hour journey to Trebizond, they said, and the port police office there might be closed when I arrived. And then I would have a five-hour bus ride to get back. The officials conferred and decided to telephone the governor for help, but he was absent, attending a ceremony. The Argonauts waited on the quayside the whole afternoon, surrounded by our kit barrels which were open for customs inspection. Eventually the governor or his deputy must have returned to his office, because the officials came hurrying down to the quay, beaming with satisfaction.

Argo had clearance to proceed. I did not have to go to Trebizond. The customs man was satisfied. So was the harbourmaster. So was the local policeman. What about our passports? I asked politely. Shouldn't they be regularized? They had been stamped with an inward stamp on our arrival in Turkey – wasn't it necessary to have an outward stamp from Hopa?

'No, no,' I was told, 'that will not be needed. You have very special clearance. And anyhow we cannot stamp your passports because no ship has been cleared from Hopa since the Second World War. In fact no one has given us any stamps! Have a safe journey. *Gule! Gule!*'

So we left Turkey with their farewell ringing in our ears. Translated, it means, 'Go laughing!'

9
Georgia

Two enormous stone pylons mark the sea frontier between Turkey and the Soviet Union. Painted with red and white bands, the two pylons loom starkly on the shoreline, one behind the other, and behind them rise the dramatic slopes of the Little Caucasus mountains. When the two pylons are seen in line from the sea, that is the moment the seafarer straddles the invisible boundary across the surface of the sea which divides the two countries. The two pylons also stand in direct line with a prominent mountain peak, high inland, that the government surveyors must have decided was nature's unmistakable landmark.

Argo, travelling at a sedate 3 knots, crossed that imaginary line in the grey half-gloom of early morning. If, as we had been told, we were the first boat in nearly forty years to have permission to cross that frontier, going direct from the last Turkish port at Hopa to the first Soviet port at Batumi, I did not want to go blundering across the line in the dark, so for most of the previous night we had been experiencing the unusual sensation of trying *not* to make any progress. We had said goodbye to our Turkish Argonauts at Hopa, and then we rowed for half an hour up the coast and anchored in a small, stony cove to eat a late supper, to rest and wait for the night breeze off the land to carry us towards the Soviet Republic of Georgia.

There was a feeling of real excitement and curiosity on board. What would the next day bring? What would Soviet Georgia be like? What sort of reception would we have? Would there be a great difference between the Georgians and the Turks? The frontier was only 80 miles short of our final goal, which was the mouth of the

River Rhioni, called by the Greeks Phasis, on whose bank had stood the sacred oak tree where Phrixus had hung the Golden Fleece. The Georgians lay claim to one of the oldest continuous civilizations in the world; they are the direct descendants of the Colchians who had lived in the Rhioni valley in Jason's time, and some of them still speak much the same language that the first Argonauts would have heard. How would these people view our twentieth-century quest? What would be the final outcome for all our grinding labour – the blistered hands, sore buttocks, uncomfortable nights on hard rowing benches, sweat-stained clothes, putrid bilges, and night watches when, bleary-eyed, one longed to sink back into the warmth of a sleeping bag instead of having to stand at the helm while the minutes dragged by.

One by one, the crew settled down to catch a brief nap before we headed for the frontier. Nothing could diminish their accomplishment in getting so far. They had succeeded in rowing and sailing a vessel of the late Bronze Age for nearly 1500 sea miles, a voyage which Homer and his contemporaries had regarded as a heroic feat by men brought up in a tradition of hard physical toil and sustained effort. In the modern age our only extra advantage was that we knew where we wanted to go. With charts and geographical knowledge, we could avoid the fear of the unknown that the Mycenaean explorers must have experienced. Nevertheless we had suffered from a different sort of ignorance. When we set out from Greece, we had no idea of whether or not our vessel would stand up to the conditions of the voyage. We did not know when to take shelter, what to do when caught by a storm, how to recognize a good galley anchorage or what parts of the vessel were most vulnerable. All this, which the first Argonauts would have known, we had learned the hard way. The new Argonauts, I felt, had reason to be proud of themselves.

As *Argo* nuzzled at her anchor rope in the darkness, I thought of all those who had helped us to get so far, and who would only vaguely know where *Argo* lay at that moment: Uncle John in Athens; Costas, the sixty-one-year-old former airline pilot, and the other Greek voluteers; Erzin, Umur and the Turks; Trondur, back in the Faeroes with his portfolio of sketches to remind him of warmer lands. I regretted very much that they could not be here to see Georgia for themselves, after they had done so much to get us to the final lap of the journey.

Many others were waiting to hear what we had discovered: Colin Mudie, whose design for *Argo* had proved so successful; Tom Vosmer would want to know how the ancient shipwright's techniques had withstood the rigours of three months' voyaging; and there was of course Vasilis. The taciturn Greek shipwright was probably even then sound asleep on Spetses before beginning the new day when like every other day of his working life, he would surely go putt-putting down to his little boatyard on his motor scooter, feed the cats, pick up a *skipani* and go to work on one of his usual wooden fishing boats. Vasilis would never see his masterpiece sail across the Soviet frontier, but at least we still had his favourite *skipani* with us, just as he had asked on the day we left Spetses. The tool was no longer attached to *Argo*'s sternpost, because we had found its razor edge a danger to men climbing over the stern, but Peter Wheeler had it stowed safely in the tool barrel and used it often when carrying out running repairs.

Everything that had gone into creating the Jason Voyage was approaching a climax. Tomorrow we would venture across into new, totally unknown territory. All my planning and scheduling ended on the Turkish frontier; beyond that line the expedition was entirely in the hands of our Soviet hosts. Yet somehow I felt that everything would go smoothly. My confidence had been shared months ago by Sarah Waters, the key member of the team who from the start of the original idea for the expedition had run the project's only 'office'. 'Oh, you'll be well looked after by the Soviets,' she had said. 'There won't be anything for me to do once you cross the border. I think I'll take my holiday then and close the office for a couple of weeks. Just send me a cable when you are on your way back.'

Now *Argo* was poised for those last few miles. The sea grumbled on the beach shingle. The crew slept. At midnight the expected night breeze came, blowing from the land. Cormac hauled up the anchor and the sail was set. *Argo* gathered way, and we headed onwards. Here the coast ran almost north and south, for we were creeping round the farthest limit of the Black Sea, the shore which the Greeks called the 'uttermost bourne', the limit of their seaborne travels. Indeed our longitude was farther east than Mecca. The night breeze was so favourable that *Argo* bustled along too quickly. There was a risk that we would be on the frontier before dawn, so I ordered the sail to be doused, and for three hours *Argo* lay patiently in the water, at right-angles to the wind, and drifting sideways towards the USSR.

Dawn revealed the two pylons, and we unfurled the mildewed sail again. The three red Mycenaean warriors painted on it were worn and faded, but they still marched forwards stiffly towards Colchis, bearing their shields with the ram's head symbol. On the

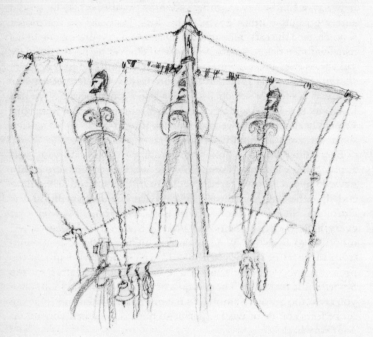

seventy-eighth day since leaving Volos they were about to enter the kingdom of the Golden Fleece. At 0634 hours the two pylons came precisely in line, and we sailed into Soviet waters. There was not a single vessel to be seen; we were quite alone. *Argo* swam stolidly across the surface of the sea, pitching softly to the swell. The early visibility was so poor that one could see scarcely half a mile through the murk. A drizzling rain shower drifted a grey, impenetrable curtain across our path. Something in the dark curtain moved slightly, a darker patch in the general gloom. Squinting forwards, we wondered if there was anyone there to meet us.

For six weeks there had been no contact with the Soviet authorities. Passing through Istanbul I had visited the Soviet consulate and asked a friendly consular officer to inform Moscow that the expedition was going well. He had promised to do this, and had known all about *Argo*, and that was a good sign. But of course it had been impossible to foretell exactly when *Argo* would reach the Soviet frontier; everything depended on wind and weather, and what happened to us on the long haul along the north Turkish coast. It was more than six months since I had written to Yuri Senkevich, the Russian doctor-traveller, and explained to an executive committee of Soviet television my hopes of tracking down the legend of the Golden Fleece in Soviet Georgia. The committee had promised to help, to arrange for me to visit the archaeological sites of Georgia and to discuss my theories with Georgian scholars. There was even talk of bringing a squad of Soviet oarsmen out to *Argo* while she was still at sea, and putting them aboard to help us row up the Georgian coast and into the mouth of the Rhioni River, if that was still navigable. But I knew just how tricky it is to arrange a rendezvous at sea between boats, especially when one vessel is as small and low in the water as *Argo*, and travelling in fits and starts at the mercy of the fickle wind.

The black patch behind the rain curtain took shape. It was a patrol boat, grey ship on a grey background, and it was heading straight towards us. *Argo* was now well within Soviet waters. The patrol boat came down on us, circled us once, and then a second time. The bridge crew stared down at us impassively. We waved. There was no response. The uniformed figures scrutinized us as if we were some dull piece of driftwood. Only a Soviet sailor, hidden from the view of the officers, peeked out of a porthole and waved back surreptitiously. Abruptly the patrol boat engines roared to full thrust. She put over her helm and swung away, heading back into the mist, leaving a white furrow of wake behind her. We saw her resume station, a sentinel lurking against the shoreline. *Argo* sailed forwards, past her. The little galley might no longer have existed.

Suddenly the little walkie-talkie burst into life. '*Argo*! *Argo*! Do you hear me?' a voice said clearly. 'This is *Tovarisch* calling you.'

I grabbed the little radio and answered, '*Tovarisch*, *Tovarisch*. This is *Argo*. Read you loud and clear. Go ahead.' I released the control button, and waited.

There was no reply. The radio hissed gently in my hand, and the voice repeated: '*Argo*! *Argo*! Do you hear me? Please answer.'

I tried again to respond, but without success. It was clear that, while we could hear the mystery ship, *Argo*'s radio was too weak for them to hear us. We could only plod forward in the water, listening to the voice of the unknown radio operator dutifully trying every ten minutes to establish contact. It was like playing a game of blind man's buff.

'Well, at least someone's expecting us,' I commented.

'If that's the *Tovarisch* I'm thinking of,' said Adam, 'then I know her. She's the big Soviet training ship that took part in last year's Tall Ships Race. She's a square-rigger.'

We moved on. The wind was holding fair, and *Argo* was making almost 4 knots through the water. The sun burned off most of the mist and, as the light strengthened, the water around us turned a beautiful opaque pale green, where the shallows and silt altered its texture. It was like sailing through liquid jade. The sunlight gave a pearl-grey tint to the distant cloudbanks, and the rain-washed air had a luminous, limpid quality that one sometimes sees after a thunderstorm has passed. Very faintly, in the far distance, three tiny lines emerged from the horizon. I peered through the binoculars, and the three tiny lines became the topmasts of a ship, advancing in our direction. A quarter of an hour later the masts were visible to the naked eye. They began to blossom with white petals – sails.

Then the hull of the stranger came over the horizon, as she sailed down to intercept us. She was indeed *Tovarisch*, the three-masted square-rigged barquentine of the Soviet training fleet. She was a ship that has appeared on thousands of postcards and calendar pictures, sailed all the world's oceans, and competed in most of the tall ship races. *Tovarisch* is known to every aficionado of the tall sailing ships, and today she was looking her best, the morning sun reflecting off her pyramids of canvas and her white hull set off against the grey clouds and the pale green sea. She looked stunning. And it was quite obvious that she was coming to greet us.

'Now that,' said an appreciative Argonaut from an oar bench, 'is what I call a reception committee.'

Tovarisch adjusted her course to sail by *Argo* no more than 100 yards away. Small figures scurried up the square-rigger's shrouds and spread out along her yards. The upper sails vanished one by one, and were neatly stowed. Then *Tovarisch* turned a half circle and took up station off our port side. The silhouettes of her cadets stayed on the crossyards. A whistle blew – we heard it quite distinctly across the waves – and the Soviet cadets whipped off their white hats and gave three cheers, a neat, orchestrated aerial ballet. The Argonauts, sitting on their grubby oar benches in their ripped and tattered clothes, their motley collection of belongings stuffed in barrels and bags under their feet, the galley scruffy and travel-worn, gazed at the immaculate square-rigger, gleaming with new paint, polish and the meticulous maintenance performed week after week by two hundred or so cadets.

More boats came hastening over the horizon. Yachts were hurrying out of Batumi which had come into sight to the northwest. The lead boat had its name written in 4-foot-high letters along its blue hull – *Kolkhida*, the Georgian version of Colchis. The old legend was obviously well remembered. *Kolkhida* came rushing down at us, tacked smartly and drew level on the opposite side of *Argo* from *Tovarisch*. The yacht's crew were waving. 'Welcome, *Argo*! Welcome to Georgia!' they yelled across to us in English. The helmsman was busily shaking a bottle. It had to be Georgian champagne, for there was a sudden spurt of foam and glasses were being handed along the deck. The yachtsmen raised their glasses in a toast, drained the champagne and tossed the glasses into the sea.

'Hey! How about some for us?' called Tim Readman. There were grins and nods, *Kolkhida* sidled to within 10 yards, and three bottles of champagne were lobbed across to us.

I looked away to port, towards *Tovarisch*. Her rail was lined with spectators, waving and cheering. I could see television camera crews pointing their lenses at *Argo* and in the waist of the ship a block of blue-clad figures all dressed in tracksuits. They looked like a football team posing for a photo. I remembered the promise made to me: they had to be the squad of Soviet oarsmen who were going to help row *Argo* up the Rhioni River. They looked suitably massive.

Our rubber dinghy began a shuttle service to *Tovarisch*. Among the first to scramble over *Argo*'s stern rail was a stocky, fresh-faced man with twinkling eyes. He put out his hand with a grin, and and I recognized him from his photograph.

'You must be Yuri Senkevich,' I said. 'Thank you so much for organizing such a wonderful welcome. It's terrific!'

'I'm glad you like it,' Yuri replied. 'We've been waiting for you for the last couple of days, and everyone is very keen to greet you.'

Suddenly blue tracksuited figures were tumbling aboard from the rubber dinghy – big, powerfully built men in running shoes. They went down *Argo*'s central gangway, shaking hands with the Argonauts. On each man's tracksuit was sewn the emblem of the Georgian republic. They could not wait to get started on the rowing.

'May we row, please?' asked their leader.

Mark Richards rolled his eyes in mock astonishment at such a request. 'Here! Be my guest! Have my oar!' He scrambled off his oar bench and gave his position to the superfit-looking Georgian athlete, who took a few expert strokes to get the feel of the 14-foot blade. All the newcomers, it turned out, were physical training instructors, trained athletes. Every one was a master of sport of the Soviet Union. Some were specialists in rowing; two were expert kayakists; their team leader had won the Spartakid Championship of the Soviet Union. Even the jovial, slightly less lean figure who ducked under the stern crossbar and offered to take over the steering for me was a competition-class helmsman.

With such a surge of visitors there was scarcely room to stand on *Argo*'s stern deck. Officialdom arrived in the uniformed shape of a senior officer of the Soviet Frontier Guards, with a great deal of braid on his shoulder boards and a galaxy of gold stars on his lapels. He was less interested in checking our documents than in collecting souvenirs of *Argo*'s own rubber stamp – a little outline of the galley – to take back and distribute in his office. Yuri's son, Nikki, arrived to join his father, and I was then introduced to a small, alert man with a very crisp and efficient air about him. By his dark eyes and black hair I guessed him to be a Georgian, and he turned out to be Nugzar Popkhadze, chairman of the Georgian State Committee on Broadcasting and the man responsible for our forthcoming visit. He was a dynamo of activity. How far did I think *Argo* would sail that day, he asked me. Could we get as far as the harbour of Poti at the mouth of the Rhioni River?

No, it was too far, I replied, but if the wind held we should be able to reach Poti the following day. 'Good,' said Nugzar, clapping his hands together briskly. 'We'll be waiting for you.' He did not elaborate any further, but the gleam in his eye should have warned me that I was in for a surprise.

With Nugzar came another visitor whose profession one could have spotted at 50 yards. He looked exactly what he was – a distinguished scholar – but rarely does one see a bespectacled, donnish academic beaming with such obvious pleasure on the heaving stern deck of an open boat. It was Professor Othar Lordkipanidze, whose name had been familiar to me for the past three years, ever since I had first begun to study in depth the archaeological background to the legend of Jason and the Golden Fleece. Othar Lordkipanidze was the name which had signed many of the articles I had read concerning the early Greek contacts with Colchis. He directed a famous excavation at the ancient Colchian city of Vani on the bank of the Rhioni, presented highly regarded papers at international conferences and was head of Georgia's prestigious Institute for Archaeological Research.

'We've been looking forward to greeting you to Vani,' he said, 'Everyone is very excited, and all has been prepared. I'll be able to take you around Georgia, and show you the archaeological sites that you want to see.'

What would have happened, I wondered as I absorbed the evidence of all this careful preparation, if *Argo* had failed? It was never certain that we would get as far as Georgia. We might have been defeated by the Bosphorus or sunk in a gale off Sinop. Yet it was obvious that here in Georgia, and at a higher level in Moscow, enormous efforts had been made to prepare for our visit – months and months of planning had been made and checked, resources delegated, schedules dovetailed, oarsmen selected and prepared, *Tovarisch* put on standby, an entire apparatus set in motion. All for a small open boat manned by a handful of volunteers, bobbing along at a snail's pace towards Soviet Georgia. I was glad that I had not even imagined the responsibility while *Argo* was at sea: it made it that much easier to enjoy the welcome.

That night we got as far as Kobuleti, a small coastal settlement some 25 kilometres south of Poti, where the low delta lands of the Rhioni give way to a sandy shoreline covered with pinewoods. The Georgian volunteers were rather disappointed that the breeze was behind us and we could sail onward until the sun went down, until in the darkness the hissing waves warned us that we were running into shallows. *Tovarisch* had earlier stood clear to avoid this shallow zone, and the other yachts went ahead to Poti's harbour for the night. Six Argonauts went with them, whisked away by enthusiastic Georgians. Where they went or whom they were with I had no idea until they showed up next morning, announcing that they had spent the night in Poti being wined and dined. 'There was a woman in the restaurant, at least six and a half feet tall!' announced Tim Readman wonderingly, as he came back like some grizzled mariner too long at sea and full of exaggerated tales for his shipmates.

The enthusiastic masters of sport, who had replaced my missing Argonauts that night, had been introduced to the yoga-like delights of sleeping on hard wooden oar benches and taking turns on anchor watch to see that *Argo* was not driven ashore in the dark. A couple of them had been thoroughly seasick, but that did not dampen their energies. As we began to row the last few miles towards Poti there was a resounding crack and a loud cheer. This time it was not the steering oar breaking, but one of the 1¼-inch diameter wooden thole pins which pivoted the oars. The former Soviet Spartakid champion had pulled so hard that he had snapped his thole pin in half.

Tovarisch now reappeared as our guide and was seen heading into a port which had to be Poti. Dutifully we followed. Half a mile short of the entrance we paused in order to tidy up the boat and make *Argo* half-presentable – sail neatly furled, ropes coiled and our jumbled kit tucked out of sight. Then, with British, Irish and Soviet oarsmen rowing shoulder to shoulder, we made our entry into Poti harbour, past workaday arrays of cranes, gantries, piles of scrap metal and half-built boats on the stocks. As we rowed around a corner and entered the main basin Yuri Senkevich, standing beside me, gave a grunt of surprise. The far side of the harbour was black with people, thousands upon thousands. They crammed the quay wall, overflowed into the public square and clustered on the balconies of the large port office which dominated the harbour. Every window, every ledge, even the high cabins of the dock cranes were packed to capacity. Lying against the quay, already moored, was *Tovarisch* with her three towering masts, together with all the yachts which had greeted us the previous day, even one flying the Bulgarian flag which had crossed the Black Sea to see *Argo*.

'Smartly now! Watch your timing! Keep your eyes in the boat!' As crisply as we could manage, *Argo* rowed the last hundred yards. 'Let go the anchor!' Cormac tossed the anchor down into the harbour mud. 'Starboard side, hold her. Port side, row on.' The Georgian rowers did not need a translation; they all knew what to do. With her oars beating evenly, *Argo* spun end for end. 'Back her down all.' The port side oarsmen reversed their stroke and *Argo* backed into her slot. A stern line was caught by a longshoreman and made fast to the quay. 'Oars inboard!' With a satisfying, thumping clatter the Argonauts slid their oars inboard and rested them across the boat. Then we rose to go ashore, to set foot for the first time in Georgia.

A line of officials was holding back the spectators. As we stepped onto the quay they let through a scampering horde of children, small girls with pigtails flying as they raced one another to reach us first. Each carried a bunch of flowers which was thrust eagerly into the hands of an Argonaut until we were almost submerged in blooms. A resplendent figure loomed up ahead of me, moustachioed and garbed in a long coat like a dragoon, complete with soft leather boots and a silver-mounted dirk at his belt. He seized me by the elbow, and flinging out one arm in a formal gesture he began to declaim sonorously.

'It's a speech of welcome,' said Othar in my ear. 'He's speaking Old Georgian.'

Then I was led forward to meet the mayor of Poti. Wine was poured into two shallow earthenware bowls and fruit was offered. 'These are the traditional welcome gifts for the guest,' explained Othar. Loudspeakers on the balconies boomed out a Georgian anthem, and the jostling crowd began to join in the words in a deep, full-throated chorus. Everyone turned to face one section of the encircling crowd. There, in the front rank, stood perhaps twenty men, most of them in their late fifties or sixties, and posed to great effect in the same sort of dragoon costume – black, long-skirted coats with silver trim, black boots, crossed cartridge bandoliers and white headclothes. They struck a suitably proud stance and their leader stalked forwards. Then he turned towards his attentive men, raised one arm, and the troupe burst into song. The astonishingly complicated, intricate, emotional art of choral song has been brought to its finest pitch with the traditional singers of Georgia. It was a sound which I was hearing live for the first time in my life, a sound which the new Argonauts would hear again and again over the next ten days, and which none of us could ever forget.

Jason and his men did not enjoy anything like such a colourful and heartfelt reception when they came to King Aeetes' realm. They approached the Colchian kingdom with great caution, closing the coast under cover of darkness. The four young Colchian nobles whom they had rescued from the island of Ares had warned them that their grandfather, the cunning and ferocious king, was intensely suspicious of all strangers who came uninvited to his kingdom; he was likely to arrest the adventurers and have them put to death. So the Argonauts made their landfall in Colchis like burglars reconnoitring a well-protected mansion. They rowed quietly into the mouth of the River Phasis during the night, and went a short distance upriver before ducking into the marshes and hiding *Argo* among the reeds. There they held a council to decide how best to tackle the problem of obtaining the Golden Fleece from its owner, the Colchian king.

According to Apollonius, Jason wanted to respect the laws of hospitality. He felt that since Aeetes had offered sanctuary to Phrixus when he had arrived in Colchis years before as a refugee, it was only right that the Argonauts should now openly state the purpose of their mission to the king, and wait for his reaction. They would then learn if he intended to treat them as guests or as enemies. So Jason set out for Aeetes' palace, carrying a herald's wand to show that he came in peace, and accompanied by two Argonauts, Augeais and Telamon, and the four grandsons of King Aeetes who were to explain *Argo*'s mission.

The royal palace, Apollonius said, lay on the right bank, that is the north shore, of the River Phasis. The path there from *Argo*'s hiding place among the reedbeds lay through gloomy thickets of osiers and willows from which dangled the corpses of dead Colchians. By local custom only the bodies of women were buried in the ground. When a Colchian man died, his corpse was wrapped in an untanned oxhide and hung in a tree to decompose in the open air. A thick mist lying over the marshes must have made the approach to the royal palace even more forebidding, but it did successfully conceal the arrival of the strangers until Jason and his companions were at the gates of the royal stronghold.

The king's residence was an imposing structure with several courtyards leading from one to the other, overlooking balconies, side buildings and folding doors opening onto the various offices of the royal household. These included the apartments of the king, his son and heir Prince Apsyrtus, and the building reserved for the palace women, in particular King Aeetes' daughter, the royal princess Medea. When Jason and his companions arrived, the great gates of the royal enclosure stood open, and they walked in to find the king's household engaged in its daily routine: chopping firewood, butchering the carcass of a bull for the royal kitchens and heating water for baths.

The precise details of Aeetes' palace may be something which Apollonius dreamed up: no more than how he thought the palace of the dreaded Colchian king would have looked. Equally, they could have been based on a dimly remembered account of how a traditional Colchian royal stronghold was laid out and organized. Apollonius' claim that King Aeetes, the same man who had ruled Colchis when Phrixus got there, was still alive is a little doubtful, and historians believe that in fact the king's title was a perpetual one, at least as far as the Greek writers were concerned. They seemed to call all the early Colchian kings Aeetes.

Jason's frank approach to the Colchian ruler now led him into great danger. King Aeetes invited the strangers to eat with him and, after the meal, questioned his grandsons as to why they had returned so soon from their voyage, bringing strangers with them. Argus, the oldest of the grandsons, explained how he and his brothers had been shipwrecked on Ares Island, rescued by the Argonauts and brought home to the Phasis. The visitors, he told his royal grandfather, had come to seek the Golden Fleece from Phrixus' sacred ram, and to carry it back to Greece with them. To recompense Aeetes for the Fleece, Jason and the Argonauts were offering to help the Colchian army in their war against their northern neighbours and traditional enemies, the Sauromatae.

King Aeetes exploded in rage. He rounded on Jason, Augeias and Telamon and swore that if they and their companions did not leave his kingdom immediately they would suffer. Their story about the Golden Fleece, he thundered, was a lie. They had really come to attack him and seize the throne of Colchis. They were no better than pirates. But for the fact that they had eaten at his table and were protected by the laws of hospitality he would have torn out their tongues and cut off their hands, sending them back to their companions waiting on *Argo* as a warning not to trespass on his kingdom.

In the face of this outburst, Jason kept his head. He repeated his offer that if they could be given the Fleece, the Argonauts would fight alongside the Colchians against the Sauromatae. And if Aeetes could be generous enough to hand over the Golden Fleece, then Jason and his men would cause the name of Aeetes to ring with praise throughout Greece.

The hapless Jason now tumbled into exactly the same sort of trap that had started the quest for the Fleece in the first place: Pelias' cunning proposition that he would be given the throne of Iolcos if he brought back the Golden Fleece. This time it was King Aeetes who set the snare. He told Jason that he could indeed have the Fleece, if he successfully accomplished a special task: he would have to yoke two fire-breathing bulls that grazed on the sacred plain of Ares, on the opposite bank of the river, where stood the sacred oak bearing the Golden Fleece. Once Jason had succeeded in yoking the two bulls he had to drive them to plough a 4-acre field in a single day. Then he was to plant the furrows with the teeth of a monstrous serpent. From these teeth would spring armed men, and Jason's task was to kill them all before nightfall. The deed, said Aeetes, was not impossible. As king of Colchis, he himself knew how to yoke the bulls, sow the teeth and kill the warriors. If Jason showed himself equally capable, then he could have the Fleece the same day.

Secretly, however, King Aeetes resolved to kill the Argonauts. Even if Jason succeeded in his ordeal, a Colchian war party was to put *Argo* to the torch and burn her crew with her. To punish his four grandsons for their rashness in bringing these dangerous strangers to Colchis, Aeetes proposed to send them into exile.

Princess Medea now enters the story. Apollonius tells how the Princess had already caught sight of Jason as he first entered the palace. That first glimpse of the Mycenaean prince threw her into turmoil, and she fell completely and helplessly in love with the young man. Even as the visitors were parleying with Aeetes Medea was in her rooms, tormented by her burning attraction to the stranger and by a foreboding that something appalling would happen as a result. She already knew that, whatever happened, she could not resist her infatuation. She could not let Jason leave Colchis without helping him, even against her father.

Medea was already known in Colchis as a young woman with magic powers, but she did not have the evil reputation she was to acquire in Greece. In Colchis she was a virgin priestess, and it was said that she knew all the magic herbs, how to prepare them, and how to weave spells and enchantments. The terrible mutation of her role in the Jason story, from love-struck maiden in Colchis to death-dealing queen in Greece, was to become one of the best-known transformations in Greek tragedy. But for the moment the young Colchian princess was a wholly attractive figure. When Jason and his companions returned to *Argo* the young Colchian noble, Argus, told them about Medea's magic powers and exhorted them to enlist her help against King Aeetes. He offered to lead Jason to a place where he was sure to meet Medea, for he knew that the princess would be at the temple sacred to the Underworld Goddess, Hecate.

Jason agreed, and he and Argus set out for the sacred place, accompanied by Mopsus, the seer. Just short of the grove, Mopsus held Argus back, knowing that if the meeting was to succeed, Jason and Medea would have to meet alone. When Medea saw Jason coming through the woods towards her, Apollonius says, 'her heart stood still, a mist descended on her eyes, and a warm flush spread across her cheeks. She could neither move towards him nor retreat; her feet were rooted to the ground.' Jason spoke to her gently, asking her not to be afraid of him. He had come humbly to seek her help. If she could have it in her heart to assist him, he said, then her name would be immortalized for her kindness. He reminded her about the high-born Ariadne who had helped Theseus unravel the maze and locate the Minotaur. She had been rewarded by the gods with her own ring of stars, Ariadne's Crown, set among the heavenly constellations. Medea's beauty, said Jason, was a sign of the warm and tender heart within.

'Jason's homage,' Apollonius wrote, 'melted Medea. . . . At one moment both of them were staring at the ground in deep embarrassment; at the next they were smiling and glancing at one another with the love light in their eyes.' Now Medea revealed to Jason the secret of how he could yoke the fire-breathing bulls, plough the field and defeat the crop of armed warriors. She had already prepared for him a magic salve, an ointment made from a blood-red plant that grew in the Caucasus mountains. If Jason performed a midnight ceremony in honour of Hecate, then smeared his body with the salve, it would render him invulnerable for a day. He could yoke the bulls, plough the field and sow the serpent's teeth. When the armed men rose up from the furrows, he was to throw a boulder among them so that they turned in confusion on one another and fought amongst themselves, until Jason rushed in and finished off the survivors.

Possessed of the secret to succeed with Aeetes' challenge, and swept off his feet by Medea's beauty, Jason asked that when *Argo* left Colchis to return to Greece, she should go aboard with him. Together they would sail to Iolcos, where she would become his wife and they would rule the kingdom. It was his proposal of marriage to Medea that was eventually to lead to the bloody events that came later to be associated with her name.

One of the first questions I put to Professor Othar Lordkipanidze was whether there was any archaeological evidence that such a figure as King Aeetes had existed in Georgia in the late Bronze Age, and whether his capital, known to the Greeks as the city of Aeae, had been located by the archaeologists. Othar replied that the mysterious city of Aeae had been sought by Georgian archaeologists and historians for a very long time, but without definite conclusions. In the next few days he planned to take me to see several places that were possible candidates, though some scholars thought that Aeae was not really the name of a specific place but a general name applied to the whole kingdom ruled by King Aeetes, whose own title meant the 'ruler of Aeae'. But I still needed some exact point on the banks of the River Rhioni to symbolize the end of our own journey in the wake of the Argonauts, so I asked Othar how far up the river lay the first, positively identified, Bronze Age site that had existed in the thirteenth century BC. It was, he told me, at a place called Jaladidi or Great Valley, 15 kilometres inland from the delta mouth of the Rhioni. That spot, I decided, would mark the end of the new *Argo*'s voyage. Othar promised that next day he would go to Jaladidi by car and station himself on the riverbank. *Argo* would row upriver, and Othar would sound his car horn when we reached the crucial spot.

So after the ceremony in Poti harbour we rowed *Argo* to the northern arm of the Rhioni delta where the river runs out through sandbanks and shallows into the Black Sea. The Rhioni delta land stretched out flat under a grey sky. Cattle grazed on the saltings, and the children who had been playing on the beach waded out into the shallows and stood there, with the last of the sea swell surging around their legs, to watch *Argo* come in from the sea. They gazed in wonder, puzzled by the strange newcomer, her painted eyes still staring forwards as she headed eastwards up the great river that the early Greeks had used as their highway into Colchis. As the little galley turned in from the salt water, just ten strokes brought us from the rocking motion of the waves to the calm of the river. And *Argo*, from being a creature of the sea for the past two and a half months, became an animal of the river, quieter and more restrained.

The coastal sand gave way to earth on the riverbank, first pale yellow-grey, and then increasingly dark and silty. Clumps of reeds and low bushes invaded the brackish backwaters. They had provided the hiding place where the first *Argo* had moored, her crew not knowing what kind of reception they would have from King Aeetes and the Colchians. Beyond the reeds grew small, slender trees that our Georgian oarsmen called *tkhelma*, and here and there an isolated willow fluttered its leaves to the breeze which came off the sea. Summer and winter, the Georgians said, the same wind blew in across the land, always from the same direction. Seasonal river floods rose and fell; the channels in the river bed altered and then went back to their former courses, and the central island of the delta inexorably pushed its rim seawards.

A few small houses stood on the bank of the Rhioni. They were little more than fishing shacks or summer cabins. Each had a wooden jetty on pilings, with a couple of punts tied alongside. Their occupants, holidaymakers by the look of them, waved cheerily to us. Then *Argo* came round a bend and we saw ahead of us an old-fashioned railway bridge, carried across the river on girders. The bridge was black with spectators. Hundreds upon hundreds of Georgians had come to this place, knowing that it gave them the best vantage point when *Argo* passed that way. There was a sudden hum of excitement, the buzz of human voices, as they caught their first glimpse of the galley. The sound, and the press of figures, made the bridge look as if it had been settled by a swarm of bees. As *Argo* came closer, more and more people squeezed onto the bridge to get a better view, until finally there was a loud, ominous crack as the pedestrian walkway alongside the rail tracks began to break under the weight of people. Luckily no one was hurt, and the crowd hastily retreated to safety. The bridge, which we had seen sagging under the number of spectators, sprang back to a flatter profile. The extra clearance above water level was useful. *Argo*, with her mast lowered, only just scraped under it. There was no more than 2 inches between her upswept scorpion tail and the rusty steel underdeck of the bridge as the crew manhandled the galley through, reaching up to push on the metal girders. When *Argo* squeezed out the other side, there was a burst of applause from the crowd.

Othar Lordkipanidze had already explained to me in Poti why the Georgians were so enthusiastic about the Jason Voyage. The legend of the Argonauts is embedded deep in the pride and consciousness of the Georgians. The story of the quest for the Golden Fleece is far better known in their country than anywhere else in the world. They learn the tale as young children when it is a fairy story. At school they read it as a basic text. At university they can study it as a source for Georgian history and classical knowledge. Georgia prides itself on an unbroken history that goes back at least 5000 years, and in that history the visit of Jason and the Argonauts is a landmark. It is Georgia's first recorded contact with the ancient civilizations of the Mediterranean. Georgian scholars have produced meticulous translations of the *Argonautica* from ancient Greek into the Georgian language. Art historians have published collections of all the illustrations, classical and more recent, of the events of the Jason story. Georgian girls still bear the name Medea, and a popular brand of Georgian tobacco is called 'Golden Fleece', with a picture of the first *Argo* on the packet. Jason, Medea and the Argonauts are folk heroes within the living culture of the Georgians, and so when a new *Argo* came rowing up the Rhioni the Georgians took her to their hearts. A special popular edition of the *Argonautica* had already been printed and distributed to coincide with our visit; a new brand of Georgian cognac named for the legend; and a large underground cavern, recently discovered by explorers in the Caucasus, was to be called 'The Cave of the Argonauts'.

On the first afternoon of the river journey we travelled 7 kilometres upriver and camped on the bank. Next morning we set out again, rowing up the Rhioni which led like a broad, turbid highway into the interior. The weather was unseasonably wet, and the heavy rain draining off the meadows reinforced the meltwater coming down from the headwaters in the Caucasus, and pushed up the speed of the current so that the oarsmen had to work very hard indeed to make any headway. But with ten Georgian masters of sport aboard, *Argo* had enough muscle power to nose up-current. We churned forward, determined to make every last inch of our quest by our own efforts. One crew man stood in the bows, casting the leadline, for although the Rhioni was in full flood it was spread across mudbanks and shallows, braiding its channels in cutoffs and dead ends.

Lush watermeadows now lined both banks, and the Georgian farmers and their families came down to watch us toiling up-current. Their children tried to keep pace with us, running barefoot through the clinging black mud along the bank and stopping at each little hillock to get a better view. Their excited chatter was like the chirping of sparrows. The day was warm, overcast and humid, and the air so thick that we seemed to be toiling through an endless landscape of brown river water, green fields and a lifeless grey sky. There were no villages, for the meadows were so soggy that the houses were set back out of sight. When we outpaced the children there was only the great river, an occasional heron, a skein of wild duck and the scattered herds of cattle and water buffalo. The only sounds were the plash of the oars, the swirl of water running down the sides of the hull, the panting breath of the oarsmen, and an occasional soft, sucking splash as a section of the loamy riverbank, undermined by the current, toppled into the gnawing flow. Several times *Argo* bumped on the hidden mudbanks; the impacts were harmless – the mud, mingled with river sand, was soft. We reversed stroke, let the current help, and disentangled the boat so that we could grope our way back into the channel and row onwards.

With each kilometre the gentle collisions became more frequent. Every five minutes now we were hitting mudbanks. The effort of extricating ourselves sapped the energy of the crew. By mid-morning I could see that they were tiring. Scanning the surface of the river for the telltale slicks and eddies that warned of more shallows, I began to wonder just how far we could actually get with *Argo* before we finally ran out of water and had to abandon the river journey. Then we came round another meander, and I could see that we had entered a crucial sector. The river spread so wide that a permanent island had formed in midstream. Neither channel on either side of the island looked very promising, so I steered to port and *Argo* plodded past. When we reached the tip of the little island I put the helm over and cut back to starboard, seeking a central channel again. I felt a gentle pluck at the steering oar. In the same moment *Argo* gave a whispering shiver as the whole length of her keel ran softly onto the swell of a submerged sandbar. Not feeling the touch, the crew continued to row for a few strokes. The river current, sliding past the hull, tricked the senses and gave them the impression that *Argo* was still making progress. Then the crew, too, realized that *Argo* was well and truly aground. Gratefully, the tired crew rested on their oars. I was just about to say that it was time to take a rest and break for lunch when a car horn began to blow, steadily and insistently. It was a strange sound in that waterlogged, bucolic landscape. Looking to my left, I saw a mud-spattered car bumping across the meadow; its horn was still blowing a fanfare. In it was Othar Lordkipanidze, and he was signalling to say that we had reached the first Bronze Age settlement on the banks of the Rhioni – Jaladidi. It was exactly the spot where *Argo* had run aground definitively.

I changed what I was going to say. 'Ship your blades!' I called, 'That's it! That's the end of the Jason Voyage! We've made it.'

Pandemonium broke out. Oarsmen jumped up from their benches. There were shouts of: 'No more rowing! Let's celebrate! Where's the wine?' For a few moments we were sufficiently composed to dig out three red rocket flares which we fired into the sky, one after another, to symbolize the end of our journey, and then the celebrations began in earnest. Hastily I put away my notebook, for I knew what traditionally happened next. Two burly Argonauts advanced purposefully down the gangway, ducked under the crossbar, picked up the skipper and hurled me over the rail and into the river. It was shallow enough to stand, and I watched a succession of oarsmen leap, fall or be thrown into the water until not a soul was on board *Argo*. Her entire crew was floundering in the current, cheering themselves hoarse. Most had abandoned ship clutching bottles of Georgian wine, and these were passed from hand to hand. Then we hauled ourselves soggily back on board and there, in midriver, held a victory party that summed up our delight.

A launch caught up with us, bringing a tremendous picnic – chicken, bread, cheeses, grapes, apples, plums, melons, fish – and this feast was spread down the central gangplank. Othar Lordkipanidze, Nugzar Popkhadze and Ilya Peradze, the Georgian boat club official who had been coaching the Georgian oarsmen, came aboard to share the triumph with the drenched but happy oarsmen. Peter the cook vowed he had prepared his last Argonaut meal and would henceforth exist on Georgian bounty, and the visitors watched attentively as one of the Georgian oarsmen demonstrated how to thump the base of a wine bottle with the flat of one's hand until the mounting pressure eventually sends the cork flying out without recourse to a corkscrew. But that was nothing. The most awesome demonstration was when one huge Georgian sportsman extended rigid the little finger of his right hand, placed the tip of the finger against the cork, and with one controlled movement literally forced the cork down through the neck and into the bottle. It was enough to make one's hand flinch in sympathy.

Then the toasts began. Every member of the visiting crew was toasted by name, then every country of every crew member, and those absent Argonauts who had helped row *Argo* on her trip but were not aboard for the final sector of her voyage. The Georgian manner of toasting was boisterously suitable for the occasion: whenever anyone thought of a good subject for a toast he called for the attention of the others, raised his glass and named his theme, and then began the syllables '*Gau . . . ma . . .*' and the rest added with a full-throated roar '*. . . Jous!!*' as they tossed off their wine. In Georgian it translates as 'Good health!' and was to become the watchword for our visit to Colchis. Then the singing began: first with Georgians, with traditional songs, and then the Argonauts with their well-rehearsed rowing choruses which they had sung from Greece to the far end of the Black Sea. As a symbol of the camaraderie it was difficult to improve on the sight of Cormac O'Connor, former curragh racing champion of the west of Ireland, with his arm across the brawny shoulders of Vladimir Beraija, former winner of the Spartakid cup of the USSR, and the two men joining in the chorus of a traditional Georgian song.

Three hours later, when the midriver party came to a close, Ilya announced that the plan was to move *Argo* upriver to a formal ceremony that had been arranged at the town of Vani. Everything, he said, had been organized. A towboat was standing by to assist *Argo*; the boat club had surveyed the river; and the club members had even drawn a river map showing the channels and the depth of water available. Othar and the other dignitaries left to go ahead to Vani, and the joint Georgian-international Argonaut crew leaped into the water, heaved *Argo* off her sandbar and passed a line to the river tug.

10
The Golden Fleece

The plan for the river journey, so immaculately prepared by the Georgians, went splendidly awry. When the volunteers from the boat club had surveyed the river to work out the best channel for *Argo*, no one could have foreseen that mid-July would bring freak rainstorms. The Rhioni's current was now flowing far faster than had been envisaged, and the level of the river was surging up and down by as much as 6 feet in twelve hours. It was impossible to predict the result. Sandbanks would appear and then be submerged; the main river current would switch from one side of a central island to the other; great masses of flotsam came lurching round the bends and menaced the propellors of the tugboat or got entangled in the towline.

We started out with a tow from a river motorboat, but very soon it was obvious that its engines were not powerful enough to breast the current. Someone dashed off for help. Soon afterwards another tug, larger and more powerful, appeared. It hauled *Argo* a few more kilometres upstream before it went aground with a great spewing up of silt from its propellors and a smell of overheated engines as it thrashed around trying to extricate itself from the shallows. We cast off the towline, and a swarm of small skiffs with outboard engines rushed in and took up the tow. Ilya Peradze directed operations with tremendous vigour. He waved his arms furiously and yelled urgent directions to the little squadron of tiny motorboats straining on the towline ahead of us, their engines going full blast like a mosquito fleet as they struggled against the current. The big tug reappeared briefly, helped out for a time, and then finally and noisily ran out of water. It was last seen falling out of sight behind a bend, stuck fast with its crew resignedly poking around the hull with a red and white banded sounding pole to try to find enough deep water for their vessel to escape.

But the Georgians would not give up. By hook or by crook they were absolutely determined to get *Argo* to Vani. Nothing was going to stop them, not even the Rhioni at its most capricious. So what had started as a short aftermath to the main voyage became a complete sub-plot, and one of the most enjoyable episodes in the entire project. There was simply no reining in the enthusiasm of our athletic hosts. When the lead boat of our mosquito fleet ran aground, its coxswain tossed the towline away and the next boat swerved abruptly and tried to find a better channel. Sometimes as many as three or four little boats were ahead of us, scattered across the width of the river, searching for a passage.

Argo needed only 2–3 feet of water to proceed, and yet she ran aground very frequently indeed. Then everyone would leap overboard, push and shove and haul, waist-deep in the river, and by

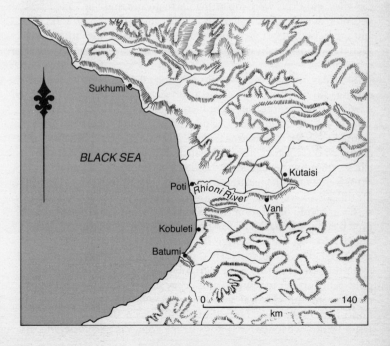

main force heave her back into deeper water. When even the mosquito boats ran out of depth, so that their little outboards could not function, all the Argonauts plunged into the Rhioni and literally manhauled the galley forward, with the water churning past their chests. We knew when we had come back into the main channel, because the lead hauliers disappeared underwater. All this was done with such buoyant excitement and panache that it was impossible not to be swept away with the spirit of the whole exercise. It was quite obvious that our Georgian strong men wanted to feel that they had really helped the expedition to reach its goal, and dragging *Argo* up the river by main force was a splendid demonstration of this. Even a torrential rainstorm that night, the wettest night of the entire voyage, failed to douse their enthusiasm. No one had a moment of sleep. *Argo* lay moored to a muddy bank in the darkness, somewhere in the middle of western Georgia, with the rain sluicing down and the lightning splitting the pitch-blackness. We had lost contact with the towboats; no one on shore knew where we had got to – the conditions were too atrocious to go and find out – and there was no towpath for searchers to find us. Instead, with no food left and the last bottles of Georgian wine to console us, the entire crew sheltered under makeshift plastic sheets and bellowed their full repertoire of songs.

Next day the weather was no better, and with *Argo*'s progress getting slower and slower against the racing current, Othar Lordkipanidze sent for me. The Georgians would look after *Argo*, I was firmly told, and bring her up to Vani. In the meantime Othar wanted to show me his archaeological site there. It would help me understand Georgia's links with ancient Greece and provide some clues as to why the legend of the Golden Fleece had survived.

One clue often lay scattered on the ground. After heavy rain on the hillside above Vani, golden objects are sometimes washed to the surface. A gold decoration from a necklace was picked up from the mud by one of Othar's chief assistants on the same day that *Argo* had sailed into the Rhioni. Over the years the local inhabitants had recovered elegant gold diadems, gold necklaces exquisitely made from thousands of tiny gold balls melded together, gold earrings, gold pendants, gold jewellery of every description. This material dated from the classical Greek period when a Greek city had flourished on the spot, but although this was many centuries after Jason's time, what mattered was that the gold was Colchian gold. It had been obtained in Georgia, and as Othar pointed out, Colchis was so famous in classical times for its gold production that the Greek writers had given it the epithet 'rich in gold', an epithet it shared with Mycenae itself. Thus the golden artefacts of Vani and other towns in Colchis kept alive the legend of a gold treasure at the far end of the Black Sea, and the place where the gold was obtained continued to be identified with Georgia.

Another clue for my research was a ceremonial bronze axehead which Othar's team had dug up three weeks earlier. It was a superb piece, the same special axe form which has lasted unchanged in western Georgia from the Stone Age until the present century; in living memory the same shape of axe was still used by Georgian farmers for clearing brushwood. The ceremonial axehead which Othar's people had found dated from the eighth century BC, and on the back of it was the figure of a mounted warrior with a spear and a conical helmet or hat. It was a Colchian war chief, and the earliest known representation of the sort of Colchian tribal lord who may have ruled in the Phasis valley at the time when Jason and his men landed there. This mounted warlord was the closest image that the archaeologists had yet come to discovering what King Aeetes and his descendants might have looked like.

Excavations up and down the Rhioni valley have revealed the nature of Colchian society in the late Bronze Age. The Colchians were farmers who built stockaded settlements and buried their kings surrounded with agricultural tools. This was most unusual, almost unique in early cultures, and Othar suggested that the story of Jason's ploughing ordeal, imposed by the Colchian King Aeetes, might relate to this respect for agricultural prowess. The story of sowing the serpent's teeth could have been copied by Apollonius from the famous tale of Cadmus, who had to face the same ordeal and who defeated the crop of warriors with the same ruse of the thrown boulder. But the fact that Aeetes expected Jason to indulge in an agricultural contest, at which Aeetes said he was expert, may equally have been connected with the early importance of Colchian kings as agricultural leaders.

But what about the fleece? I asked Othar. Granted that Colchis was 'rich in gold' and its kings were associated with crops and agriculture, why did the Argonaut legend stress the sacred nature of the ram's fleece? Othar showed me the clay figure of a ram. It had been found in Vani, and was clearly a cult object. In the next few days, he assured me, he would show me dozens upon dozens of sacred rams, and let me make up my own mind about what they signified.

The following day *Argo* had almost completed her river trek, and we were invited to attend an Argonautic gala which the people of Vani had been preparing for us. On the bank of the Rhioni they had erected a stage in a public park. By late afternoon the sun had broken through the clouds and was bathing the park in a soft, golden evening light, with the trees and bushes washed vivid green after the day's almost continuous rain. The park was thronged with Georgians dressed in their best clothes, and the whole place had a festive air like a small town fête. Othar was smiling broadly as he introduced me to my companion for the evening. It was 'Princess Medea' – a stunningly beautiful Georgian actress who had been hand-picked for her combination of fair skin and jet-black hair, now set in ringlets and held back in classical fashion with a fillet. She was dressed in a pure white Grecian costume with light sandals on her feet, and carried a bouquet of deep red roses. She was grinning mischievously, while her two attendants, equally attractive Georgian girls dressed in the traditional costume of long gold robes of a medieval cut, tried to look suitably demure.

All the Argonauts were asked to sit down in the front row before the stage, and the townsfolk of Vani crowded in behind us. Then the concert unfolded. It began, of course, with another formal speech of welcome by an elder dressed in traditional costume. Then came the choirs, drawn from the local population and singing to perfection. A flautist gave a virtuoso performance, more medieval-garbed Georgian women played gentle melodies on harp-like instruments, and at one point the entire surface of the wooden stage was crammed with forty or fifty boy dancers, about seven or eight years old, who leaped and stamped their way through their number with great gusto and discipline. There were more singers, more musicians, and a touching display when a solo dancer, a vigorous seventy-five-year-old man, was joined by a six-year-old boy who repeated and echoed the older man's steps, a fine symbol of the way in which Georgian traditions are handed down across the generations. Finally a dance troupe from the capital at Tbilisi, the only professional performers in the entire impeccable show, danced a sword dance with their blades clashing and the sparks leaping in the gathing dusk. One was left with an impression of the sheer, ebullient pride of the Georgians in their own traditions, and of the effort that had gone into our welcome. The concert must have lasted between two and three hours, and presented some twelve or fourteen different acts with no more than a twenty-second interval between each. It was a dazzlingly precise display, and kept us spellbound.

The next day the new Argonauts, our Georgian hosts and the squad of Georgian oarsmen all set out to visit the source of Colchian gold. We travelled by road, at first along the Rhioni valley and then into the rolling foothills of the mountains to the north. The valley could have been part of Burgundy. It had the same air of burgeoning fertility and age-old husbandry. There were the same crops, field after field of vines, stands of maize, orchards of plums, apples and pears. There were even tall poplars lining many of the country roads. The houses of the farmers were very distinctive; low structures, often of wood with perhaps a roof of corrugated iron, they were built on short stilts which raised them from the damp, rich earth. At every turn there was evidence of solid agricultural prosperity, good living and bucolic plenty. Vegetables grew in profusion in neatly tilled front gardens. Geese and chickens competed for their pickings with turkeys. Hogs wandered on the roadsides, leading eager clusters of spotted piglets. Even the dogs looked sleek. Fat, wet rain plashed down on the good black soil, and when we crossed the Rhioni by a road bridge the silt-laden river looked fertile enough to plant crops in.

This cornucopia was lavishly presented at table. Our hosts were not going to let their visitors starve, and even at the briefest halt they produced stopgap boxes of cold chicken, bread and fresh fruit. The planned meals could only be described as banquets. When one entered the eating room, whether it was in a private house or public meeting place, the visual impression was daunting. Long tables, seating as many as thirty guests a side, would have been set up and covered with linen, plates, glasses and cutlery, and heaped on them would be every variety and quantity of dish that the hosts could devise. The gastronomic profusion was mind-boggling. Among the selection one could identify sucking pig, sturgeon, caviar, chicken in several guises, roast pork, white fish, shish kebab, roast lamb, meat pâtés, tomatoes, cheese curd, cakes, wheat bread, corn bread, white cheese, yellow cheese and smoked cheese. All this would be washed down with Georgian wines, red or white, brandies, a curious soft drink based on tea, colas, local mineral waters or vodkas, plain or lemon-flavoured. It was like a medieval banquet. As the meal progressed, so more dishes would be carried in proudly and put before the guest until there was no more room to place them, and they would be piled on top of the previous layer of bowls.

That first day we were heading for the country of the Svans, the mountaineers of Georgia. They live mostly in the Great Caucasus range, though previously their territory extended down into the valley foothills. As we climbed upwards we saw the first Svans, immediately recognizable by their grey felt skullcaps, who were working on the road itself, for the route into the mountains was in the process of being improved and properly metalled. The terrain was a road engineer's nightmare. The flanks of the Caucasus reared upwards in great walls, riven by gorges and buttressed by impossibly steep precipices. The road wriggled back and forth, trying to penetrate the massif, following one valley until it could climb no farther, then abandoning that line of attack in order to cross a ridge and make a few more miles up a neighbouring gorge. At times it plunged through raw new tunnels, or clung to artificial ledges notched into the cliff face.

The panoramas were superb. Forests of mountain pine marched across the slopes, and far below in the valley was the river itself, dammed into a long, sinuous lake whose surface was carpeted with thousands and thousands of floating tree tunks, waiting to be collected and sawn into lumber. From the height where we saw them, these floating tree trunks already looked no larger than matchsticks. We stopped for a rest halfway up the tortuous ascent, and Nugzar's staff from the television station could all have doubled as members of a radio choir, for they took the chance to burst into song, using the immense hillsides as an echo chamber for their repertoire of Svan songs. At times it seemed almost as if they were yodelling. The Swiss comparison was even more marked as we emerged into the high plateau. Small, isolated log houses, brown cattle grazing on grass dotted with wild flowers, the distant view of snow-capped peaks, men and women cutting hay in the mountain meadows – all gave an alpine feeling to the Caucasus.

Darkness had fallen before we reached our destination, Mestia, the Svan capital. As we crossed the final pass a figure suddenly loomed up in the headlights, blocking the road. It was a young man mounted on a grey pony. In his hand he held some sort of totem, a pole with a ghostly-looking mask on the top – it was difficult to tell in the jumping shadows – and a fluttering strip of cloth was tied to the shaft. His mount skittered and fidgeted in the glare of the headlights. The car stopped, and Nugzar asked me to walk forward. Behind the rider a phalanx of men was drawn up across the road, with more riders, all dressed in Svan costume and carrying banners. Someone made a speech, and a cow's horn filled with some sort of bitter drink was thrust in my hand. It turned out to be millet beer. The men were a deputation of Svan elders waiting to greet the Argonauts, and there was a clatter and sparking of hooves on the metalled road as the little cavalcade wheeled round and trotted ahead of us to provide our escort into Mestia.

Svanetia, the country of the Svans, is crucial to an understanding of the legend of the Golden Fleece. Historians believe that the mountain culture of the Svans extends back at least 4000 years, perhaps even more, and certainly to the time when the Argonauts are said to have reached Colchis. The language, customs, traditions and beliefs of these mountain people reach into the Heroic Age. The ram appears again and again as a folk symbol, usually with magic or sacred significance. A Svan folk tale, for example, tells that somewhere in their Caucasus mountains is a secret cave in which a ram of gold, tethered with a chain of gold, stands beside a hidden treasure. No one knows how old this story is, but the Svans have been making symbols of the ram since the Bronze Age; and these

Late Bronze Age ram from Kala

symbols are generally taken to be evidence of some sort of ram cult, possibly based on the worship of the ram as a sacred animal.

In the village of Kala, near Mestia, for example, is a small bronze figure of a ram. It was made at about the same time that Jason is said to have sailed to the land of the Golden Fleece, and has a socket in the base, so that it could once have been mounted on a staff. In Kala this ram is still carefully kept in the church. From Raja, in a valley to the east of Mestia, comes an even older bronze ram symbol – a double spiral of ram's horns, found in a grave dating to the mid-second millennium BC. In Larilari, 80 kilometres west of Mestia, an archaeological team led by Schota Tzartolani, another Georgian archaeologist and himself a Svan, was excavating the contents of fifth- and sixth-century BC graves when we arrived in Svanetia. He showed me figure after figure of the sacred ram, cast in bronze and buried with the dead.

Equally important, Svanetia was the prime source of Colchian gold. Next morning we were to witness how the gold was obtained, and that has a crucial bearing on the legend of the Golden Fleece. Four Svan gold miners were awaiting us. They were standing in the shallows of the Enguri River which runs through Mestia, and they were there to show me how the Svans mine their gold. Three of them had once made their living as professional gold gatherers; the fourth, as a young lad, had helped his father in the same trade until the end of the Second World War, when the last government agent to whom these men brought their gold for sale was withdrawn.

Nugzar had arranged the demonstration. The Svans' chief tool was sheepskin. Every spring, when the snows and glaciers in the high valleys began to melt, the Svan miners would climb to the upper valleys, to the feeder streams of the Enguri. Each man went to his favourite place, where he knew by experience that the meltwater was carrying small quantities of gold washed from veins in the rock. Into these streams the Svans placed sheepskins with the fleece side uppermost. The skins were nailed out flat on wooden pallets which were sunk on the stream beds and weighted down so that the stream flowed across them, often in a series of steps from one pallet to the next. As the water ran across the fleeces, the flecks of gold, being heavier than the sand and silt, were trapped in the wool. Each Svan gold gatherer knew when to inspect his gold trap, depending on the richness of the stream and the amount of the water flow according to the season. When the time was ripe, the gold gatherer would remove the sheepskins from the stream, wash out the accumulated silt from the wool, and search through it for gold particles. Exceptionally, in the very richest area, the first fleece, the highest one in the stream bed, would be so impregnated with gold dust that it was virtually a golden fleece.

Strabo, the Greek geographer, had suspected the truth as early as the third century BC. 'It is said that in their country [Colchis] gold is carried down by the mountain torrents, and that the barbarians obtain it by means of perforated troughs and fleecy skins, and that this is the origin of the myth of the golden fleece. . . .' Two thousand years later it was astonishing to find men who still knew the ancient technique and had practised it in their own lifetimes. Standing ankle-deep in the icy cold waters of the Enguri, they showed me the tools of their craft: sheepskins pinned to a board, a mattock to spread out the silt on the wool, a scraper to clean the fleece, and a simple wooden trough to pan out the silt in a final search for gold. That afternoon, at a small but moving ceremony, the venerated father of a Svan hero, a mountaineer who had been killed in a climbing accident, presented me with a gold-gathering sheepskin and a Svan costume.

There remained, or so I thought, only one last question to ask. Was there any evidence that the Greeks, or the Mycenaeans as they were then, actually got to the land of the Golden Fleece as early as the time of Jason? No pottery, jewellery or other physical evidence of a Mycenaean presence has yet been found in Georgia, and sceptics could argue that all the tales about the Golden Fleece and the sacred ram could have been invented many centuries later, when Greek colonies were established on the banks of the Phasis; except for one all-important piece of evidence – the linguistic evidence. The Greeks used the word 'Phasis' to describe the great river of Georgia, and to know that name they must have been in touch with Colchis well before the end of the first millennium BC. Rismag Gordesiani, director of the Institute of Mediterranean Studies at Tbilisi, explained the significance of this clue.

Until the latter part of the second millennium BC, he said, the people of Colchis spoke a language known as Kartvelian. The name of the river in this language would have been 'Pati', and the Greeks must have picked up this word when they called the river 'Phasis', following the normal rules of change in pronunciation. Then, some time before 1000 BC, the Kartvelian language of western Georgia broke up. The people of the river valley began to speak a derived language called Mengrelian, and in this language the river was now called 'Poti' (a name which survives as the city of Poti on the delta). But the Greeks still retained the original name, Phasis, which they could only have acquired long before the foundation of their colonies in the Black Sea in classical times. What intrigued Rismag Gordesiani, though he could not yet find a reason for it, was that the antique Greek word for a sheepskin appeared to be related to the Kartvelian word for a fleece.

Was there, I wondered, an even earlier contact between Greece and Georgia than the voyage of *Argo*? How was it that the flying ram came to Greece in the first place to rescue Phrixus when he was threatened with death? How did Jason and the Argonauts know that they should go to Colchis to find the Golden Fleece? These were questions which lay beyond our present search. For the present, the Jason Voyage had done all it had set out to achieve. We had shown that the voyage was physically possible in a ship of late Bronze Age design. Even with only twenty oars, instead of Jason's alleged fifty men, it could row up against the current of the Bosphorus and survive the rigours of the Black Sea. All along the route we had matched the physical evidence with the geography in the ancient tale, and found that it fitted beyond the bounds of mere coincidence. Now, in Georgia, thanks to the help of the Georgian archaeologists, we had seen evidence of a very ancient ram cult, of Colchis 'rich in gold', and witnessed the actual source of a Golden Fleece. There remained, I thought, nothing more to learn about the legend of the quest for the Golden Fleece.

I was wrong. For another week we were swept along on a tumultuous outpouring of Georgian hospitality. We came down from the mountains and were taken to Tbilisi. We were wined and dined, saw monasteries and museums – in the National Museum was a pair of lovely ram's head bangles of solid gold that Othar had found at his site in Vani – and we enjoyed ourselves hugely. Tim Readman, who was to get married as soon as he got home to England, promised to wear a traditional Georgian costume of white at his wedding reception (which he did), and we began to find it difficult to make space for all the presents that were showered upon us: ornamental dirks, drinking bowls and horns, cut glass, trophies and banners and gifts of every kind. Our comrades, the Georgian rowers, accompanied the Argonauts everywhere, and it was with genuine regret that we finally had to get ready to go back down the coast and start back across the Black Sea. It was then that I stumbled, totally unexpectedly, across what I felt was the final proof that the Jason legend had to be based on fact.

Spa choke

On our very last day in Georgia, 2 August, we were taken back to the Black Sea coast towards the oil port of Batumi. On the way Othar asked if I would like to see one last archaeological site. It was near Kobuleti, where *Argo* had spent the first night at anchor off the Georgian coast. I was very keen to take a look because it would have been here on the coastal plain that Jason and the Argonauts would have landed. Here, if anywhere, would be the sort of settlement that he and his men would have discovered when they first landed in the realm of King Aeetes and sought the Golden Fleece.

It was another wet day, and Othar and I squelched up a low mound which rose like a shield boss from the marshy coastal lowland. This was the site, at Namcheduri, that the archaeologists had decided to excavate. Many similar mounds had been identified in the area but not yet dug. When we got to the top of the mound we found that its far side had been cut away, like a cake sliced in half. We looked down at the usual archaeological scene of mud, puddles and what was obviously the remains of an ancient wooden building that the excavators had uncovered in the middle of the mound.

David Khakhutaishvili, the archaeologist in charge, explained that the place had been a sacred site. There had been an outer stockade of timber posts some 10 metres high and 70 metres in diameter, a moat, and here in the centre had stood some sort of wooden structure, very probably a temple, divided into nine small rooms. Casually I asked him whether his team had found any evidence of the ram cult in the temple. By then I had seen so many figures and representations of sacred rams that I was actually shocked when he replied, 'No.' I was puzzled. What sort of cult was practised in the temple, I asked, if not the ram cult? At first his answer was disappointing. The cult here and in the immediate area during the late Bronze Age was related to the bull. The archaeologists had found caches of bull totems in several places, stone or clay tablets about a foot long and ending in a fork, the well-known representation of the horns of a bull.

Then, belatedly, I remembered something that the constant sight of the ram cult figures had driven out of my head over the past few days: Jason's ordeal with the sacred bulls. To gain access to the Fleece he had been obliged to tame the sacred bulls that lived on the plain near the holy tree in which hung the Golden Fleece. And here I was, standing unexpectedly on the edge of a temple devoted to the cult of the sacred bull, a temple located in exactly the right part of Colchis and dating back to the late Bronze Age. The details were astonishingly accurate. Had the Fleece perhaps been kept in a temple or grove sacred to the bull cult?

But there was another element to the legend. From the very first moment that he had been sent on the quest for the Golden Fleece, Jason had been warned that it was guarded by a monstrous serpent which never slept, but patrolled the holy tree on which hung the fleece. Even after Jason succeeded in taming the sacred bulls with Medea's help, he still had to get past the guardian snake. This, according to the legend, he also managed with Medea's assistance. In the night the two of them secretly went to the sacred place, and there Medea charmed the guardian snake so that its eyes closed. Hastily Jason snatched the Golden Fleece from the tree and the two lovers hurried back to *Argo*, which promptly put to sea and made all speed to escape the vengeful Colchians who had been robbed of their holy totem.

What about snakes? I put the question to the archaeologist at Kobuleti. Had his team found any references to snakes or serpents?

To my astonishment and delight, he replied, 'Oh yes, let me show you.' He took me to a nearby building where the excavators had stored their finds from the ancient temple and other sites in the area. The archaeologist pulled down from a shelf a distinctive bull's horn cult object, a clay tablet about 15 inches long and ending in the characteristic fork shape, and ran his finger down the front of it. 'Here,' he said. 'Do you see this zigzag groove? It is the symbol of a snake, a protective snake. This is from the eighth or seventh century BC, and we have found tiles, fire nozzles and bull totems even older and marked with this sign of the serpent. We think that the ancient Colchians kept snakes inside their temples as guardians. Even up to recent times it was the custom to keep guardian snakes inside Georgian houses.'

At last everything fell into place. Here, surely, was the final confirmation of the Jason story, the sort of detail which could not have been invented later by Apollonius or the authors who wrote about the Golden Fleece. The archaeological evidence shows that in the late Bronze Age there existed on the coastal plain temples sacred to the bull cult. Inside the temples were kept snakes which guarded the cult objects. The entire story of Jason's ordeal and his theft of the Golden Fleece could be explained in the light of what the archaeologists had found.

The Golden Fleece was precisely that: a fleece from the Caucasus mountains, used in the gold-washing technique, and impregnated with gold dust. It may have been brought to the lowlands, along trade routes that we know existed because pottery made in the lowlands has been found in the mountains, or it could possibly have arrived as tribute, or as a cult gift, from the people of the mountains to the most powerful king on the coast. Naturally the fleece would have been placed in the temple of the coast people, the wooden stockaded temple of their bull worship. To obtain the fleece, Jason first had to circumvent the sacred bulls themselves, and once inside the precinct he would have had to get past the guardian serpent that protected the actual enclosure.

Every single element of the legend matched the archaeology. What had seemed a far-fetched yarn when we began the Jason Voyage had found its solution in Georgia, 1500 miles away from its starting point in Iolcos. Back in Greece the mute stones of Dimini,

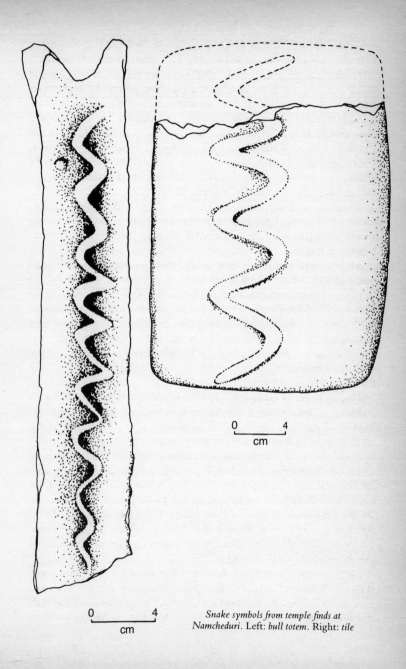

*Snake symbols from temple finds at
Namcheduri. Left:* bull totem. *Right:* tile

which the archaeologists thought was perhaps Aesonia, the royal temporary settlement of Jason's family outside Iolcos during their times of trouble, seemèd to confirm both the beginning and the end of the ancient quest. Here in Georgia the sacred place of the bull cult protected by its snakes, in the land where the ram was held sacred and the fleece was used to gather gold, was further striking evidence for the truth of the tale. For me that moment on the muddy temple mound near Kobuleti was the end of the search, as it must have been for Jason, close on thirty-three centuries earlier.

Epilogue

What finally happened to Jason and Medea and the wandering Argonauts? How did they come home to Greece, bringing with them the Fleece and the tale of their adventures? Here the original legend becomes very confused. There are as many versions of the return journey as there are poets who wrote about it.

Appollonius says that the Argonauts sailed back first to the Anatolian coast, where at the mouth of the River Halys they put ashore Dascylus, the son of the king of the Mariandyni, so that he could return to his home. Then, with a favourable wind behind *Argo*, they cut across the Black Sea to the mouth of the Danube and turned up into it, following the river until it brought them into the Adriatic by a tributary. Apollonius is confused in his geography, because such a tributary does not exist. Nevertheless, he says that the Argonauts emerged into the Adriatic. There they encountered Medea's brother, Prince Apsyrtus, and the Colchian fleet who were blockading the river mouth. Outnumbered, the Argonauts offered a truce. Apsyrtus was willing to let them go on their way on condition that Medea's fate was referred to the local king, who would decide whether she must return to Colchis, or go on to Iolcos with Jason. Jason agreed to this formula, but Medea was furious and upbraided him for his faint-heartedness. If he really loved her, he would show it by ridding her of Apsyrtus, and she persuaded him into setting a trap for Apsyrtus. She sent word to her brother that she had really been kidnapped by the Argonauts and been forced to go with Jason against her will. If Apsyrtus would come to a secret rendezvous on a deserted island, she would quietly slip away from *Argo* carrying with her the Fleece. Apsyrtus was betrayed. He came to the island alone and unarmed, and while Medea distracted his attention Jason, who had been waiting in hiding, crept up and killed the Colchian, whose blood stained his sister's clothes. This foul deed, the breaking of a truce and the murder of an unarmed man, was to bring down the retribution of the gods. Thenceforth the marriage between Medea and Jason was doomed.

A different version of the tale says that Medea lured her brother aboard *Argo* while still in the Black Sea, killed him and dismembered the body. Then, as *Argo* sailed on, she threw the pieces one by one into *Argo*'s wake, so that the pursuing Colchian ships were delayed as they paused to collect up the morsels and give their dead prince a proper burial on the shores of the Black Sea.

Yet a third version of the return route says that *Argo* continued up the Phasis until the galley reached the World River, which the Greeks at one time believed encircled the habitable world. Sailing south and west, the Argonauts came back into the Mediterranean by portaging *Argo* across the Libyan Desert. There died Mopsus, the seer, who was bitten by a poisonous snake. From the Libyan coast the surviving Argonauts sailed north past Crete where they were menaced by Talus, the great articulated giant of bronze, who patrolled the edge of the island and threw rocks at intruders. He prevented the Argonauts from landing, but Medea cast the evil eye on him and, while he was transfixed, he grazed the weak spot on his ankle so that the fluid ran out of his veins and the giant collapsed and expired. From there the Argonauts sailed home to Iolcos.

Yet other versions of the return route claim that *Argo* left the Black Sea by going northwards up the River Don, sailing around Europe, and came home either by way of the Pillars of Hercules; or down the Rhine and the Rhône; or even the River Po in northern Italy. Of course, all of these routes were fictions. Not one is feasible for a galley. They simply reflect the contemporary geographical notions of their authors who wished to show off their expertise and avoid the rather uninteresting fact that the Argonauts must have gone back the way they had come – across the Black Sea and back down through the Bosphorus, this time with the currents in their favour. No other route is possible.

One Roman author, Apollodorus, was sure that this was the correct route. He noted that in his day sailors were still making sacrifices at the headland on the Asian side of the Bosphorus at its northern end, which they called Jason's Point because it was here that Jason, as he safely left the Black Sea after his expedition, stopped and gave thanks to the gods. Another Bosphorus tradition says that when *Argo* passed southwards down the Bosphorus Princess Medea threw ashore the box containing her stock of magic drugs, which she had gathered in Colchis. Henceforth the place became renowned as a centre for medical cures.

When the Argonauts finally sailed back into the Bay of Iolcos, it was the moment to claim the throne for Jason, now that they had successfully completed the quest. King Pelias still ruled, though he was now an old man. As it was by no means sure that Pelias would honour his agreement, and Iolcos was too strong for the small force of Argonauts to capture by force, Medea, so the story goes, slipped into Iolcos in disguise. Going to the royal palace, she tricked the king's daughters into believing that she could teach them how they could restore King Pelias to his youth. She told them to kill their father and boil his body in a cauldron of a special brew she would prepare. Naturally the daughters of Pelias at first refused to believe Medea's claim, but she hoodwinked them with her witchcraft. Taking an old ram, she slit its throat and tossed it into the cauldron, from which by sleight of hand she then drew forth a young, living lamb. The credulous daughters of Pelias were duped. They went to the king's chamber, killed him as Medea had directed and threw his dismembered body into the cauldron. Even as they realized the enormity of their deed, the Argonauts marched into the city, and the people of Iolcos, without their king, surrendered and accepted Jason's claim to the throne.

That is the most gory version of the homecoming of the Argonauts. A less violent form of the tale says merely that Jason came back with his men, who had long since been given up for dead, and that Pelias peaceably handed over the throne of Iolcos to Jason, whose father and mother had died in his absence. For some unexplained reason, Jason decided not to keep the throne but relinquished it soon afterwards, handing it back to Pelias. Perhaps Jason found life in Iolcos a little dull after his foreign voyaging.

In any event, the romance with Medea cooled. Jason decided to take another wife, the daughter of the king of Corinth, and Medea is said to have exacted a terrible revenge. She sent a poisoned robe to the Corinthian princess as a wedding gift. When the girl put on the robe, it burst into flames and she burned to death in agony, even though she leaped down a well to try to extinguish the deadly flames. This ghastly tale, because it was immortalized by Euripides in his play *Medea*, is much better remembered in modern Greece than the more cheerful events of the quest itself. For that reason, unlike their Georgian counterparts, no Greek girl is likely to be called Medea. In far-off Colchis, by contrast, the daughter of King Aeetes is remembered as a young and beautiful girl who fell so madly in love with the handsome stranger that she abandoned her home and family and followed him to a foreign shore, only to live unhappily. Georgian girls, it follows, should think twice about leaving their land to go abroad with foreigners.

Jason and Medea were not the only ones to suffer a melancholy homecoming. Most Argonauts returned to their homes without incident, but a few met violent deaths. Hercules had never forgotten or forgiven Calais and Zetes for persuading the other Argonauts to sail on instead of putting back to try to find Hylas when he was lost to the water nymph. To avenge that deed, Hercules tracked down the Sons of the North Wind on their return to Greece and killed them on the island of Tenos when they were returning from the funeral games in honour of Pelias. Over their bodies he placed huge, finely balanced boulders which rocked whenever their father, the North Wind, blew across them.

Lynceus, the far-sighted, and Idas, the boaster, fell out with the twins, Castor and Pollux, their former shipmates. They quarrelled, either over two beautiful girls whom both pairs wanted to marry or, more likely, over division of the spoils from a joint plundering raid. Whatever the cause, the rivalry was deadly. The twins pursued Idas and Lynceus, and the latter, using his fabulous eyesight, was able to forestall an ambush, seeing the twins from afar as they lay hidden inside a hollow tree. In a bloody fight Idas speared Castor and killed him; then Pollux managed to revenge his twin brother by cutting down Lynceus, but he himself would have fallen to the mighty Idas if Zeus had not blasted Idas to death with a thunderbolt. This left only Pollux alive. He could not stand the thought of life without his twin, and he beseeched their father, Zeus, to let them exist together. His wish was granted when Castor and Pollux were set among the stars as the constellation identified as Gemini.

Jason himself fared little better. He had moved to Corinth, taking the immortal *Argo* with him. The great ship was dragged ashore, like most vessels approaching the end of their time, and left to decay. One day, feeling lonely and depressed, Jason went to sit in the shadow of *Argo*. The great timber of the prow, rotten with age, finally gave way. The beam fell and crushed him to death.

Nearly all the events which happened on the outward voyage, the time of exploration and hope, have remained positive and optimistic in the telling – the story of the women of Lemnos, the defeat of King Amycus the boxer, the succour given to blind Phineas, the gallant passage of the Clashing Rocks, the rescue of King Aeetes' grandsons from the island of Ares and the successful winning of the Golden Fleece itself. But when the later life of the Heroes became a favourite theme for Greek tragic poets and playwrights the legend lapsed into despondency and gloom, mirroring the events in Greece itself where the Mycenaean way of life was to suffer invasion, war and destruction.

Fortunately no such catastrophe accompanied the modern *Argo*'s return from Georgia. After we had finally succeeded in getting *Argo* upriver to Vani, she was moored beside the concert park so that the local people could have a close look at her. During the hectic adventures of the upriver journey a couple of serious accidents to crewmen had only narrowly been avoided, and I was genuinely fearful that someone would get badly hurt if we attempted the much more dangerous task of running *Argo* back down the flood-swollen Rhioni when the time came to return to the Black Sea. I voiced my fears to Nugzar, who said that he would see what could be done to get the boat down to the coast so that we could depart on our way back to the Bosphorus.

The problem was that transport by road was impracticable. Bridges across the roads were too low to let *Argo* pass underneath when loaded on a road transporter. No problem, Nugzar said with his usual briskness; how about lifting *Argo* out by helicopter? My jaw dropped. *Argo* was an 8-ton load, 54 feet long, and beyond the capacity of all but the largest helicopters. No matter – a team of helicopter pilots actually came to inspect *Argo* to see if they could help. Finally they agreed that a helicopter lift was too dangerous.

Then someone suggested loading *Argo* on a special train. Once again the Georgians were simply not going to be defeated. Engineers came and took measurements and railway officials were consulted. Peter Wheeler went off to a steel fabricating plant and with its chief engineer devised a cradle made of steel girders. *Argo* was a long, delicate load to lift by crane, and if wrongly handled she could snap in half. On the appointed day a mobile crane crawled cautiously over the soggy watermeadow. From its hook dangled the steel cradle. Slowly the cradle was lowered into the racing river, until it rested on the river bed with the tops of the steel uprights poking above the swirling water. All the Argonauts, Georgians and visitors, jockeyed *Argo* downstream with ropes and oars until she nuzzled between the uprights and was lashed in position.

Gently the crane driver wound in his cable, and *Argo* rose dripping from the Phasis. The crane lurched alarmingly as its wheels sank in the boggy ground, and the driver had to leapfrog *Argo* step by step across the meadow until he could place her upon the transporter lorry that would take her to the railhead. That night a special train carried *Argo* across Georgia, and by noon next day she was floating in Batumi harbour, ready to set out for home.

My plan had been to sail back to Turkey, and there hire a fishing boat to tow *Argo* the 800 miles back to Istanbul for winter lay-up. There was no point in rowing and sailing all the way home. The Argonauts were running out of time, people had to get back to their jobs and, frankly, most of them were physically exhausted by the labour of the outward journey. When I mentioned my plan to Yuri Senkevich he agreed.

'But before you decide,' he said, 'let me contact the Soviet Merchant Fleet and see if they can help. The Minister is very helpful. Maybe he can arrange some assistance.'

Two days later a telegram came back from Moscow. Our old friend *Tovarisch* was leaving on a training cruise in the Mediterranean. The Minister's office had arranged for her to be diverted to Batumi where she would take *Argo* in tow for the Bosphorus. The crew could hardly believe their ears: a three-master as our tug! It was a magnificent gesture, and beyond anything we had dreamed.

So from Batumi we travelled behind *Tovarisch* all the way to the Bosphorus, plucked along by the beautiful, square-rigged barquentine, with nothing to do but take turns to keep a towing watch aboard little *Argo*, bobbing along like a child's toy on a string. Finally the mouth of the Bosphorus came in sight. *Tovarisch* was travelling straight through without stopping, so we had already transferred all our kit aboard *Argo* and were just waiting to slip the tow. I thanked Captain Oleg Vandenko of *Tovarisch* and the little rubber dinghy carried me back to *Argo*. The sides of the

Bosphorus closed around us, and *Tovarisch* cut her speed to allow us to cast off the towline. As the Soviet sailing ship passed on down the Bosphorus, we waved our thanks and turned for the European shore.

Poor *Argo* was showing the scars of her travels. Both her steering oars had been snapped a second time, one during the adventures in the Rhioni, the other on the way across the Black Sea. A couple of her other oars were broken; her thole pins were wrecked; and her cotton sail was so rotten from mildew during the damp days in the eastern Black Sea as to be unusable in anything but a light breeze. Like her crew, she was distinctly bedraggled and weary. Rowing with makeshift thole pins, we sidled across the current towards the shore. I scanned the bank for somewhere to tie up, while I went in search of the Turkish customs and port officials to clear *Argo* inward-bound.

Only one person knew that we were returning: I had sent a telegram to Irgun, my loyal friend of twenty-three years standing, to say that we were on our way back. I heard the hooting of a car horn, and there, miraculously, was Irgun himself waving from the end of a jetty. A moment later he was helping us tie the mooring lines. 'Everything's arranged,' he said. 'I've got a friend in the customs office here, and he will do all your paperwork in a few minutes.' I was back with my Turkish family.

The Argonauts stayed four days in Istanbul, winding up the expedition. We unloaded the galley, packed our souvenirs of the extraordinary voyage, and prepared the boat ready for her winter lay-up. I wanted her to be well taken care of, because her voyaging was not yet done. Having unravelled the story of Jason and the Argonauts, I intended the following spring to set sail with *Argo* again, this time to try to trace the voyage of Ulysses as he came home from Troy, the voyage told by Homer in the *Odyssey*.

Dalan Bedrettin, the mayor of Istanbul, declared that *Argo* was to be the guest of the city. With unfailing Turkish hospitality he arranged for *Argo* to be brought ashore and kept for the winter on the banks of the Bosphorus in a boat park opposite Bebek, the same place where we had stood our greatest trial rowing up against the current of the straits. There I said goodbye to *Argo*, her nose peeping out from under her winter cover. One by one the Argonauts had already left or were on their way back to their homes and jobs. Peter Moran and John Egan were going to spend a few more weeks touring in Greece before returning separately to Ireland. Mark Richards and Tim Readman went off dragging a huge wooden chest of souvenirs to take the train by way of Bulgaria to England, where in a few weeks' time Tim was due to get married. The two doctors, Nick and Adam, were on their way back to find medical posts. Jonathan Cloke and Peter Warren had planes to catch. Cormac hoped to be back aboard his Irish trawler for the late summer fishery. The Argonauts were disbanding, but Peter Warren promised to organize a reunion in the New Year when we could get together and reminisce.

Finally, I too had to leave. I promised my Turkish family that I would return in the winter to check on *Argo*. Perhaps Kaan, their son, could help on part of the Ulysses Voyage? Of course, they said, and already Husnu, one of the Turks who had rowed along the Black Sea coast, was asking when I would be setting out again in *Argo*. He and several of the other Turkish Argonauts wanted to help us when *Argo* was relaunched for the Ulysses project.

Next year, I vowed to myself, I would try to bring *Argo* back to Spetses so that Vasilis, the shipwright, could see her. I packed up my belongings and got ready to leave. All my Turkish family were on hand to say goodbye. I was reminded of the day the Argonauts left Vani in Georgia. Then there had been tears in the eyes of the Georgian crew members. Perhaps next year some Georgians too could be involved with *Argo*. Certainly I would invite them. I climbed into the back seat of the car that was taking me to Istanbul airport. As the car began to move away from the kerb, there was a terrific splashing sound. Startled, I glanced back. There, standing in the street, was the maid who worked for the family. She had just thrown an entire pail of water into the road behind the car. It was an old Turkish custom, which meant that the departing guest would return. In my case I knew it to be true.

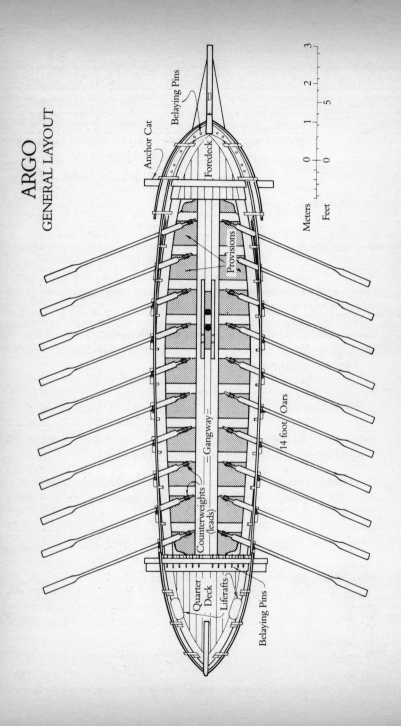

ARGO
GENERAL LAYOUT

Belaying Pins

Anchor Cat

Foredeck

Provisions

Gangway

14 foot Oars

Counterweights
(leads)

Quarter
Deck

Liferafts

Belaying Pins

Meters

Feet

0   1   2   3

0   5

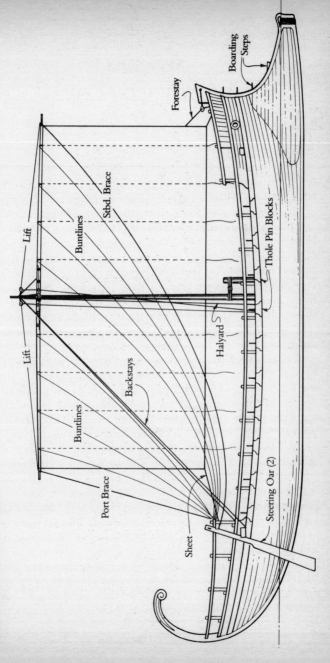

ARGO
SAIL & RIGGING PLAN

Lift

Lift

Buntlines

Buntlines

Stbd. Brace

Backstays

Port Brace

Sheet

Halyard

Steering Oar (2)

Forestay

Boarding Steps

Thole Pin Blocks

APPENDIX I
Ancestry of the Legend

In the *Odyssey*, Homer refers to 'celebrated *Argo*' which managed to evade the Wandering Rocks when 'homeward bound from Aeetes coast'. And in the *Iliad* he wrote of Euneos, Jason's son by Queen Hypsipyle on Lemnos. As Homer is our oldest surviving source of Greek mythology, this means that the ancestry of the Argonaut story is established as far back as records exist. Quite how far back that ancestry goes, we have no way of knowing, but it is evident from Homer's poetry that he expected his audience to be thoroughly familiar with at least the story of the Lemnian women, the visit to King Aeetes' country, and of course the existence of *Argo* herself.

Homer's near-contemporary, the Boeotian poet Hesiod who lived in the late 8th century BC, must have known the Argonaut story because in his writings he mentions Jason's visit to King Aeetes, his meeting with Princess Medea, and his return to Iolcos with 'the bright-eyed damsel whom he made his loving wife'. In a group of texts known as 'Hesiodic', once attributed to Hesiod himself but now believed to have been written by other authors, there are also references to Phrixus, to Jason's youth, and to the adventure with Phineas and the Harpies.

In the following century, the 7th BC, Minnermus, another Greek poet specifically mentions the Golden Fleece as the object of Jason's voyage, and a Corinthian poet, Eumelos, claims that Jason went to live in Corinth, not Iolcos, after his return from Colchis. As more and more fragments of early Greek writing survive, so the extra details emerge, although not all of them are consistent with one another: Simonides in the 6th century BC confirms the passage of the Clashing Rocks but says that the Fleece was not gold but dyed with sea-purple. In the 5th century BC there was a great flowering of

240

the legend when Jason's story became a favourite theme for poets and dramatists. Aeschylus wrote no less than six plays based on various Argonaut themes, and although most of the plays themselves have been lost, we know that there were a *Phineas*, a *Lemnian Women*, a *Hypsipyle*, and a *Kabeirii*. Sophocles wrote plays on Phrixus' father *Athamas*, on *Phrixus*, the *Colchidians, Phineas*, the fight with King Amycus, and three plays which touched on events during the return voyage of *Argo*. In total, no less than eight tragic poets tackled various Argonautic themes, but the one to survive and most influence modern perception was Euripides' *Medea*. As it was virtually impossible for any early historian or geographer to treat of the Black Sea without some reference to *Argo*, their writings are sprinkled with mentions of peoples and places visited by the Argonauts. The most famous of the early historians, Herodotus, put forward the interesting notion that *Argo* was blown down to the North African coast on the outward leg of her epic journey.

Thus, by the time Apollonius of Rhodes came to compose his epic, the main events of the Argonaut saga were well set. We do not know what sources Apollonius used for his major version of the tale, but his version of the attack on the Argonauts by the monsters of Bear Mountain is very similar to a passage in Homer's Odyssey when Ulysses' squadron is attacked by the Laestrygonians. It is possible that Apollonius also had other – now lost – Homeric material available to him because the geographer Strabo says that Homer wrote about 'the places round Propontis and the Euxine as far as Colchis, the bourne of Jason's expedition'.

The fascination of the legend continued after Apollonius' work. In 40 BC Diodorus Siculus composed a lengthy prose version which is chiefly remarkable for its unwaveringly prosaic approach to the events of the saga. Thus, he believed that the flying ram was the ram figurehead of a warship which carried away Phrixus and Helle, and that the princess fell overboard and drowned in the Dardanelles Strait while being seasick. In the first and second centuries AD there were further versions of the legend by Apollodurus and Valerius Flaccus, and then in the 3rd/4th centuries an Orphic *Argonautica* appeared which gave a major role in the adventures to the musician Orpheus.

From a very early stage, people were intrigued as to whether or not the story was true. Strabo was convinced it was. The saga of the Argonauts, he firmly stated, showed that 'the ancients made longer journeys, both by land and by sea, than have men of later time'. It was Strabo who identified the possibility that the Colchian technique of gold-gathering, using sheepskins, could have some connection with the legend of the Golden Fleece. But the more commentators thought about the tale, the wilder and more far-fetched became their interpretations of the events. The Golden Fleece became a parchment illuminated with golden writing, or even a document which contained the alchemists' secret of how to turn dross into gold. By the nineteenth century folklorists were putting forward theories that the fleece was a symbol of the sun, or it was a raincloud, depending on your choice. If it was a sun symbol, then the sunlight came from King Aeetes who was a child of the sun according to mythology, the ram was the setting sun returning to the east, and Medea was the red glow of dawn and dusk. For those who favoured the raincloud interpretation, the fleece was the purple of a thundercloud, and in Greece the clouds could be seen heading east in summer towards Colchis, and returning in spring and autumn, bearing rain. According to this idea, it was significant that many of the Argonauts were descended from watery spirits such as water nymphs, river gods, and Poseidon himself. Other ideas put forward to explain the Golden Fleece were that it symbolized the ripened corn of the Black Sea coastlands rippling in the wind or that it was a rough sea gilded by sunlight.

It was left to a Cambridge don, Janet Brown, to impose some discipline on all these ideas in her study *The Voyage of the Argonauts* (Methuen, 1925) which remains a standard work. After reviewing the evidence Janet Brown reached the conclusion that 'long before Homer voyages were made to Colchis for gold; a voyage was made by Jason. Jason was a Minyan of Thessaly; by Minyan race he was connected to Phrixus who had been saved by a golden ram and fled eastward'. Jason's voyage, she felt, was 'a real quest for real gold'.

Apollonius' text has been translated in the Loeb Classical Library Series by R.C. Seaton (Heinemann, 1912) and is also available from Oxford Classical Texts (1961). But for ease of access *The Voyage of Argo* (first published in 1959 by Penguin Classics and frequently reissued) cannot be equalled. It was translated by E.V. Rieu in his usual fluent style, and has been used for quotations in this book. Finally, between 1976 and 1981, has appeared the best critical and annotated edition to date: *Argonautiques* – Apollonius de Rhodes,

Vols. I–III, edited by Francis Vian and translated by Emile Delage. This excellent edition is in the Guillaume Bude series, Paris, Societé d'Edition 'Les Belles Lettres', and is the most comprehensive version for text and commentary.

APPENDIX II
Summary of the Text of Apollonius Rhodius

Book I

Crossing the winter-swollen Anaurus on his way to a banquet given by King Pelias, Jason lost a sandal. As soon as King Pelias saw Jason, with one foot bare, he remembered the oracle and decided to send Jason on a mission so dangerous that he hoped the young man would never return.

The ship was built by Argus, supervised by the goddess Athena, but as the tale has been told by other poets, Apollonius will content himself with providing the crew list, as follows:

Orpheus, the musician;
Asterion of Peiresiae;
Polyphemus, an old man but still valiant, from Larissa;
Iphiclus of Phylace, Jason's maternal uncle;
Admetus, King of Pherae;
Erytus of Alope, guileful son of Apollo;
Echion of Alope, his brother;
Aethalides, their kinsman and the expedition's herald;
Coronus of Gyrton, son of Caenus the unconquerable;
Mopsus, who could understand the language of birds;
Eurydamas of Ctimene;
Eurytion, son of Teleon;
Eribotes, son of Irus;
Oileus, the headlong warrior;
Canthus of Euboea;
Clytius, son of Eurthus;
Iphitus, his brother;
Telamon of Salamis;

Peleus of Phthia;
Butes, son of Teleon;
Phalerus 'of the ashen spear', only son of Alcon;
Tiphys of Siphae, an expert mariner;
Phlias of Araethyrea;
Talaus, son of Bias;
Areius, his brother;
Leodocus, his brother;
Hercules, the strongest man who ever lived;
Hylas, squire to Hercules;
Nauplius, son of Clytoneus;
Idmon the soothsayer;
Castor of Sparta, master of horse racing;
Pollux of Sparta, his twin and champion boxer;
Lynceus the sharp-eyed, son of Aphareus;
Idas, the boaster, his brother;
Periclymenus, the many-formed, son of Neleus of Pylos;
Amphidamas, son of Aleus;
Cepheus, his brother;
Ancaeus the strong, son of Lycurgus;
Augeias the wealthy Elean;
Asterius, son of Hyperasius;
Amphion, his brother;
Euphemus of Taenarum, fastest runner in the world;
Erginus of Miletus;
Ancaeus of Samos;
Meleager of Calydon;
Laocoon, his half-uncle;
Iphiclus, a good javelin fighter, uncle to Meleager;
Palaemonius the lame, alleged son of Lernus;
Iphitus, son of Naubolus;
Zetes, winged son of Boreas;
Calais, winged son of Boreas;
Acastus, son of King Pelias of Iolcos;
Argus the master shipwright;
Jason, son of Aeson, rightful heir to Iolcos.

Argo was ready and well found, and her crew made their way to where she lay waiting on the beach at Magnesian Pagasae. At their departure the townsfolk of Iolcos marvelled at such a splendid band of men, and the women prayed for their safe return. In Jason's home, where his father lay bed-ridden, his mother made a long and tearful farewell. Jason calmed her fears and then he too set out to join his companions, waiting on the beach. To their surprise, at the last moment two more volunteers were seen hurrying down from Iolcos – Acastus, son of King Pelias, and Argus the boat builder. Both men were defying King Pelias' express orders not to sail with the expedition.

Now Jason asked the assembled company to elect their leader for the venture. All eyes turned at once towards the incomparable Hercules, but immediately he declined the idea. The man who had brought them together, he said, should lead them. His suggestion was carried with acclaim.

Jason's first command was that the Argonauts should offer a sacrifice to Phoebus, and he sent to his home for oxen to sacrifice. While they were waiting for the cattle to appear, it was time to launch *Argo*.

Stripping for action, the men bound a stout rope around *Argo* to strengthen her, dug a channel down the beach, and laid smooth rollers in it. They tipped *Argo* onto the first roller and then swung the oars inboard and fastened them so their handles projected. Each man took his place, ready to shove, and at a shout from Tiphys the helmsman, the young men pushed *Argo* down into the sea, and checked her with hawsers. Next they fitted the oars to the thole pins, put mast and stores aboard, and made sure that everything was shipshape. Then they cast lots for their positions on the oar benches, by common agreement leaving the centre bench for the two strongest men – Hercules and Ancaeus. They heaped up shingle on the beach to make an altar for Apollo, and when Jason's herdsmen arrived with two oxen, the animals were correctly sacrificed to the God of Departures, with an appeal for a fair passage. Idmon the seer interpreted the flames and smoke, and announced that their mission would be successful. The expedition would undergo many trials, but they would bring back the Fleece. He himself, however, was doomed to die in some remote spot in Asia.

The young men spent the evening camped on the beach, eating, drinking wine and telling stories among themselves. But Jason, assailed by last minute doubts, sat apart from the rest and was chided by Idas. Drunkenly Idas boasted that, because he was a member, the expedition was bound to succeed. He was so skilled with his spear, that he was even ready to challenge the gods. Idas' profanity shocked the others, and he was called to task by Idmon who warned him not to blaspheme. Idas made an angry retort, and there would have been blows if Orpheus had not sprung to his feet, plucked his lyre and begun a soothing song describing the creation of the world. By the time his song was finished, the quarrel was forgotten and the men lay down on the beach to sleep.

At dawn Tiphys the helmsman awoke, and roused the crew to action. Out on the water *Argo*'s speaking beam, cut from the sacred trees of Dodona, cried out, eager to be started on the voyage. The Argonauts went aboard, libations were poured on the sea, and the hawsers hauled in. To the sound of Orpheus' music, the men rowed out, a splendid sight, while the gods looked down in approval, and Cheiron the Centaur came down from the slopes of Mount Pelion to wade out into the surf and wave farewell. As soon as they had left harbour, the Argonauts stepped the mast, tightened the stays, hauled up the sail, and unfurled it. Then, with a favourable breeze behind them, the Argonauts took their ease on the galley's benches as *Argo* ran along the coast, and Orpheus played his music so sweetly that the fishes gambolled in the vessel's wake.

Past Cape Sepcias and Skiathos, *Argo* sailed along the Magnesian coast under a clear sky, until the wind veered against them and they put in to the beach at Aphetae. Here for three days the Argonauts lingered, and on the third day set out again, sailing past Mounts Ossa and Olympus, crossing to Cape Canastra, and by dawn next day were in sight of Mount Athos. As the wind was holding fair, Tiphys decided to press on, and for another twenty-four hours *Argo* ran before a stiff breeze so that by daybreak, when a calm fell, they were able to row the remaining distance to the island of Lemnos.

On Lemnos in the previous year the women had slaughtered all the male inhabitants. Their husbands had spurned them in favour of captured girls taken in raids on the Thracian coast, and the vengeful women of Lemnos had murdered not only their husbands and their Thracian concubines, but every male on the island. The only man to escape was the aged Thoas, father of Hypsipyle. She had set him adrift in a wooden chest, hoping he would be saved. Some fishermen dragged him ashore on the island called Oenoe.

The Lemnian women found that they preferred cattle-herding, ploughing, and wearing armour to the more traditional female tasks, but they lived in constant fear of a raid from the Thracians. So when they saw *Argo* rowing in, they immediately put on their war gear and ran down to the beach.

The Argonauts sent ashore smooth-tongued Aethalidas the herald, who successfully persuaded the Lemnian women at least to allow the travellers to stay the night. Next day, however *Argo* did not cast off and put to sea.

Summoned by Hypsipyle, the Lemnian women held a meeting in the town. Hypsipyle counselled them to treat the Argonauts generously. If they sent wine and food to the ship, then the strangers would have no reason to come into the town. For if they did, they might learn the awful secret of the massacre of the males. Polyxo, Hypsipyle's old nurse, was the next to speak. It was right to welcome the Argonauts, she said. How would the Lemnians survive in the future without men? Who would defend them against foreign attack? And when the present generation grew old, how would there be children to follow them? The solution was to invite the Argonauts ashore and offer them everything – their homes, livestock, and the city itself.

Polyxo's audience was convinced. Hypsipyle sent a messenger to invite the leader of the Argonauts to come to her house, and to inform the other Argonauts that they might come ashore:

Jason, dressed in his finest clothes, made a deep impression on the spectators as he walked from the harbour to Hypsipyle's palace. There she persuaded him that the Lemnian men had only been banished – not killed – for their infidelity, and she demurely offered him the throne of Lemnos. Jason declined the throne, but he and his companions gladly moved into the city, where they were lavishly entertained. Only Hercules and a few picked companions stayed with *Argo*. Day followed day, spent in feasting and merry-making, and still *Argo* did not move. Finally Hercules called a meeting, from which all the women were barred, and rebuked his colleagues. They had forgotten the purpose of their mission, he told them. They would not win the Fleece by enjoying themselves on Lemnos. Rather, they would become the laughing stock of all Greece.

The Argonauts were repentant. They began to get ready to leave, and the women of Lemnos, guessing their intentions, came to say their farewells. Hypsipyle promised Jason that the throne of Lemnos would still be available to him on his return, if he wished; and for his part Jason asked that if Hypsipyle bore his son, then the boy should be sent to his grandparents in Iolcos.

Then *Argo* set out again, going first to Samothrace, where Orpheus instructed them in the secret rites, and afterwards rowing to the mouth of the Hellespont. There they picked up a following wind and under sail negotiated the strait in a single night, arriving at the peninsula of Bear Mountain where they landed at a harbour called Fair Haven. Here, on Tiphys' advice, they left their small anchor stone at the spring called Artacie, and replaced it with a heavier rock.

The Doliones who inhabited the peninsula, greeted the Argonauts kindly, and their king Cyzicus, a man of Jason's age, invited the travellers to join in the feasting to celebrate his recent marriage to Cleite, a princess from the mainland. The Argonauts moved their galley to the town harbour of the Doliones, and a party of them climbed to the top of Mount Dindymun, hoping to see the way they would have to travel. The route they took became known as Jason's Path.

While they were away, a group of savage, six-armed monsters from the mountain suddenly attacked *Argo*, trying to trap her by blocking the harbour mouth with boulders. But Hercules led the boat guard, and fought them off, killing many of them until the other Argonauts arrived, and the monsters were routed with heavy losses.

Putting out to sea, the Argonauts sailed on all day until the wind failed. Then it veered against them and rose to gale force, sending them running for shelter back to the land of the Doliones. At the place where they came ashore, the rock where they hastily cast their hawsers became known as the Sacred Rock.

The Argonauts did not know where they were, and in the darkness the Doliones mistook them for a raiding party, and attacked. There was a bloody fight, and in the struggle Jason killed Cyzicus, while Heracles, Acastus, Peleus, Telamon, Idas, Clytius, Castor and Pollux, and Meleager each killed at least one Doliones warrior. The rest fled back into their city and barred the gates.

Dawn revealed the tragic error, and the Argonauts were stricken with remorse. For three days they and the Doliones grieved for Cyzicus. They held funeral games, marched three times around the corpse in their bronze armour, and then buried him in a barrow – which still stands. The new bride, Cleite, unable to cope with her grief, hanged herself, and the tears which the woodland nymphs shed at her death, caused a spring to arise, called Cleite's Spring by the people of the area, who in their mourning ate only uncooked food and did not grind corn at home, a custom still observed annually in later times.

For the next twelve days the Argonauts were pinned down on the coast of the peninsula by foul weather. Then just before dawn a kingfisher appeared and fluttered over Jason's head as he lay asleep. Mopsus the seer understood the omen, and when the bird flew off and perched on *Argo*'s mascot, he awoke Jason, telling him that he must propitiate Rhea the Mother Goddess who controlled the winds. If he did so, the gales would cease.

After moving *Argo* to a safer anchorage, Jason and his companions climbed Mount Dindymun, from where they could see back to the Hellespont, across to Thrace, and onward to the Bosphorus. There they cut down an ancient vine, and Argus the shipwright skilfully shaped it into an image of the goddess which they set on a rocky eminence and built an altar nearby. Then they crowned themselves with oak leaves, and in full armour performed a high-stepping dance, beating their shields with their swords to drown out the wailing rising from the city of the Doliones. In response the goddess made the trees bring forth abundant fruit, the grass sprouted, and wild animals came out of their lairs wagging their tails. And a spring gushed forth on the mountain where there had never been a water source before. To this day the inhabitants call it Jason's Spring.

By dawn the wind had eased, and in a flat calm they moved on, competing with one another as oarsmen. By afternoon when the offshore wind began to ruffle the sea, only Hercules was left still able to row on with mightly strokes, until at last when *Argo* was in sight of the river Rhyndacus, the oar snapped in his hands, and he was left glaring in helpless fury.

They made landfall that evening on the Cianian coast, and were welcomed by the Mysians. While the rest of the Argonauts set up camp on the beach, Hercules searched the woods for a suitable pine tree to make a new oar. Finding the right tree, he loosened the roots with several blows from his club, then tore it up with his bare hands. Meanwhile his squire Hylas had set out by himself to fetch water. He came to a spring called Pegae, and the water naiad who lived there, seeing Hylas in all his beauty, was filled with desire for him. As Hylas leaned over to fill his bronze ewer with water, the naiad reached up to kiss him. Placing one arm around his neck, with the other she drew him down into the depths.

The Argonaut Polyphemus, going to meet Hercules, was the only one to hear the lad's last cry. Thinking him attacked by wild beasts or brigands, Polyphemus ran towards the sound but could find no one. Drawing his sword, he was searching the woods and calling out Hylas' name when he met Hercules returning with his tree. At once Polyphemus told him of the missing squire, and Hercules, mad with worry, rushed off in search of Hylas. With the morning star a favourable wind arose, and on the beach Tiphys urged the crew to embark without delay. They went aboard at once and put out to sea, and were soon sailing fast before a following breeze. At daybreak they realized that Hylas, Hercules and Polyphemus were missing, and a fierce argument erupted whether or not to turn back. Jason himself was sunk in indecisive gloom, and Telamon accused him of deliberately marooning Hercules, and would have forced Tiphys to turn the boat around, but Zetes and Calais stopped him. Just then the sea god Glaucus arose from the sea and told the Argonauts to sail on. Zeus, he said, had ordained that Hercules should finish his labours, not to go to Colchis, while Polyphemus would settle in Cius, and Hylas was now the husband of the naiad. Telamon apologized to Jason for his outburst, and his apology was accepted with good grace. On shore Hercules obliged the people of Cius to continue the search for Hylas while he went off to continue his labours, and Polyphemus stayed on to found a city.

All that day and the next *Argo* sailed on, until land appeared ahead, and they ran the galley ashore on a wide beach.

Book II

They had landed in the territory of Amycus the arrogant king of the Bebryces, the world's greatest bully. His barbarous habit was to allow no one to leave his kingdom unless they first fought a boxing match against him. Already he had killed several of his neighbours. Coming down to the ship, he issued his usual challenge so rudely that Pollux took it as a personal affront, and immediately accepted the fight. The two men removed their cloaks and prepared to box. Physically they were complete opposites: Amycus like an ogre, Pollux slim and lithe. They donned gloves of hardened rawhide, and immediately set to. Amycus adopted his customary style of rushing at his opponent, attempting to overwhelm him by massive blows, and at first Pollux used his superior technique and ability to avoid the charges, but once he had the measure of his man he stood up to the attack, and the two men traded blow for blow until they drew apart to catch breath. They went at it again, until Amycus tried to batter his opponent with a great downward swing. Pollux turned the blow on his shoulder, and stuck Amycus a deadly blow behind the ear, smashing the bones so that the Bebrycian king collapsed and died.

At this, the watching Bebryces launched an attack on the Argonauts but were beaten off and fled, leaving several dead.

The Argonauts staunched their own wounds and celebrated their victory, and the next morning proceeded up the Bosphorus. Tiphys' skill at the helm saved them from being swamped by a huge wave, and they came ashore at the home of aged Phineas the blind seer. He had been punished with blindness by Zeus because Phineas had been too accurate and comprehensive in his prophecies. As an additional burden Zeus had sent the Harpies to torment him. At every meal the Harpies would sweep down and snatch food from Phineas' table, leaving such a stench as to befoul any food they did not carry away. Phineas knew at once who the Argonauts were, for Zeus had told him that he would be delivered from the Harpies by a band of men seeking the Golden Fleece. Tottering with age, Phineas went to greet the travellers, and inquired if Zetes and Calais were among them, because these two sons of the North Wind were the only men capable of ridding him of the dreadful Harpies. Zetes and Calais took up guard by Phineas as his table was spread for the welcoming banquet. Sure enough, the Harpies immediately swooped in and snatched away the food, leaving an appalling smell. But as the Harpies flew away, Calais and Zetes – using their own power of flight – chased after them with drawn swords. They were overhauling their prey and had even touched them with their fingertips when Iris, messenger of the Gods, intervened. Hastening down from Olympus, she intercepted Calais and Zetes as they flew over the Floating Islands and told them not to harm the Harpies, as they were the hounds of Zeus. She promised that the Harpies would never again torment Phineas. So Calais and Zetes turned back, and from that day the Floating Islands, where they abandoned the chase, were known as the Islands of Return.

Meanwhile Phineas had been entertaining the other Argonauts at his banquet, and explaining the way they now had to go. Their greatest danger was the Clashing Rocks which they would encounter as soon as they set out again on their travels. No ship had ever succeeded in passing between the Rocks which constantly collided together smashing any ship caught between them. But, said Phineas, if the Argonauts were prudent, they would release a dove as they approached the Rocks, and if it flew safely between them, they should take this as a sign and follow the dove's example. Should they succeed in passing the Clashing Rocks, the Argonauts were to turn east and follow the coast for as far as it would lead them. Phineas listed the tribes and places they would pass until finally they reached the mouth of the river Phasis in Colchis. But what would happen there, Phineas refused to say. That, he said, would be to prophesy too much.

For some days the Argonauts were delayed at Phineas' home by adverse winds, but finally they were able to row out, taking with them a dove. Soon they found themselves entering the narrowest part of the straits and heard the clash of the moving Rocks and the thunder of the surf. Rowing on, they rounded a corner and saw the Rocks were beginning to move apart. Euphemus released the dove and it flew at the gap. The Rocks snapped shut with a great crash which sent a massive wave that spun *Argo* right round, but the dove had slipped through between the Rocks, unharmed except for the tips of her tail feathers which were nipped off by the Rocks. Tiphys shouted at the oarsmen to row for the gap as the Rocks drew apart again, and the rowers made a terrific spurt. But even as they entered the gap, they were menaced by a great wave which overhung them. Tiphys' helmsmanship saved them again, and Euphemus ran up and down the galley calling on his companions to row with all their might. But the backwash from a second powerful wave gripped *Argo* and held her back just at the fatal point where the Rocks were due to meet, and it seemed that they were doomed. Just then Athena, who had been watching the terrible ordeal, intervened. With her left hand she held back a Rock, and with her right she thrust *Argo* through the gap like an arrow. The boat sped through, and only the tip of her stern ornament was clipped off by the Clashing Rocks, which from that day forth remained rooted firmly to the ground, as had been foretold would happen when the first ship passed between them successfully.

Now the Argonauts turned eastward, passing the river Rhebus and the Black Cape, and the mouth of the river Phyllis where

Phrixus and the flying ram had halted on their way to Colchis. Sometimes they sailed, often they had to row, labouring like oxen at the plough. At the island of Thynias, they had a vision of Apollo flying through the sky, and so there they built an altar in the God's honour and sacrificed upon it. On the third day a fresh wind brought them to the Acherusian Cape, behind which lies the glen which contains the mouth of Hades. Here an icy breath emerges at dawn and covers everything with rime, and the constant rustling of the leaves of the trees mingles with the rumble of the sea. In this place they were greeted by Lycus, chief of the Mariandyni tribe, and royally entertained. The Mariandyni were enemies of Bebryces, and so paid particular honour to Pollux and his twin for the defeat of the brutal boxer-king Amycus. Lycus promised to erect a monument to them, overlooking the sea where it would be seen by passing sailors.

At dawn, returning from Lycus' feast, the crew were crossing the marshes to reach their ship when a wild boar charged out from the reed beds and gored Idmon savagely. Idmon fell, mortally wounded, and his companions carried him back to *Argo*, where he died, thus fulfilling his own prophesy that he would never return from the expedition. Idmon was buried on a barrow close to the Acherusian height, and soon afterwards Tiphys too died after a short illness, and was buried in a second barrow beside his shipmate. The double loss plunged the Argonauts into deep gloom, and they seemed paralysed by their grief until, at last, Ancaeus chided them into action. Unless the expedition moved on, he said, they would never see their homes again. Electing Ancaeus as their helmsman to replace Tiphys, the Argonauts waited for a favourable breeze, and on the twelfth day took up their voyage once more.

Pausing to pay homage at the tomb of Sthenelus, son of Actor, they sped along the coast under sail guided by Dascylus, son of Lycus. At Sinop they picked up three more recruits – Deileon, Autolycus and Phlogius, stragglers from Hercules' expedition against the Amazons – and at the mouth of the Thermodon went ashore hoping to do battle with the warlike Amazons. But another favourable northwest wind encouraged them to push on, and by the next day they were passing the iron-bearing lands of the Chalybes who never till the soil or pasture flocks but spend their time in endless toil to extract the metal they sell for their living. In turn the Argonauts passed by the lands of the Tibareni, then the mountains of the Mosynechi who live in wooden houses and do openly what other peoples do in private, even coupling together in public. Farther on, they came to Ares island, and as they rowed towards it, saw approaching one of the ferocious birds which infested the place. The bird darted a sharp feather at Oileus, which wounded him in the left shoulder. Eribotes pulled out the feather and bound up the wound, and when another bird was seen flying to the attack, Clytius shot it down with a well-aimed arrow. At Amphidamas' suggestion, the crew put on full armour, and while half of them rowed, the others stood ready to protect the oarsmen with their shields. When *Argo* reached the island, the Argonauts raised such a din by banging on their shields, that all the birds fled in panic, discharging a shower of feathers which rattled off the roof of shields.

On the island of Ares the travellers found four castaways – the sons of Phrixus. These young men had been bound from Colchis, heading for their father's homeland to claim their inheritance – when their Colchian ship foundered in a northerly gale. Clinging to the wreckage they had been washed ashore on Ares Island, and now they approached the Argonauts for succour. When Jason found he was related to the castaways, they resolved to join forces. They went to sacrifice at the temple of Ares where an altar of small stones stood outside a roofless temple. Inside was a black rock fixed to the ground, which was held sacred by the Amazons who came to sacrifice horses there. Jason revealed the purpose of his mission to the four Colchian princes, and they promised they would help the Argonauts reach Colchis and there intercede with their grandfather King Aeetes on Jason's behalf. But even with such help, the princes warned, Jason's quest was perilous. Aeetes was a powerful king, his tribesman were very numerous, and there was no chance of taking the Fleece by force. Moreover it was constantly guarded by a huge serpent which never slept.

Pushing on with a fair breeze, *Argo* next passed the island of Philyra, the lands of the Macrones, Sapeires and Byzeres, and finally came in sight of the Caucasus mountains where Prometheus lay bound while the eagle fed on his liver. At nightfall they reached the mouth of the Phasis river and piloted by Argus, Phrixus' son, turned into the estuary. Lowering the yard and sail, they took down *Argo*'s mast and stowed them all, and then rowed up-river. There Jason poured a thanksgiving libation of sweet wine and, advised by

Argus, ordered his men to row *Argo* into the reedbeds and conceal her for the night.

Book III

The goddesses Hera and Athena, observing that *Argo* had reached her destination, now took counsel together as to how to help Jason obtain the Golden Fleece. They decided to ask Aphrodite for assistance. If Aphrodite could arrange for Medea, Aeetes' daughter, to fall in love with Jason, then a way could be found to obtain the Fleece. Aphrodite agreed to ask Eros, her son, to shoot Medea with an arrow of love, and as Eros was notoriously capricious, bribed him with the promise of a present – a splendid ball made of interlocking hoops of gold – if he would fulfill the mission at once. Eros agreed, and flew off to set his ambush.

Meanwhile the Argonauts, too, had been holding council. They decided that Jason, together with Telamon, Augeias and Phrixus' four sons should go openly to Aeetes' palace and explain their mission. The small group set off through the thickets of willow and osiers near the river where the Colchians hung the corpses of their dead and, shrouded by a convenient mist, reached the gates of Aeetes' palace unobserved. The main courtyard of the palace had soaring columns and was decorated with marble, and there were four fountains wrought by Hephaestus which gushed out wine, milk, oil and water, the latter changed from hot to cold with the alternation of the seasons. For Aeetes, too, Hephaestus had forged a plough of hardened steel and had made bulls with bronze feet and bronze mouths from which spouted blazing fire.

The inner courtyard of the palace was surrounded by rooms and galleries, and the apartments reserved for the queen, for Prince Apsyrtus the son and heir to the throne, and for Aeetes' two daughters – Chalciope and Medea. The latter saw the entry of the travellers and her cry alerted Chalciope who came hurrying out to upbraid her four sons for leaving her in order to go off to seek their father's homeland. By now Eros had flitted in, and was waiting with an arrow notched to his bow. When Medea first laid eyes on Jason, Eros fired the arrow and it struck the mark. Medea was transfixed with love for Jason.

After the visitors had bathed, King Aeetes' servants prepared a banquet for them, and once they had eaten, the king asked his grandsons to explain what had happened. Argus, the eldest, told of their shipwreck and rescue by the Argonauts, and explained how Jason had come to seek the Fleece on the orders of a cruel king. But Aeetes refused to believe the tale. In a rage he accused his grandsons of bringing men to Colchis whose real intention was to seize the throne. But for the laws of hospitality he would have chopped off the hands and torn out the tongues of the impudent visitors. As it was, he commanded them to leave Colchis at once.

Jason replied soothingly that he and his men would earn the Fleece by fighting alongside the Colchian army against the King's enemies. But his offer had little effect. Aeetes, after considering, proposed that Jason could have the Fleece only if he passed a mortal test: he would have to yoke two fire-breathing bulls which grazed on the plain of Ares on the river bank and with them plough a four-acre field. In the furrows he was to sow dragons' teeth from which would spring a host of armed men, all of whom he would have to cut down by nightfall. Only then could he have the Fleece.

Despite this terrible condition, Jason accepted the terms and went back with his companions to *Argo* to inform his crew. There Argus counselled them to enlist the aid of Medea, for she was adept in the magic arts, and her skill might yet save them. This was agreed, and Argus returned to the palace to speak with Chalciope his mother. She, fearing that Aeetes' wrath would now be turned against her sons, also begged Medea for her help. But already Medea was so smitten with love for Jason that she knew she would have to assist him even though it would mean betraying her own father.

After passing a sleepless night Medea, accompanied by her handmaidens, went at dawn to the shrine of Hecate the goddess she served. Alerted by Argus, Jason too set out from *Argo* for the temple precinct, and they met as if by chance. Medea's handmaidens withdrew to leave them alone together, and Jason humbly asked Medea for her help. When he finished, Medea handed him an ointment that she had prepared. Jason, Medea instructed, was to sacrifice to Hecate at midnight, then in the morning smear his body with the salve, and for one day it would render him invulnerable. When he had ploughed the field and the crop of armed men sprang up, he was to throw a boulder among them so that in confusion they fought among themselves. Then he could finish off the survivors. As Jason's and Medea's eyes met, it was Jason who knew he was falling in love. If he survived the ordeal, Jason said, he wanted Medea to return to Greece with him and be his Queen.

The two parted, and that night Jason followed Medea's instructions. He made his sacrifice to Hecate, and in the morning anointed himself with the magic ointment, also sprinkling a few drops on his shield and spear. When his companions tested the effect, they found that even the hardest blow could not damage his equipment. Next the crew rowed *Argo* up river to the plain of Ares where Aeetes and his warriors were waiting to witness the ordeal. Jason leapt ashore, carrying the serpent's teeth he was to plant, and the two fire-breathing bulls rushed out to the attack. Impervious to their fiery breath, Jason seized and yoked them, and with the steel plough drove them to plough the field until by late afternoon all the four acres were planted with the dragon's teeth. Up sprang the crop of earth-born warriors and, as Meda had predicted, a boulder Jason threw among them caused such confusion that they fought among themselves until Jason could hack down the remainder. By nightfall the ordeal was done, and the Argonauts returned to their vessel, while Aeetes withdrew to his city, pondering how he could get rid of the intruders.

Book IV

That night, as Aeetes plotted the destruction of the Argonauts, Medea slipped out of the palace and hurried down to the riverbank where *Argo* lay moored. She urged the crew to row to the sacred grove where hung the Fleece. There, going ashore with Jason, she led him to the sacred spot. The huge serpent heard them coming, and hissed in alarm. But Medea soothed the snake with a gentle song, and as its coils relaxed, sprinkled its eyes with a magic drug so the reptile slept. Jason snatched the Fleece from the oak, and the two lovers fled back down the path to the waiting galley, Jason carrying the shimmering fleece. As soon as they stepped aboard, *Argo* dropped down river in a race to clear the Phasis before Colchians barred their passage.

They were just in time. King Aeetes in his war chariot was already leading a host of Colchian warriors to the river bank, and they arrived only to see *Argo* standing out to sea. In fury Aeetes threatened his people with dire punishment if Medea and the Fleece were not brought back. The very same day the Colchian fleet was equipped and sailed in pursuit of *Argo*.

Hera sent a favourable breeze for the Argonauts, and in just three days she was once again on the Paphlagonian coast where Dascylus, Lycus' son, was set ashore to rejoin his people. At a council the crew of *Argo* decided that their best chance to escape the Colchian pursuit was to return home, not past the Clashing Rocks, but up the Danube and thence down its tributary into the Adriatic Sea. So *Argo* crossed the Euxine to the delta of the Danube and turned into its northern arm. But Prince Apsyrtus, leading the chase, had split his forces, and while one Colchian squadron went by way of the Clashing Rocks, the other had also headed for the Danube. This squadron took the shorter southern arm of the delta, and so emerged into the Adriatic ahead of *Argo*. There they trapped the Argonauts, and in face of overwhelming odds Jason prepared to parlay. But Medea, hearing that his fate was to be decided by the judgement of a local king, upbraided Jason for his faint-heartedness. She proposed a treacherous ambush for her brother Apsyrtus, and pretending to him that she had been taken away on *Argo* against her will, lured him, alone and unarmed, to a secret meeting. There Jason murdered the Colchian prince, a deed so foul that only Circe, the great sorceress and sister to Aeetes, could expiate the crime. But as yet the Argonauts did not know this, until, trying to sail south, they were struck by a gale and *Argo* herself cried out, her speaking beam telling them that they should sail to Circe's island. So, sailing up the Eridanus river and then down the Rhone, they came to the Tyrrhenian Sea and there sought Circe's help. She cleansed the guilt as best she could with her black arts, and *Argo* sailed for home. As they passed the Sirens, Orpheus drowned out their bewitching song with music from his lyre, and Hera arranged a safe passage past the dangers of the Scylla and Charybdis and the raging surf of the Wandering Islands.

But off the island of Phaecia the Argonauts found themselves face to face with the second Colchian squadron which had been lying in wait for them, and they would have been destroyed if King Alcinous of Phaecia had not intervened. He decreed that Medea should stay with Jason if they were truly man and wife. Since Arete, Alcinous' wife, had forewarned Medea of the judgement, she and Jason celebrated their wedding in the sacred cave of Macris'. So the Colchians gave up the chase, though *Argo*'s tribulations were not yet at an end. She was blown to Libya by a northerly gale, and stranded in the shallows of the Gulf of Sirte. Searching for water in the desert the Argonauts were guided to a spring by the Hesperides, bewailing the theft of the gold apples by Hercules. Canthus, stealing a flock of sheep to feed his famished companions, was killed by a stone thrown by the shepherd, and Mopsus died from the poisonous bite of a snake. Finally, with the help of a Triton, *Argo* was extricated from the sandbars of the Gulf, and sailed north to Crete. There Talus the bronze giant kept them from landing by breaking off great lumps of rock and hurling them at the strangers, until Medea fixed him with the evil eye and caused him to graze his ankle on a rock. This was Talus' only vulnerable spot, for the vein broke beneath his brazen skin and the icthor flowed out so that Talus collapsed and died.

The Argonauts spent that night on Crete and then sailed on, only to run into a strange pitch-black night. In the darkness they would have been wrecked, if Apollo had not suddenly appeared and lit the danger so that *Argo* found anchorage off Anaphe island. So, by way of Aegina, where the Argonauts took on water, *Argo* finally came back home to the beach at Pagasae.

Acknowledgements

It will be clear from the preceding tale that the Jason Voyage was made possible through the help of a great many people spread across several different countries. The following list of such 'friends of the Argonauts' is by no means complete, but gives some idea of the international spirit of cooperation which helped us reach our goal.

First to be thanked must be Sarah Waters who once again was the all-important project coordinator. With the help of Constance Messenger in Windsor, Sarah ran the expedition's office with her customary finesse. Her role in the Jason Voyage was vital to the final outcome of the expedition, and it was – as always – immensely reassuring to know that Sarah was at the expedition base handling the day-to-day workload faultlessly. On the other side of the Atlantic the staff of the *National Geographic Magazine* once again provided encouragement and the photographic assistance for which they are justly renowned.

In the British Isles help was given by Lord Killanin; Dr John Harvey; Arthur Beale Ltd; E. P. Barrus Ltd (outboard motor for the rubber dinghy); Beaufort Air-Sea Equipment (the very generous loan of liferafts and lifejackets); Henri-Lloyd (oilskins); Munster Simms Engineering (hand pumps); the London office of Olympic Airways; Seafarer Navigation Ltd (emergency radio and other equipment); Telesonic Ltd; and Zodiac UK (rubber dinghy).

In Greece, Wendy Vosmer was splendid in the role which one visitor aptly described as 'house mother' to the building crew, and very many thanks are due to Clem and Jesse Wood for their unfailing hospitality, and also to Andy and Metula. In Greece, too, there were Richard Arnold-Baker; Edward Hekimian; Pandelis Kartapanis, shipwright of Pefkakia; Angelos Kilaidonis; Lance

Rowell; Anastasis Rodopoulos; Harry Tzalas; and Sotiris Zeibekis, harbour master of Limnos. Among official bodies we received help from Olympic Airways and the National Tourist Organisation of Greece, as well as the Mayor and Council of Volos.

In Turkey, I would like to thank the Turkish Navy and in particular four of its admirals: Mustafa Turumcoglu commanding the Turkish Coastguard; Yasar Onkal commanding the Naval College; Sadun Ozturk Commander of the Bosphorus, who very thoughtfully provided a complete set of the Turkish Navy's Black Sea charts, and retired admiral Nejet Serim. At Milliyet newspaper, Sevin Okyay went to great lengths to support the expedition, and it was always wonderful to see her when she came to visit us at various ports during *Argo*'s journey along the Turkish coast. Yelman Emcan at the Ministry of Tourism and Culture thoughtfully directed his staff to assist the Argonauts, and they did so with typical Turkish hospitality and kindness, in particular at Canakkale (Meryem Basli and Lale Sumer), Erdek (Vural Menteseoglu), Istanbul (regional director Cengis Taner) and Samsun (Erdopan Istankoylu). In Istanbul Bill Bauer, manager of the Sheraton Hotel, made our stay far more comfortable than we had ever expected, and Mayor Bedrettin Dalan not only looked after us outward bound but then took care of *Argo* on our return. In Erdek, my thanks also to another hotelier, the proprietor of the Avelok Hotel for his help and hospitality. The Governors and Mayors of regions and towns all along our Turkish route were unstinting in their hospitality, and there are notably happy memories from Akcakoca, Amasra, Cide, Samsun, Sinop and Zonguldak. In Istanbul we were guests of the Fenerbache Yacht Club; in Eregli we were guided round the Caves of Hades by Cengiz Guceri and entertained by Turgut Goray, introduced to me by Alpay Cin the President of the Turkish Yachting Federation whose members maintained the best traditions of comradeship between sailors. When we broke steering oars, Ayhan Demir (Sinop) and Hilmi Gurler (Samsun) came to our assistance during shore-based repairs. Expert archaeological counsel was provided by Necmettin Akgunduz (Sinop) and Nihat Sumer (Samsun). Sevim Berker, working with the BBC-TV team in Turkey, helped us, as did the on-shore film crew, led by John Miller from the Manchester TV Centre, who somehow found time to bring out mail and supplies as well as carry out their filming duties to make a documentary record of the Voyage. The same extra-curricular help was provided by Stephen Phillips, arts correspondent for ITN, during his visits to report the progress of the expedition.

In the USSR, I would like to thank the Ministry of Mercantile Marine for putting *Tovarisch* at our disposal for the return to Istanbul as well as our memorable greeting to Georgia. In advance of our visit to the Soviet Union it was Soviet TV who laid the groundwork. The team at the Foreign Relations department, headed by Lev Korolyev, put me in touch with the producers of Yuri Senkevich's Voyage Club programme (particularly Stas) and the Committee comprising Boris Semyonov, Nina Sevruk, Irina Zhelezova and Zinaida Yevgrafova. Later Sergey Skvortsov and Pavel Korchagin then came from Moscow to Georgia to smooth our paths.

I hope the text has already given some idea of the tremendous welcome given us by the Georgians, and much credit for this must go to Nugzar Popkhadze and Othar Lordkipanidze. Among many helpful scholars Vachtang Licheli and Alexandre Alexidze must stand as representatives for their colleagues. While David Shalikashvili and Tamar Makharoblidze must do the same for our many friends at Georgian TV and Radio. I would also like to make a special mention of the three Svan gold-gatherers who were so kind as to show me the age-old technique of gold-gathering with the use of sheepskins. They were: David Dzaparidze, Walo Gulbani and Alexandre Dzaparidze.

I hope that those 'friends of the Argonauts' whose names have neither been mentioned above nor introduced in the book itself will forgive the omission. By recompense I hope they enjoy the story of the Jason Voyage, and feel that the results have repaid their efforts in our support.

Finally my thanks to Monique Kervran in Greece, Turkey and France where her perceptive analysis of archaeology and her tireless support were deeply appreciated.